Praise for Fast Track Astrologer

"Mike Grabarek has presented a view of astrology that serves the beginner as well as those who are more advanced. His presentation of the facets of astrology come together in a way that invites all of us to enjoy it at a deeper level. I found his book hard to put down. It contains a blend of his precise engineering background and his ability to write in a heartfelt manner."

  Jimmy Davis, writer
  Santa Fe, NM

"*Fast Track Astrologer* is a wonderful book for astrologers, from beginners to seasoned experts. I found Mike's explanations to be clear, concise, and easy to grasp. His enthusiasm for the subject is contagious as he takes the reader on a fascinating journey of discovery covering every aspect of the discipline. Mike's voice is engaging, often humorous, and enthusiastic. His obvious passion for astrology shines through in every sentence. I highly recommend this book to everyone who has an interest in this ancient discipline."

  Lynn Cline, copy editor and astrology aficionado
  Santa Fe, NM

"This book is one of a kind. Although this is a common saying, it definitely applies to this new astrological guide. Mike Grabarek truly accomplishes what he set out to do, provide a single source that gives you all the necessary tools for getting acquainted in delineating a chart. You'll love studying this fast track to astrology, which is short and concise with a fresh and to-the-point writing style. He does not hide the fact that astrology is complex and he wants you to be a committed and curious student. Study this book if you really want to get into astrology, and you will be greatly rewarded."

  Joy Hansen, astrologer
  Fort Collins, CO

"I really enjoyed going through *Fast Track Astrologer* and found its methodical approach very useful. It showed me that I knew more than I thought and added some sense of organization to that knowledge. It offers a clear and concise description of a sometimes difficult, albeit fascinating, subject. Mike's objective to bring forth a book that was missing among the thousands of works available will undoubtedly delight astrologers at all levels."

  Dominique Chevaucher
  Santa Fe, NM

"I love your book! For me, it is a real chance to start to learn about astrology. When I looked at the other astrology books before, I always felt intimidated by the inaccessible knowledge they carry. Your book feels easily accessible to a novice. It is also well-structured and cross-referenced. What I love the most is the idea that everyone's astrology is just their potential, and it is up to the person's free will to make full use of their unique gifts."
 Irina Osechinskaya
 San Clemente, CA

"This user-friendly book provides a much-needed, refreshingly simple introduction to the basics of chart reading and astrology for the layperson and serious student. I have found it more helpful than any other astrology book for laying the foundations of knowledge needed for more serious inquiry and practice."
 Jennifer Ferraro, author & student of astrology
 Santa Fe, NM

"Absolutely amazing! All these years of being curious about the whole astrology subject, but never actually having the time, or a guide, to fathom all the mind-numbing charts. This book not only put the whole subject into an easy to understand, step-by-step guide on how to read and decipher your natal chart, but it made the charts seem accessible. Mike did such a great job of taking each part of the chart and explaining it in a clear and concise method, that it's a great read. What I really appreciated was that he made numerous references to material covered in previous chapters, so you don't find yourself having to go back and search. If you've ever harbored a curiosity about astrology, but found it too overwhelming, then this is your book. It's *the* essential guide to learning this fascinating field."
 Lisa Bougoulas
 Sudbury, MA

"Mike Grabarek has indeed written an astrology book that is both user-friendly and accessible. With a hint of humor, clear and abundant examples, and impeccable logic, he takes a good deal of the struggle out of understanding how to read or interpret a chart, especially for a totally inexperienced student of astrology like me."
 Jose Luis Stevens Ph.D.
 Santa Fe, NM

"Finally! A book to understand and use astrology in a clear, concise and useful way! I've already incorporated astrology into my life and I'm seeing changes. This book is a MUST HAVE for those wishing to understand, incorporate and harness the power of the universe into their lives, NOW."
 Nancy Hutchison, retired CFO
 Santa Fe, NM

Fast Track Astrologer

The Book I Wish I Had When I Became an Astrologer

Mike Grabarek

Fast Track Astrologer by Mike Grabarek

Copyright © 2012 by Mike Grabarek,
Manifesting Intentions LLC
http://www.usefulastrology.com
mike@usefulastrology.com

All rights reserved. No part of this book may be used or reproduced in any manner without written permission of the author.

ISBN-13: 978-1468057713

ISBN-10: 1468057715

All astrology charts were created using Sirius software produced by Cosmic Patterns, Inc.

All other pictures were purchased at fotolia.com

3-D diagrams in the celestial geometry chapter were photoshopped by Mike Grabarek

Acknowledgements

Writing any book involves help from the generosity of others. This book was no exception. I am especially grateful for all the people who reviewed this book and provided useful feedback, much of which I incorporated in the final editing of this book.

Joy Hansen, a European-trained astrologer, spent many days carefully reading this book and providing a wealth of valuable suggestions and comments. Bogdan Krusiński, inventor of the Krusiński house system, helped me ensure that my treatment of the geometry of his house system is accurately detailed in this book. Lynn Cline, an astrology aficionado and copy editor, ensured my language was clear and grammatically correct. Jewel Alexander, my life coach, helped me stay centered and present throughout this process.

I am also grateful for Tom Brady who inspired me to become an astrologer and included me as part of his working group.

Others who spent considerable time reviewing this book include Bruce Hutchison, David and Fei Cochrane (creators of Sirius astrology software), Patrick Foley, Jennifer Ferraro, Jose Stevens, Vera Neufeld, Mary Jonaitis, Rebecca Wolle, Dominique Chevaucher, Irina Osechinskaya, Vera Neufeld, Nancy Hutchison, Lisa Bougoulas, Jimmy Davis, and Lucy Garrity.

Finally, a great big hug goes to my wife, Astrid, for supporting and nurturing me throughout this whole process. To her credit, this project was a "labor of love."

Table of Contents

1. Introduction 1

Astrology Fundamentals

2. Four Major Components 7
3. Natal Chart 15
4. Planets and Personal Points 25
5. Aspects 31
6. Zodiac Signs 37
7. Houses 49
8. House Activity 55
9. Fate Versus Free Will 61
10. Growth in Maturity 65

Exploration of the Major Components

11. Exploration of Planets 71
12. Exploration of Aspects 77
13. Two Planet Combinations 81
14. Exploration of Personal Points 89
15. Exploration of Zodiac Signs 91
16. Exploration of Houses 97

Delineating Natal Charts

- 17. Delineating Individual Components 105
- 18. Approaching Natal Charts 129
- 19. Delineation Methodology 137

Other Astrology Methods

- 20. Transits 143
- 21. Relocation 151
- 22. Compatibility 161
- 23. Mundane (World) 165

Finale

- 24. Now It's Your Turn 181

Bonus Section

- 25. Birth Time Uncertainty 189
- 26. Advanced House Activity 195
- 27. Celestial Geometry 207
- 28. House Systems 235

Appendix

- Useful Tables 249

1 Introduction

Being an astrologer has given me a personally rewarding career. My internal "batteries" get recharged when I help people explore their unique potential in practical ways. While astrology is a complex discipline that takes a long time to fully learn and appreciate, it is well worth the effort.

This book is for people at all knowledge levels of Western astrology who want to fast track their learning and use it like the professionals. It is relatively short, and yet provides everything you need. I have no doubt that even professional astrologers will garner many insights from this book.

Step by step, we will go through the myriad of components in astrology and learn to use them like the professionals. We will cover five types of astrology. Specifically:

1. **Natal (birth):** Every person is born with a unique combination of energetic potential and has a lifetime to mature in effectively directing this potential. Becoming more aware of your unique makeup and possibilities allows you to accelerate your growth.

2. **Transits:** Life is abundant with cycles, as depicted in the Bible's Book of Ecclesiastes and also in the 1965 song recorded by the Byrds: "To everything there is a season; turn, turn, turn; and a time for every purpose under heaven." Transits help you gain insights about the parts of you that will be resonating and alive over a specific time period.

3. **Relocation:** We all have had dreams of moving to a new area to start a new chapter in our lives. Relocation charts help you explore places to live that will emphasize the parts of your life that are the most important for you.

4. **Compatibility:** Relationships start with an attraction between two people who then decide to spend time with each other. Compatibility analysis helps a couple get to know each other at a much deeper level, which then opens the opportunity for personal growth and mutual nurturing and support.

5. **Mundane:** We all can sense that we are going through a period in history that is far from ordinary. Mundane astrology helps us make sense of the worldwide energies in play. It allows us to better understand our times and prompts us to explore our own options and choices.

This book also provides a much-needed exploration of House systems and how they relate to the three-dimensional (3-D) cosmos from the perspective of the birth time and location. Included is an exploration of the Krusiński House system, which is rapidly being adopted by astrologers for its accuracy and geometric simplicity.

The mechanics of astrology are fairly straightforward and can be learned and memorized in a reasonable amount of time. We will learn these mechanics using a methodical and organized approach.

Learning to interpret and communicate the information provided by astrology charts takes a while. It requires an ability to synthesize information and communicate it meaningfully. This book provides numerous examples to accelerate your learning in this area.

Throughout this book, I have chosen to capitalize words that have unique astrological meaning. Examples are Planets, Houses, Aspects, Taurus, Scorpio, Pisces, Sun, Moon, Earth, Trine, Square, Ruler, Retrograde, Intercepted, Cusp, Ascendant, and Midheaven. I did this to emphasize that while the word is typically not capitalized, its definition from an astrological perspective is different from its generic definition. I hope this misuse of grammar aids in your learning.

Let's get started.

Astrology Fundamentals

2 Four Major Components

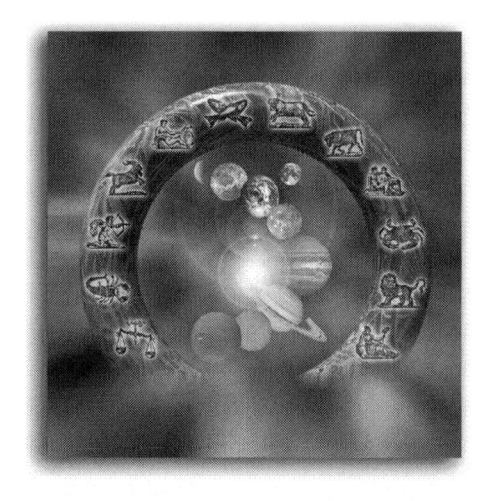

The practice of astrology is several thousand years old. At its foundation lies an observation that there is a correlation between life on Earth and the Planets and stars. The first evidence of this correlation goes back 25,000 years to the discovery of the rhythms of the Moon and tides, and the Sun and seasons. The earliest known astrological records are from Babylonia around 2300 BCE. Astrology's origins can also be traced to ancient Persia, Mesopotamia, Assyria, India, Egypt, Greece, and Rome. As astrology grew in practice and experience, it was brought to the individual level through the use of horoscopes, with the earliest recorded horoscope dating back to around 200 BCE, likely in Hellenistic Egypt. Astrology continued to evolve and branched out in a variety of forms including Vedic (India), Medieval (Europe, Middle East), and contemporary Western astrology.

An often used ancient phrase in astrology is "as above, so below."

A principle in current Western astrology is that you are born with a unique combination of energy. Throughout your life, you use your free will to direct your unique combination of energy, sometimes in ways that are helpful and other times in ways that are not helpful. With time, you mature in directing your energetic gifts, which leads to greater effectiveness. When you understand your unique energetic makeup and how to direct it more effectively, your growth accelerates.

There are four major components within astrology: Planets, Zodiac Signs, Aspects, and Houses. Below is a brief description of these four components. We will delve into each of these major components throughout this book.

Planets can be thought of as the actors within you that are a part of you. Each Planet represents a different role you play in your life. For example, Jupiter is the part of you that wants to optimistically expand your territory. Saturn is the part of you that wants to have boundaries and structures so you can get results or protect yourself. If you have felt, at times, like there were conflicts within yourself (i.e. one part of you wanted to do one thing and another part wanted to do something different), then from an astrological perspective, you were sensing the different Planets (actors) within you wanting to be heard. For those of you who have been led to think there might be something wrong with you when these internal conflicts occur, from an astrological perspective you are perfectly normal.

Zodiac Signs give personality to each of your Planets (actors). For example, Taurus provides a personality of practicality, predictability, and grounding, while Libra is focused on beauty, harmony, and balance (and sometimes extreme imbalance). When you were born, each of your Planets was in a particular Zodiac Sign. The backdrop of stars behind the Planets is divided into 12 equal segments, each of which corresponds to a particular Zodiac Sign. To determine the specific Zodiac Sign for a Planet, you view the backdrop of stars behind the Planet and identify the Zodiac Sign associated with that portion of the backdrop of stars.

Aspects indicate which Planets (parts of you) tend to play their roles at the same time, similar to cliques in high school. When Planets are approximately aligned (Conjunct - 0°), opposite each other (Opposition - 180°), one-third of a circle (Trine - 120°), or one-quarter of a circle (Square - 90°) apart, they will form strong cliques. There are other important angles as well that will be covered later. Part of the growth in maturity you experience throughout your life is directing these combinations of Planets (parts of you) to cooperate with each other instead of competing. For example, if Jupiter was Conjunct (next to) Saturn when you were born, there are two parts of you wanting to be heard simultaneously. One part wants to expand and grow (Jupiter) while the other wants to have structure and control (Saturn).

Houses indicate the areas of life in which Planets will have an emphasized role. The Houses are simply numbered from one to 12. The beginning of the 1st House (Cusp) is on the eastern horizon at the time and place of your birth. In astrology, examples of Houses (areas in life) include relationships (7th House), career (10th House), and spiritual growth (12th House). Planets emphasize their energy in the various Houses by a variety of means, which we will cover in detail later.

Example

Let's illustrate the concepts in this chapter with an example. Suppose you have your Mars (Planet) in Taurus (Zodiac Sign) in the 6th House (area of life) and your Moon (Planet) in Capricorn (Zodiac Sign) in the 2nd House (area of life). Furthermore, these two Planets (Mars and Moon) are almost exactly 120° apart (Trine), which means these two parts of you are active in unison.

First we will look at each Planet in its Zodiac Sign and House separately. Then we will see how the combination of the two Planets may play out when you are less evolved and more evolved in the development of these parts of yourself.

Mars in Taurus in the 6th House

Mars is the part of you (actor) that takes action to get what you want. When the Mars part of you is less evolved, you use aggression (sometimes passive aggression) to get what you want. When Mars is more evolved, you use assertiveness.

Taurus gives your Mars characteristics of being practical, pragmatic, and predictable, and having a need for safety and security. When these characteristics are expressed in a less-evolved way, you are stubborn, complacent, and hard to change. When evolved, these characteristics are expressed as being grounded, feeling peaceful, translating ideas into practical results, and being someone who can be counted on when making commitments.

The **6th House** is the area of life associated with your daily routines and habits, including how you approach your activities, how you take care of your health, and the services you provide for others.

With **Mars in Taurus in the 6th House** when less evolved, you avoid and actively sabotage new ideas, which will disrupt your rigid patterns. When you are evolved, you will be the "go to" person for practical problem solving, finding the simplicity in the complexity, and creating a peaceful and predictable atmosphere.

Moon in Capricorn in the 2nd House

The **Moon** is the part of you (actress) that taps into the world of feelings, emotions, and moods. When less evolved, you frequently feel off balance and overwhelmed by your feelings. You may express this as irritability, frustration, or ill-temperedness. When evolved, you recognize your feelings as something to be honored and explored, and as valuable signals to yourself. You use this information to be more aware and to guide yourself to a centered state.

Capricorn provides characteristics to your Moon of having boundaries, structure, and discipline. With less-developed Capricorn characteristics, you may either have boundaries that are stifling or vague and unpredictable. With well-developed Capricorn characteristics, your boundaries are wide enough to invite creativity and openness, and focused enough to ensure results.

The **2nd House** is the area in life associated with your need for security and safety as well as with the possessions you accrue. This area is also closely tied to the development of your self image, self worth, and self confidence.

With your **Moon in Capricorn in the 2nd House** when less evolved, you may suppress your feelings and emotions by attempting to bottle them up inside and refusing to express yourself from the heart with others. When well evolved, you use your feelings as valuable information, and then using a structured approach, address the cause of the feelings in an environment that feels safe.

Combination of Mars and Moon Acting in Unison

Now we can put this combination of two Planets together and imagine how you may express these parts of yourself.

Suppose you are at work and your boss calls you into his office. He is visibly upset because one of your co-workers came to him and complained that you were not being a team player.

In a **less-evolved state**, you receive this harsh feedback and your feelings inside start running wild. Rather than express your feelings, you attempt to bottle them up inside and become defensive, stating all the reasons why you were right and the other person was wrong. After the conversation is over, your boss feels like he wasn't heard. You then create an internal story that both your boss and co-worker are idiots. Because your ego naturally wants to prove your stories are right, you become attuned to all the dumb things your boss and co-worker do, and even find subtle ways to highlight their incompetence. As much as possible, you avoid your boss and co-worker and limit your communication with them.

In an **evolved state**, you walk into your boss's office and receive the harsh feedback. You let your boss know that you are very concerned about this and invite him to explore it further with you. Together, you gather the facts surrounding the actual event. You share how you feel about the situation and invite your boss to do the same. You acknowledge your contribution to the situation and explore with your boss what you learned, how it could have been handled differently, and how you will approach these situations differently in the future. After your meeting, you approach your co-worker and go through a similar conversation, resulting in the "air being cleared." The internal story you create is that you are human, and thus prone to making mistakes. Furthermore you are learning from your mistakes and becoming a better person as a result.

Notice that this Planetary combination is neither good nor bad. What makes it work or not work for you is your maturity in directing these parts of yourself (Planets).

Planets are parts of you (actors) playing specific roles. They have characteristics provided by the Zodiac Signs. Your Planets emphasize their roles in areas of life depicted by the Houses. Furthermore, your Planets interact simultaneously when Aspected.

We are now ready for an introduction to the Natal chart.

3   Natal Chart

The Natal chart, often referred to as the Birth chart, is a depiction of the location of the Planets relative to the backdrop of stars (Signs of the Zodiac) and the Earth's orientation (Houses) at the time and location of a person's birth. The picture on the next page is an example of a Natal (birth) chart. The picture on the following page is the same, but with important features noted.

In the upper left hand corner, you'll find the person's name, Karen Raven (name changed), birth date, birth time, birth location, and the House system used. We will explore more detail on the various House systems in chapters 27 and 28.

In the Natal chart on the next page, a large circle in the center contains lines, glyphs, and numbers. At the bottom are grids and tables. If you've never seen a Natal chart before, it will look confusing. Let's explore this Natal chart piece by piece.

16

Karen Raven
March 17, 1955
10:37 PM
New Haven, Connecticut
Standard Time
Time Zone: 5 hours West
Tropical Krusinski

NATAL CHART

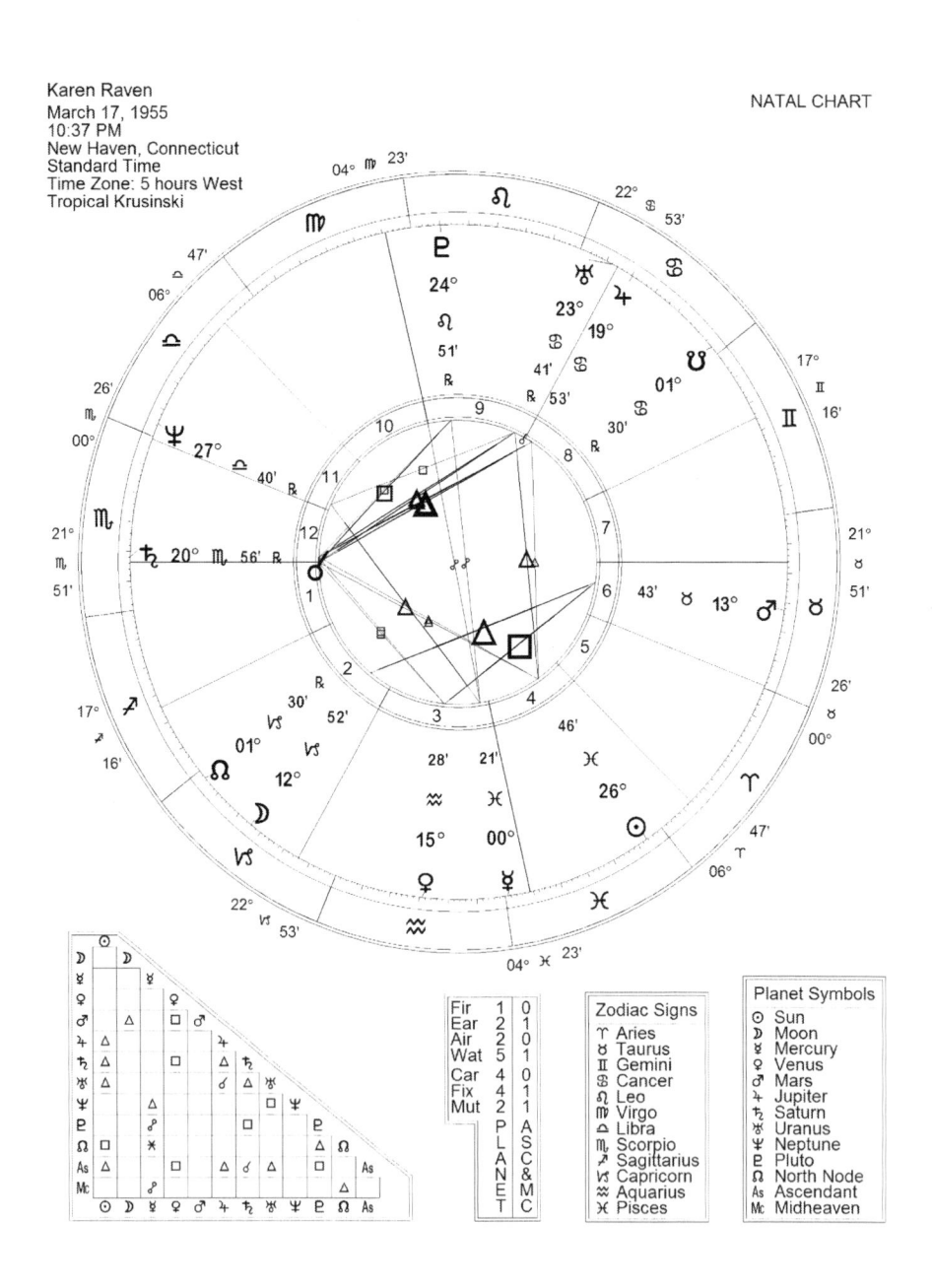

Fast Track Astrologer

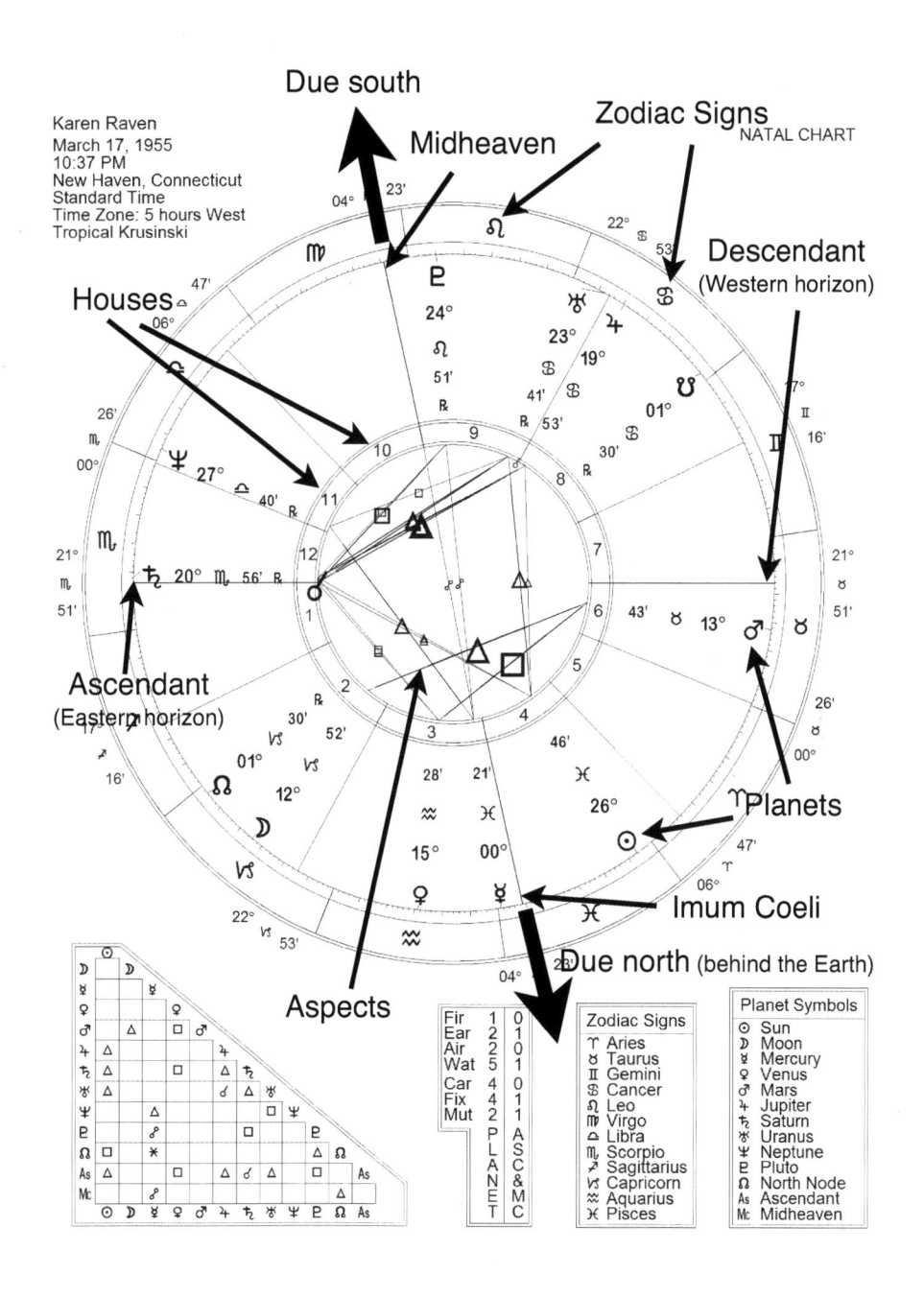

Natal Chart

Large Center Circle

The large center circle with multiple rings in the Natal chart on the previous page is a picture of where the Planets were relative to the backdrop of stars (Signs of the Zodiac) and the orientation of the Earth (Houses) at the time and location of Karen's birth. Do you remember the four major components of astrology from the previous chapter? These four major components are the Zodiac Signs, Planets, Houses, and Aspects. Each of these four major components are depicted in the Natal chart. Let's take a closer look.

Zodiac Signs: In the outer ring of Karen's Natal chart, you can view the Signs of the Zodiac depicted by the 12 glyphs. At the bottom right side of the previous page, a table indicates which Sign of the Zodiac corresponds to each of the 12 glyphs. You can also view a summary of all glyphs used in this book in the appendix. As mentioned earlier, the backdrop of stars are divided into 12 segments, each of which is represented by a Sign of the Zodiac. So this outer ring tells us the orientation of the backdrop of stars that are divided into the 12 Zodiac segments. The Zodiac Signs give characteristics to each of the Planets. We will cover more detail on the Signs of the Zodiac in chapters 6 and 15.

Planets: In Karen's Natal chart on the previous page, the second ring in from the outside depicts the positions of the Planets. These are shown as glyphs. At the lower right side of the page, another table depicts the Planets associated with each glyph. Note that the table includes the glyphs for what are referred to as the conventional Planets (Sun, Moon, Mercury, Venus, Mars, Jupiter, Saturn, Uranus, Neptune, and Pluto). The Planets are the actors within you that are a part of you. Each Planet represents a role you play in your life. We will explore more on the Planets in the next chapter as well as in chapters 11 and 13. The Planet Symbol table contains the Personal Points (North Node, Midheaven, and Ascendant). These Personal Points will be discussed in more detail in the next chapter as well as in Chapter 14.

Houses: In Karen's Natal chart, the third ring in, which is quite thin, has numbers from one to 12. These are the Houses, which begin with the 1st House at the left side of the chart. Houses are numbered consecutively in a counterclockwise direction. The Houses represent the areas of life in which your Planets (actors that are a part of you) have an emphasis. We will cover Houses in more detail in chapters 7, 8, 16, 26, 27 and 28.

Aspects: At the very center of Karen's Natal chart, numerous lines connect the Planets. These are the Aspect lines. When Planets are connected by these lines, they tend to interact together in unison (cliques). The lines with a square connect Planets, which are approximately 90° apart (one-quarter of a circle). Lines that have triangles connect Planets that are approximately 120° apart. There are other lines representing other Aspects that we will explore later. The grid on the far lower left of Karen's Natal chart depicts all these Aspects in a matrix form. We will go into more detail on Aspects in chapters 5 and 12.

Remaining Table in the Natal Chart

There is an additional table in the Natal chart that you will find useful. At the bottom center, a table lists the number of Planets in the Fire, Earth, Air, and Water Zodiac Signs (Elements) as well as the number of Planets that are Cardinal, Fixed, and Mutable Zodiac Signs

(Qualities). We will explore Elements and Qualities more closely in Chapter 6.

Orientation of the Natal Chart

If you were to take Karen's Natal chart, orient it so it is facing south (top of the chart points south), and then tilt the top of the chart slightly upward, you would have an approximate visual picture of where the Planets were at the time and location of Karen's birth.

Because you are facing south, the top of the chart points in a southerly direction and up toward the sky. Technically, if you were to put an upward pointing arrow on the 10th House Cusp (the line separating the 9th and 10th Houses), then that arrow would point due south. The 10th House Cusp in a Natal chart is referred to as the Midheaven or the Medium Coeli, and sometimes the M^c. In Chapter 27 on celestial geometry, we will explore how the three-dimensional (3-D) cosmos relates to the two-dimensional (2-D) Natal chart. For the sake of simplicity, you can think of the top of the Natal chart as being in the southerly direction and looking up.

The bottom of the Natal chart is north and down (behind the Earth). To be exact, a downward pointing arrow on the 4th House Cusp (the line separating the 3rd and 4th Houses) would point due north and down (behind the Earth). The 4th House Cusp is referred to as the Imum Coeli, or simply I^c. For the sake of simplicity, you can think of the bottom of the Natal chart as pointing northerly and behind the Earth. By definition, the 10th House Cusp is opposite (180°) the 4th House Cusp.

The 1st House Cusp (beginning of the 1st House) is on the left side of the Natal chart. This represents the eastern horizon. With rare exceptions, it is actually somewhat north or south of due east on the eastern horizon. The reason for this will become clear when we explore Chapter 27 on celestial geometry. The 1st House Cusp is also referred to as the Ascendant, or simply A^s. For the sake of simplicity, you can think of the 1st House Cusp (Ascendant A^s) of the Natal chart as representing the eastern horizon.

The 7th House Cusp (beginning of the 7th House) is on the right side of the Natal chart. This represents the western horizon. As with the left side of the Natal chart, the right side is almost always somewhat north or south of due west at the horizon. The 7th House Cusp is also referred to as the Descendant, or simply D^s. For the sake of simplicity, you can think of the 7th House Cusp (Descendant D^s) as representing the western horizon.

Note that the orientation of a Natal chart is upside down compared to a traditional map. In a Natal chart south is up, north is down, east is left, and west is right.

Imagine slicing the circular Natal chart into two halves: an upper half (Houses 7-12) and a lower half (Houses 1-6). Planets in the upper half were visible in the sky (sometimes with the aid of a telescope) at the time and location of Karen's birth. Planets in the bottom half were behind the Earth.

Example from the Previous Chapter

In the previous chapter, we explored a Planetary configuration that included Mars ♂ in Taurus ♉ in the 6th House Trine △ Moon ☽ in Capricorn ♑ in the 2nd House. I've included the glyphs for the Planets and Zodiac Signs here and will continue to do so for the remainder of this book. Through repetition, you will gradually become more familiar with these glyphs.

Karen's Natal chart on page 17 has this Planetary configuration. The arrow I placed in her Natal chart depicting "Aspects" is pointing to this particular configuration. Notice that Mars ♂ is in the 6th House and in the Zodiac Sign of Taurus ♉. The Moon ☽ is in the Zodiac Sign of Capricorn ♑ in the 2nd House. Furthermore, Mars ♂ and the Moon ☽ are almost exactly 120° apart (Trine △). Since Mars ♂ and the Moon ☽ are Aspected (through a Trine △), they will interact simultaneously.

We went through three pages of interpretation for this single combination of two Planets in the previous chapter. Viewing Karen's Natal chart on page 17, you can see there are numerous other combinations that we could also explore. We will do this exploration later in the book in Chapter 17.

Create Your Own Natal Chart

For the next several chapters, we will be using Karen Raven's Natal chart to dig into the details of astrology. While you may enjoy learning the basics using Karen's Natal chart, you may also want to create your own Natal (Birth) chart and analyze it while going through the upcoming material.

There are a number of sites on the web where you can create and print your Natal chart for free. One very useful website is Astrodienst (www.astro.com). Another is Astrolabe (alabe.com/freechart/). While these free Natal charts will not have the same look as the charts in this book, you will easily be able to draw the parallels.

Another option is available at my web site: www.usefulastrology.com. For $19.00 USD, I will create the charts you will need for this book in high-resolution color graphics in pdf format. These charts include your Natal chart, BiWheel chart, Transit chart, and Relocation chart. These charts will be in the same format found throughout this book. NOTE: On the final PayPal page before submitting your payment, select the "note to seller" option. Please include the following information: your name, birth date, birth time, birth location (town, state, country), current location (town, state, country), and your email. When I create your charts, I will email the pdf files for you to print out.

Next, let's look at the first of the four major components of astrology: Planets. We will also explore the Personal Points.

4 Planets and Personal Points

Planets are the actors within you that are a part of you. Each Planet represents a role you play in your life.

Astrological Planets most commonly include the Sun ☉, Moon ☽, Mercury ☿, Venus ♀, Mars ♂, Jupiter ♃, Saturn ♄, Uranus ♅, Neptune ♆, and Pluto ♇ (sometimes shown as ♇).

Yes, Pluto ♇ has been demoted to a dwarf Planet. Richard Tarnas (*Cosmos and Psyche*), among others, has done thorough research on the Pluto ♇ cycles. They are there and real. I don't think there is a single astrologer not using Pluto ♇ because of this reclassification.

Some astrologers include additional "Planets" such as Chiron ⚷ (comet) as well as asteroids including Ceres ⚳, Juno ⚵, Pallas ⚴, and Vesta ⚶. For the sake of simplicity, this book will not include further information on these additional Planets.

Even though the Sun ☉ and the Moon ☽ are not technically Planets, they are referred to as Planets in astrology and sometimes called Luminaries. Glyphs associated with each Planet are included above and you also can view them in the box labeled Planet Symbols in the lower right portion of Karen's Natal chart on page 29. These glyphs are also included in the appendix. Furthermore, I have included the Planet glyphs throughout the remainder of this book so you can eventually memorize them through repetition.

Each Planet represents a part of you that plays a particular role in your life. For example, Mercury ☿ is associated with your thinking and communicating, while the Moon ☽ is that part of you that wants to nurture yourself and others.

In addition, there are four Personal Points that, while not Planets, are significant places in the Natal chart. These include the Ascendant A^s, Midheaven M^c, North Node ☊, and South Node ☋.

The table on the next page lists the key words associated with the Planet roles as well as the Personal Point characteristics.

You may find it useful to visit Chapter 11 (page 71) and view more information on the specific roles each Planet represents within you. You can also view the Personal Point details in Chapter 14 on page 89.

Key Words for Planets and Personal Points

Planet or Personal Point	Glyph	Key Words
Sun	☉	Your main actor, coming out in the world
Moon	☽	Nurturing, receiving, feeling
Mercury	☿	Thinking and communicating
Venus	♀	Attracting and relating, sensuality
Mars	♂	Initiating, getting what you want, passion
Jupiter	♃	Expanding, projecting optimism
Saturn	♄	Structuring, controlling, promoting realism
Uranus	♅	Breaking free, being unique, social change, rebel
Neptune	♆	Growing spiritually, transcending the ego
Pluto	♇	Transformation, using power, sexuality
Ascendant	A^s	Personality you portray to others
Midheaven	M^c	Characteristics of your career and reputation
North Node	☊	Areas for lifetime growth that are not instinctual
South Node	☋	Areas for lifetime growth that are instinctual

Viewing Karen's Natal chart on the next page, notice the location of the Planets and Personal Points. For example, Neptune ♆ is at the end of the 11th House, Venus ♀ is in the 3rd House, and Pluto ♇ is in the 9th House. We will cover much more on Houses later.

In most Natal charts, you will not find the symbol for the Ascendant As. This is because the Ascendant As, by definition, is at the Cusp (beginning) of the 1st House. Because of this, its position is generally not included in the Natal chart and is just assumed to be at the 1st House Cusp. The same goes for the Midheaven Mc, which, by definition, is at the Cusp (beginning) of the 10th House. The Imum Coeli Ic (4th House Cusp) is, by definition, opposite the Midheaven Mc. Similarly, the Descendant Ds (7th House Cusp) is, by definition, opposite the Ascendant As. I have marked these points in Karen's Natal chart on the next page.

Notice that each Planet in Karen's Natal chart has its position identified within its Zodiac Sign (backdrop of stars behind the Planet). For example, in Karen's Natal chart, we see that her Sun ☉ is at 26° 46' in Pisces ♓. Each Zodiac Sign is 30° in arc. Twelve Zodiac Signs multiplied by 30° each equals 360°, which is a full circle. Since Karen was born on March 17, she is just a few days away from the Sun ☉ moving from Pisces ♓ into Aries ♈, which occurs at the time of the spring equinox (northern hemisphere), around March 22. So you would expect her Sun ☉ to be toward the end of the Zodiac Sign of Pisces ♓. As we see, her Sun ☉ is at 26° 46', which is near the end of Pisces ♓ (30°).

29

Karen Raven
March 17, 1955
10:37 PM
New Haven, Connecticut
Standard Time
Time Zone: 5 hours West
Tropical Krusinski

NATAL CHART

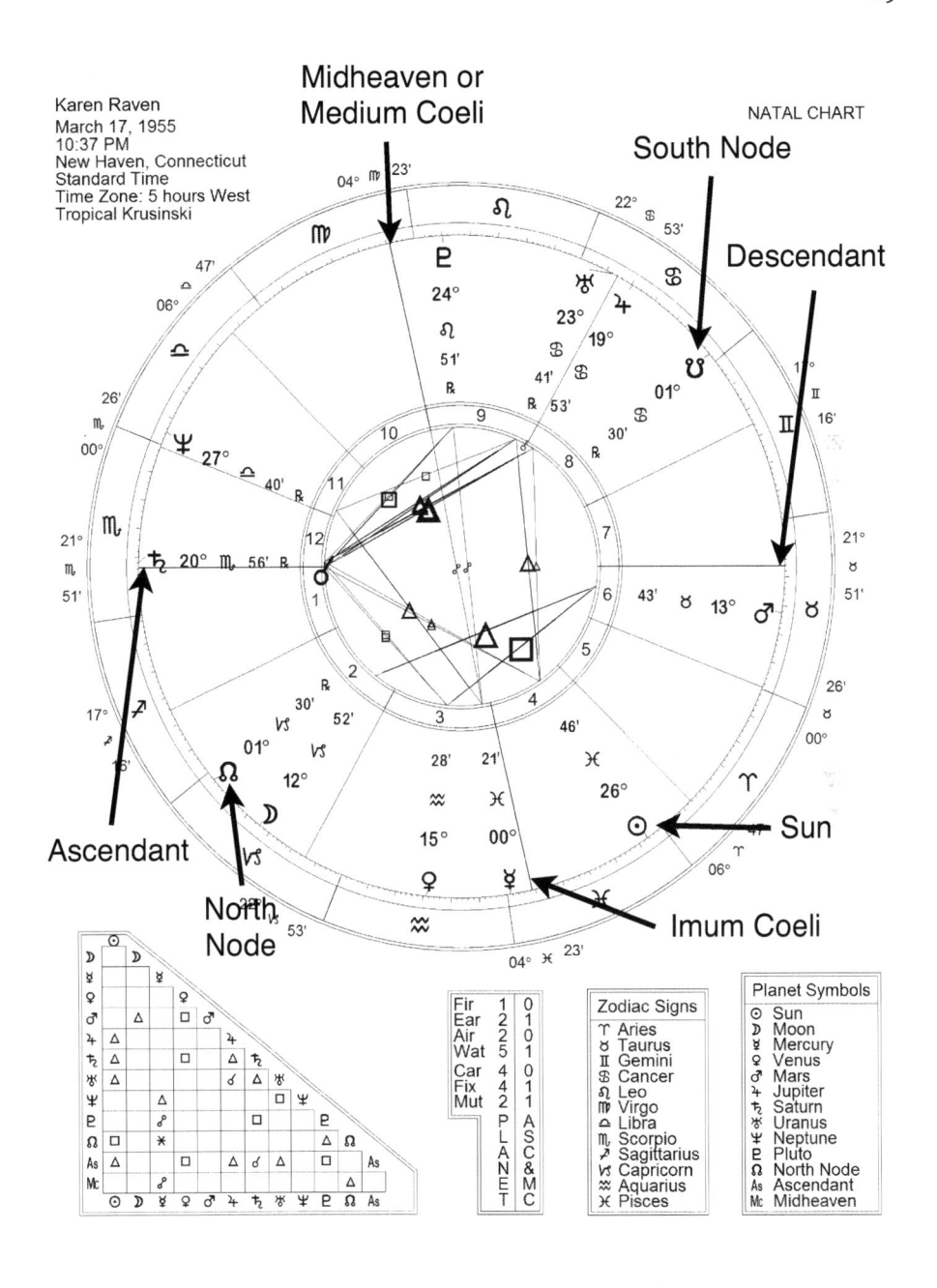

Labels on chart:
- Midheaven or Medium Coeli
- South Node
- Descendant
- Sun
- Imum Coeli
- North Node
- Ascendant

Fir	1	0
Ear	2	1
Air	2	0
Wat	5	1
Car	4	0
Fix	4	1
Mut	2	1
	P	A
	L	S
	A	C
	N	&
	E	M
	T	C

Zodiac Signs
- ♈ Aries
- ♉ Taurus
- ♊ Gemini
- ♋ Cancer
- ♌ Leo
- ♍ Virgo
- ♎ Libra
- ♏ Scorpio
- ♐ Sagittarius
- ♑ Capricorn
- ♒ Aquarius
- ♓ Pisces

Planet Symbols
- ☉ Sun
- ☽ Moon
- ☿ Mercury
- ♀ Venus
- ♂ Mars
- ♃ Jupiter
- ♄ Saturn
- ♅ Uranus
- ♆ Neptune
- ♇ Pluto
- ☊ North Node
- As Ascendant
- Mc Midheaven

Planets and Personal Points

Similarly, all the other Planets and Personal Points are located at specific points in the Zodiac. Note that the unmarked locations of the Ascendant A^s (Cusp of the 1st House) and the Midheaven M^c (Cusp of the 10th House) are at 21° 51' in Scorpio ♏, and 4° 23' in Virgo ♍, respectively. We'll cover the Zodiac Signs in Chapter 6.

One other facet of the Planet locations in Karen's Natal chart above can be illustrated by observing Saturn's ♄ position at the end of the 12th House. Specifically, you observe Saturn's ♄ position is depicted as 20° ♏ 56' ℞. The symbol ℞ indicates that Saturn ♄ was Retrograde ℞ at the time of Karen's birth. Because we observe Planets from the perspective of the Earth ⊕, they (with the exception of the Sun ☉ and Moon ☽) periodically appear to move backward relative to the backdrop of stars (Zodiac). In fact, the word Planet means wanderer, which characterizes the apparent erratic movement of the Planets from the perspective of Earth ⊕.

Going back to Karen's Natal chart, we see that several of her Planets are Retrograde ℞: Saturn ♄, Uranus ♅, Neptune ♆, and Pluto ♇. Also, her North ☊ and South Nodes ☋ are Retrograde ℞. In a Natal chart, a little less than half the Planets are typically Retrograde ℞. I don't read much into Retrograde ℞ Planets in a Natal chart, although some astrologers do.

Next we will look at the Aspects, which identify the Planets that are active in unison.

5   Aspects

Many insights from an astrological investigation come from a discussion of the interplay between Planets (parts of you). When two or more of your Planets are separated by important angles, these parts of you interact in ways that create interesting and significant dynamics.

Remembering basic geometry, points on opposite sides of a circle are 180° apart, one-quarter of a circle is 90°, one-third of a circle is 120°, and right next to each other is 0°.

These important angles in astrology are referred to as Aspects, and they are divided into Major Aspects and Minor Aspects. The Major Aspects are:

Conjunction ☌ : Planets next to each other.

Opposition ☍: Planets approximately 180° apart (half a circle).

Trine △: Planets approximately 120° apart (third of a circle).

Square □: Planets approximately 90° apart (quarter of a circle).

There are numerous Minor Aspects, a few of which include:

Sextile ✶: Planets approximately 60° apart (sixth of a circle). Some astrologers consider the Sextile ✶ to be a Major Aspect.

Semisquare ∠: Planets approximately 45° apart (eighth of a circle).

Inconjunct ⚻: Planets approximately 150° apart (five-twelfths of a circle).

Sesquiquadrate ⚼: Planets approximately 135° apart (three-eighths of a circle).

The Major Aspects tend to create stronger interactions between Planets (parts of you) when compared to the Minor Aspects. The table on the next page summarized the Aspects.

Let's look at examples of Aspecting Planets. In Karen's Natal chart on page 34, we see a number of lines in the innermost circle. Where we see the Square symbol □, we have Planets that are approximately 90° apart. For example, Mars ♂ is Square □ Venus ♀. Lines with larger squares mean that the two Planets are closer to being exactly 90° apart. Thinner lines with smaller squares correspond to Planets a bit further from being exactly 90° apart. This exactness is referred to as the Orb. In the case of a Square □, a 0° Orb would mean that the two Planets are exactly 90° apart. A 1° Orb would correspond to the Planets being either 89° or 91° apart. The smaller the Orb, the more strongly the Planets (actors) interact.

Similarly, Planets Aspected by Trines △ include Mars ♂ Trine △ Moon ☽. Planets in Opposition ☍ include Pluto ♇ Opposition ☍ Mercury ☿. Finally, note that Uranus ♅ is Conjunct ☌ Jupiter ♃ with an Orb of about 4°.

Aspects		
Aspect	**Glyph**	**Angle**
Conjunction	☌	0°
Opposition	☍	180°
Trine	△	120°
Square	□	90°
Sextile	✶	60°
Semisquare	∠	45°
Sesquiquadrate	⚼	135°
Semisextile	⚺	30°
Inconjunct	⚻	150°

34

Karen Raven
March 17, 1955
10:37 PM
New Haven, Connecticut
Standard Time
Time Zone: 5 hours West
Tropical Krusinski

NATAL CHART

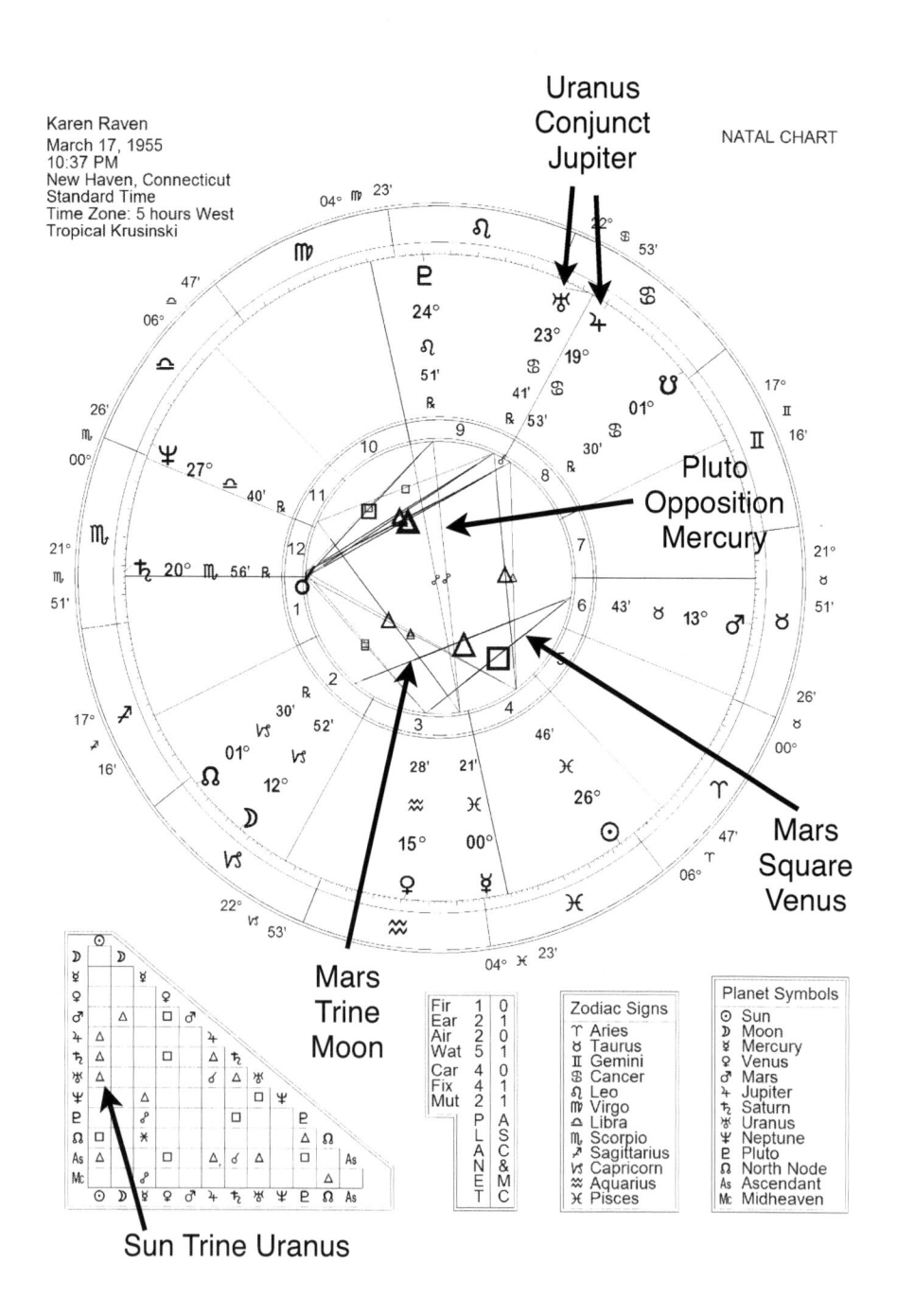

Uranus Conjunct Jupiter

Pluto Opposition Mercury

Mars Square Venus

Mars Trine Moon

Sun Trine Uranus

Fir	1	0
Ear	2	1
Air	2	0
Wat	5	1
Car	4	0
Fix	4	1
Mut	2	1

PLANET / ASC&MC

Zodiac Signs
♈ Aries
♉ Taurus
♊ Gemini
♋ Cancer
♌ Leo
♍ Virgo
♎ Libra
♏ Scorpio
♐ Sagittarius
♑ Capricorn
♒ Aquarius
♓ Pisces

Planet Symbols
☉ Sun
☽ Moon
☿ Mercury
♀ Venus
♂ Mars
♃ Jupiter
♄ Saturn
♅ Uranus
♆ Neptune
♇ Pluto
☊ North Node
As Ascendant
Mc Midheaven

Fast Track Astrologer

In Karen's Natal chart, the matrix on the lower left provides a summary of the Planets that Aspect each other. As an example, looking down the leftmost column for the Sun ☉, we see that when the Sun ☉ part of Karen is active, Jupiter ♃, Saturn ♄, and Uranus ♅ are simultaneously active as all three of these Planets are Trine △ the Sun ☉. The table on the next page summarizes all the Planet Aspects for Karen's Natal chart.

Note that the Aspects that appear on the Natal chart depend on the maximum size of the Orb I allow. Typically for Natal charts, I use a maximum Orb of 7° for the Major Aspects and a 2° Orb for the Minor Aspects. Other astrologers use different maximum allowable Orbs. This is not a big deal, as an astrologer generally focuses on the Major Aspects with the smallest Orbs anyway so the conversation with a client can be kept to an hour or so.

When your Planets (actors) are in Aspect, those parts of you interact simultaneously. In other words, when one of your Planets (a part of you playing a specific role) wants to be heard, the other Aspected Planets (other parts of you) want to be heard at the same time. It's like having the same people frequently hanging out together. Sometimes the Planetary interactions you direct don't feel helpful to you and sometimes they do. As life goes on, you grow and mature to the point where your Aspected Planets (actors within you) collaborate with each other more than they compete.

We will explore Aspects further in Chapter 12. Let's next turn our attention to the Zodiac Signs.

Aspected Planets for Karen's Natal Chart

Planet	Planet Aspects
Sun ☉	Sun ☉ Trine △ Jupiter ♃ Sun ☉ Trine △ Saturn ♄ Sun ☉ Trine △ Uranus ♅
Moon ☽	Moon ☽ Trine △ Mars ♂
Mercury ☿	Mercury ☿ Trine △ Neptune ♆ Mercury ☿ Opposition ☍ Pluto ♇
Venus ♀	Venus ♀ Square □ Mars ♂ Venus ♀ Square □ Saturn ♄
Mars ♂	Mars ♂ Trine △ Moon ☽ Mars ♂ Square □ Venus ♀
Jupiter ♃	Jupiter ♃ Trine △ Sun ☉ Jupiter ♃ Trine △ Saturn ♄ Jupiter ♃ Conjunct ☌ Uranus ♅
Saturn ♄	Saturn ♄ Trine △ Sun ☉ Saturn ♄ Square □ Venus ♀ Saturn ♄ Trine △ Jupiter ♃ Saturn ♄ Trine △ Uranus ♅ Saturn ♄ Square □ Pluto ♇
Uranus ♅	Uranus ♅ Trine △ Sun ☉ Uranus ♅ Conjunct ☌ Jupiter ♃ Uranus ♅ Trine △ Saturn ♄ Uranus ♅ Square □ Neptune ♆
Neptune ♆	Neptune ♆ Trine △ Mercury ☿ Neptune ♆ Square □ Uranus ♅
Pluto ♇	Pluto ♇ Opposition ☍ Mercury ☿ Pluto ♇ Square □ Saturn ♄

Fast Track Astrologer

6 Zodiac Signs

The backdrop of stars are divided into 12 30-degree segments, each represented by one of the 12 Signs of the Zodiac. The Zodiac Signs are Aries ♈, Taurus ♉, Gemini ♊, Cancer ♋, Leo ♌, Virgo ♍, Libra ♎, Scorpio ♏, Sagittarius ♐, Capricorn ♑, Aquarius ♒, and Pisces ♓. Each Zodiac Sign has its own glyph, which I've included above and also in the table labeled "Zodiac Signs" in the lower right portion of Karen's Natal chart on page 40. I've also included these glyphs in the appendix. As with the Planets and Personal Points, I have added the glyphs for the Zodiac Signs throughout the remainder of this book so you can eventually memorize them through repetition.

Western Versus Vedic Astrology

In Western astrology, the Zodiac begins, by definition, at 0° Aries ♈. This is defined as the point in the backdrop of stars behind the Sun ☉ when viewed from the Earth ⊕ at the time of the spring equinox, around March 22, each year. Because the Earth ⊕ has a very slow 25,920-year wobble (like the wobbling of a spinning top as it slows down), the 0° Aries ♈ point changes its position relative to the backdrop of stars by about 1° every 72 years. Thus, 0° Aries ♈ in Western astrology is tied to the spring equinox and, as a result, is always in sync with the four seasons.

In Vedic astrology, the 0° Aries ♈ point is fixed to a particular place in the backdrop of stars and never changes. Over time, in Vedic astrology the date when the Sun ☉ is at 0° Aries ♈ drifts forward in time relative to the spring equinox.

About 1,700 years ago, 0° Aries ♈ was at the same point for both Western and Vedic astrology. Since then, the 0° Aries ♈ points for both systems have slowly separated such that today, 0° Aries ♈ in Western astrology corresponds to about 6° Pisces ♓ in Vedic astrology. This 24° shift in the last 1,700 years is due to the wobble of the Earth ⊕. Today, the 0° Aries ♈ point in Vedic astrology occurs about 24 days after the spring equinox.

This brings up the natural question of which astrology system is the correct one: Western or Vedic. There are proponents on both sides of this question. Interpreting a Vedic chart is significantly different than interpreting a Western chart. My experience is that each system provides different and useful information, most of which is consistent. Philosophically, Vedic Astrology has a significantly more fatalistic interpretation when compared to Western Astrology. Those who tend to believe in a strong free will component within their lives are often drawn to Western Astrology. Those looking for specific events at specific times are drawn toward Vedic astrology

Back to Karen's Natal Chart

In Karen's Natal chart on the next page, notice the Zodiac Sign glyphs on the outermost ring and the distribution of the Planets on the next ring in. Observe, for example, that the Moon ☽ in the 2nd House is in the Zodiac Sign of Capricorn ♑. This means that the backdrop of stars behind the Moon ☽ at the time of Karen's birth corresponds to the Zodiac Sign of Capricorn ♑. In fact, Karen's Moon ☽ was at 12° 52' in Capricorn ♑. In this example, we say that Karen's Moon ☽ is in Capricorn ♑.

People are familiar with their Sun ☉ Sign. In Karen's Natal chart, the Sun ☉, which is in the 4th House, is in Pisces ♓. This means that the background portion of the sky behind the Sun ☉ viewed at the time of Karen's birth corresponds to the Zodiac Sign of Pisces ♓. Thus, we say that Karen's Sun ☉ is in Pisces ♓.

When someone asks you, "What is your Sign?" they are technically asking you, "What Sign of the Zodiac was behind your Sun ☉ when you were born?" If you read your horoscope in the morning paper or on the Internet, this only represents a very general description of only one (Sun ☉) of the numerous Planets in your Natal chart. It's like looking at one-tenth of a painting and trying to get some meaning from it. That is why daily horoscopes are found by many people to be useful, but limited in information.

40

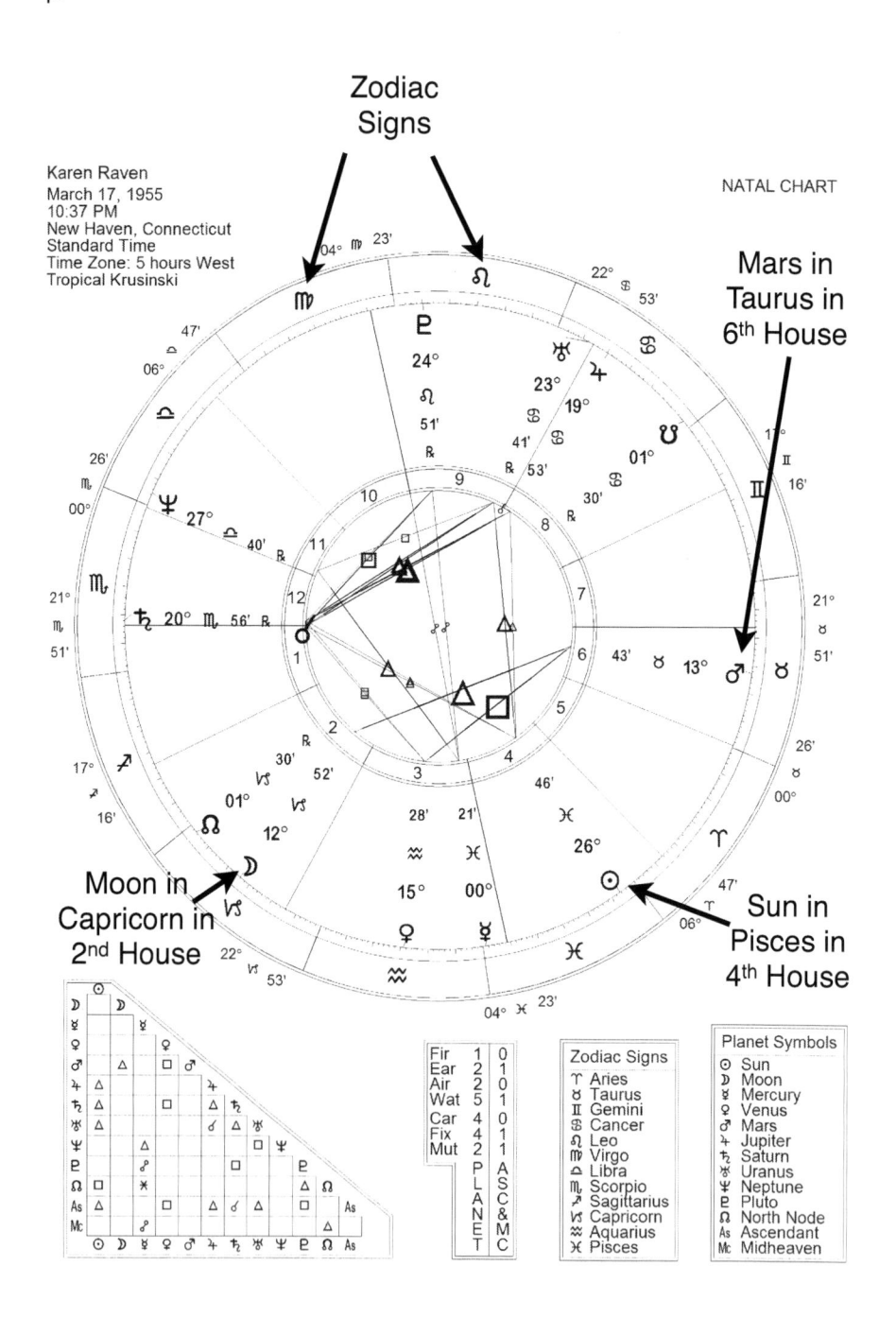

Karen Raven
March 17, 1955
10:37 PM
New Haven, Connecticut
Standard Time
Time Zone: 5 hours West
Tropical Krusinski

NATAL CHART

Zodiac Signs

Mars in Taurus in 6th House

Moon in Capricorn in 2nd House

Sun in Pisces in 4th House

Fir	1	0
Ear	2	1
Air	5	0
Wat	5	1
Car	4	0
Fix	4	1
Mut	2	1

PLANET / ASC&MC

Zodiac Signs
♈ Aries
♉ Taurus
♊ Gemini
♋ Cancer
♌ Leo
♍ Virgo
♎ Libra
♏ Scorpio
♐ Sagittarius
♑ Capricorn
♒ Aquarius
♓ Pisces

Planet Symbols
☉ Sun
☽ Moon
☿ Mercury
♀ Venus
♂ Mars
♃ Jupiter
♄ Saturn
♅ Uranus
♆ Neptune
♇ Pluto
☊ North Node
As Ascendant
Mc Midheaven

Fast Track Astrologer

The Zodiac Signs can be thought of as adding character or personality to each Planet (actor within you).

The table on the next page summarizes the key characteristics for each Sign of the Zodiac.

If you are inclined, you can jump ahead and read the detailed characteristics associated with each Sign of the Zodiac in Chapter 15 (page 91).

Let's use the example in Karen's Natal chart of her Sun ☉ in Pisces ♓. Karen's Sun ☉ is that part of her that wants to shine out in the world. Pisces ♓ adds characteristics to her Sun ☉ of being compassionate, idealistic, and connected. One way we can view Karen's Sun ☉ in Pisces ♓ is a desire to seek out the best in people and to help uplift them to a better place.

Whether Karen chooses to direct her desire to compassionately help people in a less evolved way (becoming a magnet for people who habitually take more than they give) or in a more evolved way (seeking to uplift people while respecting her own boundaries) is all part of Karen's life path toward growth and maturity. We will further explore this idea in chapters 9 and 10.

As another example, let's look at Karen's Venus ♀ in Aquarius ♒. Venus ♀ is associated with her role in having relationships with people and things, and Aquarius ♒ provides characteristics of uniqueness, innovation, and originality. Thus, Karen's approach in relationships will tend to draw out the differentness in people. This can show up as either judging or embracing the uniqueness of people. It is her free will to choose how she directs this energy.

Zodiac Sign Characteristics

Zodiac Sign	Glyph	Characteristics
Aries	♈	Pathfinder, action-oriented, spirited
Taurus	♉	Predictable, pragmatic, sensual, practical
Gemini	♊	Quick, communicative, collector of knowledge
Cancer	♋	Feeling, intuitive, nurturing, giving & receiving
Leo	♌	Creative, fun, ego balance, magnanimous
Virgo	♍	Improvement-focused, discriminating, service
Libra	♎	Harmony, balance, relationship-oriented
Scorpio	♏	Exploring the hidden depths, use of power
Sagittarius	♐	Wide-ranging, philosophical, distant ventures
Capricorn	♑	Structured, ambitious, achiever, disciplined
Aquarius	♒	Innovative, altering social paradigms, original
Pisces	♓	Spiritual connectedness, idealistic, visionary

Elements (Triplicities)

We often refer to each Zodiac Sign as having an Element of either Fire, Earth, Air, or Water (Triplicities).

Fire Signs have characteristics of projecting into the world. They include Aries ♈ (pathfinder), Leo ♌ (creative), and Sagittarius ♐ (wide-ranging). Karen's only Planet in a Fire Sign is Pluto ♇ in Leo ♌.

Earth Signs have characteristics of grounded reality. They include Taurus ♉ (practicality), Virgo ♍ (improvement), and Capricorn ♑ (results). Her Planets and Personal Points in Earth Signs are the Moon ☽ in Capricorn ♑, Mars ♂ in Taurus ♉, Midheaven M^c in Virgo ♍ (Zodiac Sign at the Cusp of the 10th House), and North Node ☊ in Capricorn ♑.

Air Signs have characteristics of thinking and communicating, such as using intellectual reasoning and logic. Air Signs include Gemini ♊ (gathering and disseminating), Libra ♎ (relationships), and Aquarius ♒ (the collective). Karen's Planets in Air Signs are Venus ♀ in Aquarius ♒ and Neptune ♆ in Libra ♎.

Zodiac Signs

Water Signs have characteristics associated with feelings, emotions, and moods. They include Cancer ♋ (nurturing), Scorpio ♏ (deep exploration), and Pisces ♓ (higher consciousness). Karen's Planets and Personal Points in Water Signs are the Sun ☉ in Pisces ♓, Mercury ☿ in Pisces ♓, Jupiter ♃ in Cancer ♋, Saturn ♄ in Scorpio ♏, Uranus ♅ in Cancer ♋, Ascendant As in Scorpio ♏ (Zodiac Sign at the Cusp of the 1st House), and the South Node ☋ in Cancer ♋.

Notice that every fourth Zodiac Sign on the outer ring of the Natal chart is in the same Element. This is an easy way to quickly remember the Elements.

In a Natal chart, we typically count the number of Planets in each Element. In Karen's Natal chart (page 40) on the bottom center, we see a table that lists the number of Planets in each Element. This saves you the trouble of counting the Planets spread throughout Karen's Natal chart. The table also shows the Elements associated with the Ascendant As and Midheaven Mc (right column).

Notice that in Karen's chart, five of her 10 Planets are in Water Signs (Sun ☉, Mercury ☿, Jupiter ♃, Uranus ♅, and Saturn ♄). This abundance of Planets in Water Signs will offer Karen a heightened ability to tune into feelings, instincts, moods, and emotions. As she matures, she will likely develop the ability to sense the emotional states of others, even when they are attempting to hide their feelings. This is a powerful gift for creating strong relationships and connections with others.

Qualities (Quadruplicities)

In addition to the Elements associated with the Zodiac Signs, we also consider the Qualities, sometimes referred to as Quadruplicities. There are three Qualities: Cardinal, Fixed, and Mutable.

Cardinal Signs have characteristics of initiating, making the first moves. They include Aries ♈, Cancer ♋, Libra ♎, and Capricorn ♑. Planets in Cardinal Signs are considered to be more powerful than those in Fixed and Mutable Signs as they are catalysts for change.

Fixed Signs have characteristics of building and maintaining. They include Taurus ♉, Leo ♌, Scorpio ♏, and Aquarius ♒. Planets in Fixed Signs tend to have momentum and staying power, sometimes even when conditions warrant a new direction.

Mutable Signs have characteristics of detaching from the old, exploring, and preparing for the new. They include Gemini ♊, Virgo ♍, Sagittarius ♐, and Pisces ♓. Planets in Mutable Signs are able to explore mentally, physically, or spiritually during nebulous times after letting go of the past and not yet knowing what comes next.

Notice that every third Zodiac Sign on the outer ring of Karen's Natal chart is in the same Quality. This is an easy way to quickly remember the Qualities.

At the bottom middle of Karen's Natal chart on page 40 is a table listing the number of Planets in each Quality. There are four Planets in Cardinal Signs (Jupiter ♃ and Uranus ♅ both in Cancer ♋, Neptune ♆ in Libra ♎, and Moon ☽ in Capricorn ♑), four in Fixed Signs (Mars ♂ in Taurus ♉, Pluto ♇ in Leo ♌, Saturn ♄ in Scorpio ♏, and Venus ♀ in Aquarius ♒), and two in Mutable Signs (Sun

☉ and Mercury ☿ both in Pisces ♓). Karen has quite a bit of Planetary energy in initiating, building, and maintaining (Cardinal and Fixed). For her, the nebulous times between endings and new beginnings may not feel as energizing as other times (Mutable).

Polarities

Finally, you may have heard of Polarities, which consist of Masculine and Feminine Signs of the Zodiac. This is not to be confused with gender. Whether we are male or female, we all have parts of us that are Masculine in character and Feminine in character.

Feminine Signs have characteristics in which the focus is from within. The Feminine Signs are all the Water and Earth Signs of the Zodiac. These are easily identified by walking our way around the Zodiac (outer ring in Karen's Natal chart), starting with Taurus ♉ and selecting every other Zodiac Sign. Thus, the Feminine Signs are Taurus ♉, Cancer ♋, Virgo ♍, Scorpio ♏, Capricorn ♑, and Pisces ♓. With Water Signs, the focus is on feelings, moods, emotions, and what we refer to as our sixth sense, which are all internal to ourselves. With Earth Signs, the focus is on our five senses, what works for us, what is realistic and practical, and what brings us peace and comfort, which again are all internal to ourselves.

Masculine Signs have characteristics in which the focus is outside ourselves. The Masculine Signs are all the Fire and Air Signs of the Zodiac. These are easily identified by walking our way around the Zodiac (outer ring in Karen's Natal chart), starting with Aries ♈ and selecting every other Zodiac Sign. The Masculine Signs are Aries ♈, Gemini ♊, Leo ♌, Libra ♎, Sagittarius ♐, and Aquarius ♒. With Fire Signs, the focus is on projecting out to the world. With Air Signs the focus is on our thoughts. While it's tempting to think that thoughts come from within ourselves, thoughts are just thoughts and not real. It's up to us to determine what to do with our thoughts. Sometimes we are curious about them, sometimes we bury them, and sometimes we create stories (both good and bad) to make sense of them. If this idea comes across to you as bizarre or if you are curious to explore this further, I highly recommend you read *You Can Be Happy, No Matter What*, by Richard Carlson. This is an easy read and gets the point across that your thoughts exist outside of yourself. This book also explores ways you can reduce stress in your life by recognizing thoughts for what they actually are.

The table on the next page indicates the Elements, Qualities, and Polarities for each Zodiac Sign. You'll also find this table in the appendix at the end of this book.

So far, we have discussed the Planets, which are the actors within you and part of you, and the Zodiac Signs, which add character and personality to your Planets. We also explored the interaction of Planets which are Aspected. We will now explore the Houses in the next two chapters.

Zodiac Signs

Zodiac Sign / Glyph	Element	Quality	Polarity
Aries ♈	Fire	Cardinal	Masculine
Taurus ♉	Earth	Fixed	Feminine
Gemini ♊	Air	Mutable	Masculine
Cancer ♋	Water	Cardinal	Feminine
Leo ♌	Fire	Fixed	Masculine
Virgo ♍	Earth	Mutable	Feminine
Libra ♎	Air	Cardinal	Masculine
Scorpio ♏	Water	Fixed	Feminine
Sagittarius ♐	Fire	Mutable	Masculine
Capricorn ♑	Earth	Cardinal	Feminine
Aquarius ♒	Air	Fixed	Masculine
Pisces ♓	Water	Mutable	Feminine

7 Houses

The Houses represent the areas of your life. The 12 Houses are simply numbered one through 12. Be happy we don't have to learn 12 new glyphs. You can see these Houses depicted in the slim inner ring of Karen's Natal chart on page 53, and note that the Houses are numbered counterclockwise from one to 12.

Houses are calculated such that the 1st House Cusp (beginning) is at the Ascendant A^s on the eastern horizon. Technically, the Ascendant A^s is the point where the Ecliptic (the circle formed around the Earth's surface if you were to slice the Earth in equal halves with the plane formed by the Earth ⊕ revolving around the Sun ☉) crosses the eastern horizon at the time and location of your birth. This will become clear in Chapter 27 on celestial geometry. The Ascendant A^s generally deviates north or south from due east, as described in Chapter 3. For simplicity, view the 1st House Cusp (Ascendant A^s) as at the eastern horizon.

Remember from Chapter 3 that a Natal chart is oriented such that south is up, north is down (behind the Earth ⊕), east is left, and west is right. The Ascendant A^s is on the left side of the Natal chart at the 1st House Cusp (eastern horizon).

The 7th House Cusp (beginning) is at the Descendant D^s, which is the point where the Ecliptic intersects the western horizon when and where you were born. The Descendant D^s is, by definition, 180° from the Ascendant A^s. This point will not generally be due west. You can think of the 7th House Cusp as at the western horizon.

The 10th House Cusp (beginning) is at the Midheaven M^c, which is the point in the sky at the intersection of the Ecliptic and an arc formed by pointing straight up at the birth location and sweeping your arm to the south. Because south is up in a Natal chart, the Midheaven M^c is toward the top of the Natal chart at the Cusp (beginning) of the 10th House. The Midheaven M^c generally will not be vertical in a Natal chart because of geometrical considerations portrayed in Chapter 27 on celestial geometry. Again, for simplicity, think of the top of the Natal chart as south (up).

The 4th House Cusp (beginning) is at the Imum Coeli I^c. The Imum Coeli I^c is simply 180° (opposite) the Midheaven M^c. The 4th House Cusp is toward the bottom of a Natal chart, but not exactly vertical for the same reasons that the 10th House Cusp is not exactly vertical. For the sake of simplicity, think of the bottom of the Natal chart as north (behind the Earth ⊕).

If you were born at sunrise, you would see your Sun ☉ on the Cusp (beginning) of your 1st House. If you were born at sunset, your Sun ☉ would be on the Cusp of your 7th House. If you were born around midday, you would see your Sun ☉ near the Cusp of your 10th House

(Midheaven M^c), and if you were born around midnight, your Sun ☉ would be near your 4th House Cusp (Imum Coeli I^c).

Observe that the Houses have differing sizes. This apparent distortion occurs because of the way Houses are calculated, which often involves geometric projections from one curved surface to another. The chapter on celestial geometry will clarify this.

There are a variety of House systems, each with its own unique philosophy and method of calculation. For Karen's chart, I used the Krusiński House system. We will hold off on more exploration of House systems until chapters 27 and 28.

Another quirk associated with the Houses is that the time from sunrise to sunset is greater or less than 12 hours. For example, in the northern hemisphere around the time of the summer solstice, the time from sunrise to sunset may be 15 hours, and from sunset to sunrise nine hours. If we simulate the movement of the Planets in the Natal chart over the course of 24 hours in this situation, the Sun ☉ would take 15 hours to traverse from the Ascendant A^s to the Descendant D^s (Houses 12, 11, 10, 9, 8, 7) and only nine hours to traverse from the Descendant D^s to the Ascendant A^s (Houses 6, 5, 4, 3, 2, 1). This is because the tilt of the Ecliptic changes throughout the day, which has the effect of changing the Zodiac positions of the Ascendant A^s and Descendant D^s throughout the day.

Viewing the positions of the Planets in Karen's Natal chart, Uranus ♅ and Jupiter ♃ (both near the 9th House Cusp) were toward the south-southwest and next to each other (south is up and west is to the right in a Natal chart). Saturn ♄, which is close to the 1st House Cusp (Ascendant A^s), had just risen from the eastern horizon. With Karen's birth at night, you would expect the Sun ☉ to be in the bottom half of Karen's Natal chart, and it is, in fact, in the 4th House.

The Houses represent the areas in life and are summarized in the table on page 54. **You might want to now explore all 12 Houses in more depth (Chapter 16 on page 97).**

Let's go back to Karen's Natal chart and get a partial taste of how the Houses work. The 4th House is the area of life associated with Karen's home and her roots. She has her Sun ☉ in Pisces ♓ in her 4th House. Since her Sun ☉ is her main actor, this would indicate that Karen's home life is important to her and that she may even find herself preferring to spend significant time in her home.

Now let's take a look at Karen's 7th House. Oops! There are no Planets. That does NOT mean that Karen will have no hope for relationships (7th House area of life). We will explore this in more detail in the next chapter and in Chapter 26. Note that there are also no Planets in the 1st, 5th, and 10th Houses in Karen's Natal chart.

Up to this point, we understand that a Planet is an actor within you, part of you playing a specific role; has characteristics given by its Zodiac Sign; and emphasizes its role in the House it resides. Furthermore, Planets (parts of you) which are Aspected will play their roles in unison.

Let's focus next on the basics of House activity.

53

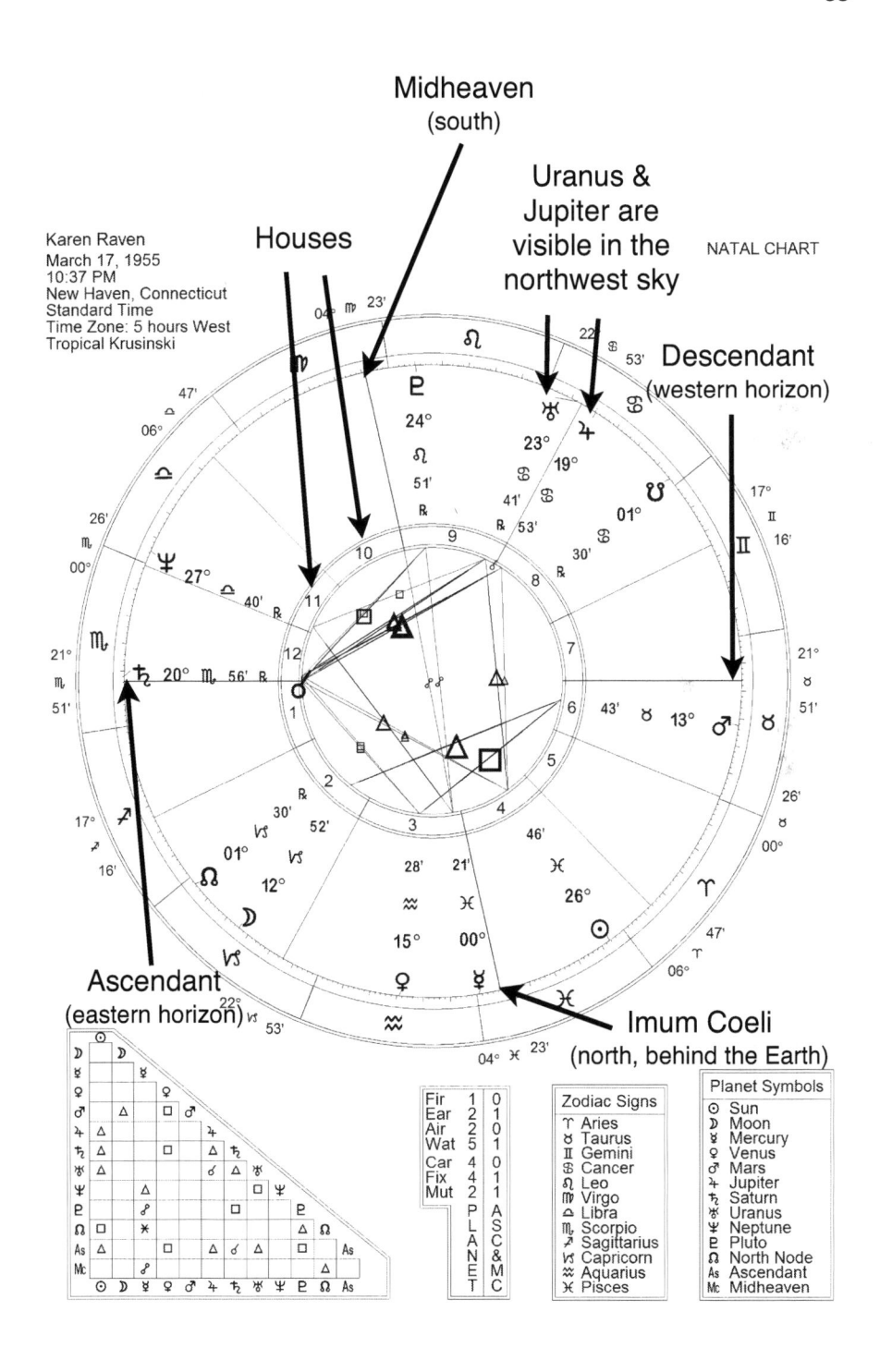

Karen Raven
March 17, 1955
10:37 PM
New Haven, Connecticut
Standard Time
Time Zone: 5 hours West
Tropical Krusinski

NATAL CHART

- Midheaven (south)
- Houses
- Uranus & Jupiter are visible in the northwest sky
- Descendant (western horizon)
- Ascendant (eastern horizon)
- Imum Coeli (north, behind the Earth)

Fir	1	0
Ear	2	1
Air	5	0
Wat	4	1
Car	4	0
Fix	4	1
Mut	2	1

PLANET / ASC & MC

Zodiac Signs
- ♈ Aries
- ♉ Taurus
- ♊ Gemini
- ♋ Cancer
- ♌ Leo
- ♍ Virgo
- ♎ Libra
- ♏ Scorpio
- ♐ Sagittarius
- ♑ Capricorn
- ♒ Aquarius
- ♓ Pisces

Planet Symbols
- ☉ Sun
- ☽ Moon
- ☿ Mercury
- ♀ Venus
- ♂ Mars
- ♃ Jupiter
- ♄ Saturn
- ♅ Uranus
- ♆ Neptune
- ♇ Pluto
- ☊ North Node
- As Ascendant
- Mc Midheaven

Houses

Areas of Life for each House

House	Areas of Life
1st	How you convey yourself to other people
2nd	Possessions, how you earn money, self-confidence
3rd	Your thinking and communicating, short-term travel
4th	Home, psychological roots, family patterns
5th	Creativity, recreation, hobbies, pleasure, fun, romance
6th	Daily routines and habits, health attitudes
7th	Close relationships, influence, diplomacy, intimacy
8th	Cycles of death and rebirth, resource sharing, sexuality
9th	Long-distance travel, philosophy, higher education, ethics
10th	Career, reputation, status, achievement
11th	Your dreams and aspirations, friends and associations
12th	Your inner sanctuary and how you care for it

8 House Activity

House activity gets a little complicated, even for many astrologers. For me, this was the hardest part of astrology to learn. There is so much going on in each House that it can be overwhelming for the beginner. Because of this, in this chapter I have provided the basics of House activity used by the majority of astrologers. Some astrologers also use more advanced techniques, which we will cover in Chapter 26. Don't let this fool you though. The basics of House activity covered in this chapter provide a wealth of information.

As a review, there are 10 Planets representing our internal actors that each have a unique role to play, 12 Zodiac Signs providing characteristics to each of the Planets, and 12 Houses signifying the areas of life emphasized by the Planets.

With 10 Planets and 12 Houses, at least two Houses, and usually more, will be empty since more than one Planet typically lies in some Houses. In Karen's Natal chart on the next page, notice that there are no Planets in the 1st, 5th, 7th, and 10th Houses.

56

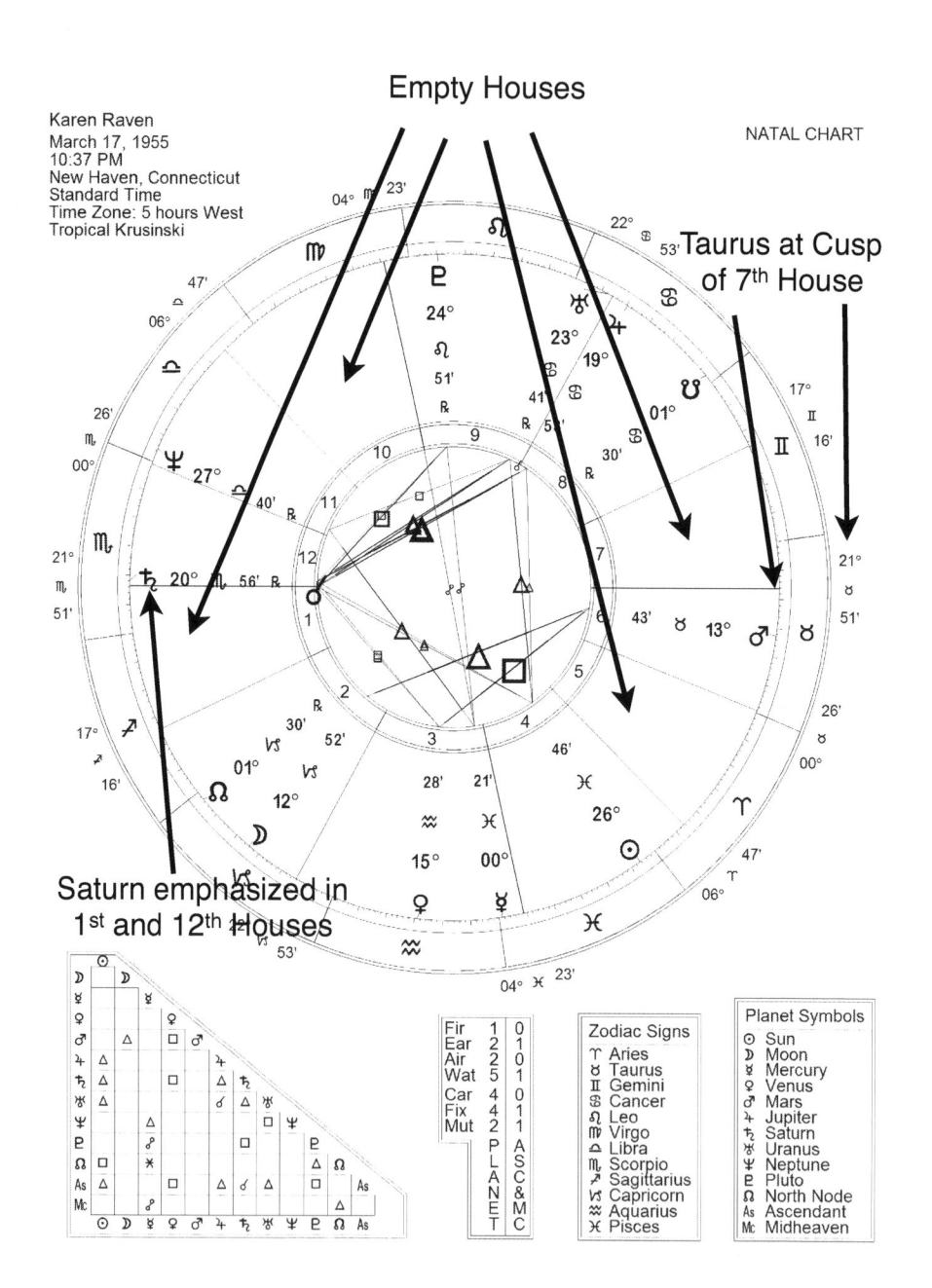

Empty Houses

Karen Raven
March 17, 1955
10:37 PM
New Haven, Connecticut
Standard Time
Time Zone: 5 hours West
Tropical Krusinski

NATAL CHART

Taurus at Cusp of 7th House

Saturn emphasized in 1st and 12th Houses

Fir	1	0
Ear	2	1
Air	2	0
Wat	5	1
Car	4	0
Fix	4	1
Mut	2	1
	P L A N E T	A S C & M C

Zodiac Signs
♈ Aries
♉ Taurus
♊ Gemini
♋ Cancer
♌ Leo
♍ Virgo
♎ Libra
♏ Scorpio
♐ Sagittarius
♑ Capricorn
♒ Aquarius
♓ Pisces

Planet Symbols
☉ Sun
☽ Moon
☿ Mercury
♀ Venus
♂ Mars
♃ Jupiter
♄ Saturn
♅ Uranus
♆ Neptune
♇ Pluto
☊ North Node
As Ascendant
Mc Midheaven

Fast Track Astrologer

So, how do we figure out the activity in a House (area of life)?

This activity comes from seven sources: (1) All Planets, (2) Planets within a House, (3) Planets near the borders of a House, (4) the Zodiac Sign at the Cusp of the House, (5) Planets that Rule the House, (6) Natural Rulers of Houses, and (7) Intercepted Houses.

In this chapter, we will look at the first four of the seven sources. We will cover the remaining three sources in Chapter 26 on advanced House activity. My suggestion is that you initially only use the four sources covered in this chapter. At some point in the future, you can then experiment with the remaining three sources in Chapter 26.

1. All Planets

It is important to recognize that all your Planets (parts of you) play their roles in all Houses (areas of life). While a particular Planet emphasizes its role in particular Houses, that same Planet is also active in all other Houses, though with not as much emphasis.

2. Planets within a House

A Planet in a particular House has an emphasis in that area of life. For example, Karen's Natal chart has her Moon ☽ in Capricorn ♑ in her 2nd House. While her Moon ☽ is active in all Houses, it has an emphasized role in her 2nd House of possessions, values, and self confidence.

3. Planets near the borders of a House

A Planet in a neighboring House (on either side) and close to the border of the House will emphasize its role in both Houses. In Karen's Natal chart, her Saturn ♄ in Scorpio ♏ is in her 12th House and also very close to her 1st House. In this situation, Saturn ♄ will also be emphasized in Karen's 1st House as well as her 12th House. I generally consider a Planet within 3° from a House border to emphasize its role in both Houses.

4. Zodiac Sign at the Cusp of a House

The Zodiac Sign at the Cusp of a House will indicate the characteristics for that House (area of life). For example, in Karen's Natal chart above, Taurus ♉ is at the Cusp (beginning of) of her 7th House (close relationships). Viewing the characteristics of Taurus ♉ (see appendix), Karen will, in part, desire close relationships (7th House) that offer practicality, security, safety, predictability, and peace.

Example

Let's look at an example of Karen's 8th House of transformation and show how the first four sources of activity play into that House.

1. **All Planets:** All Planets play their roles in Karen's 8th House.

2. **Planets Within a House:** Jupiter ♃ is in Karen's 8th House, so the Jupiter ♃ role within Karen (expansion and optimism) will be emphasized in her 8th House.

3. **Planets Near the borders of a House:** Uranus ♅ is in Karen's 9th House, about 1° from the end of her 8th House. So the Uranus ♅ role played out by Karen (unique, original) will also have an emphasis in her 8th House of transformation.

4. **Zodiac Sign at the Cusp of a House:** Gemini ♊ is at the Cusp of Karen's 8th House. Her approach toward transformation (8th House) will involve rapid and frequent changes (Gemini ♊).

Using Karen's Natal chart, I've summarized the House activity for the four sources in the table on the next page. While it is a bit complicated, it will be worth it for you to examine this chart to be sure you can make sense of all the entries. Notice that Taurus ♉ is at the Cusp of both the 6th and 7th Houses, and that Scorpio ♏ is at the Cusp of both the 12th and 1st Houses. Also, Aquarius ♒ and Leo ♌ are not at the Cusps of any Houses. We will explore this more in Chapter 26 on advanced House activity.

Chapter 26 covers the remaining three sources for House activity. Most people new to astrology are best served by first practicing the four sources described in this chapter, and then at some time in the future, learning the remaining three sources. **If you are comfortable in your understanding of the four sources described in this chapter and you are curious about the three additional sources, this is a good time to jump to Chapter 26 on advanced House activity.**

Next we will get to the very important area of fate versus free will as well as growth and maturity.

House Activity for Karen's Natal Chart

House	Planets & Personal Points in House	Planets near the House borders	Zodiac Sign at Cusp
1st		Saturn ♄	Scorpio ♏
2nd	Moon ☽ N. Node ☊		Sagittarius ♐
3rd	Venus ♀ Mercury ☿		Capricorn ♑
4th	Sun ☉		Pisces ♓
5th			Aries ♈
6th	Mars ♂		Taurus ♉
7th			Taurus ♉
8th	Jupiter ♃ S. Node ☋	Uranus ♅	Gemini ♊
9th	Uranus ♅ Pluto ♇	Jupiter ♃	Cancer ♋
10th			Virgo ♍
11th	Neptune ♆		Libra ♎
12th	Saturn ♄	Neptune ♆	Scorpio ♏

Fast Track Astrologer

9   Fate Versus Free Will

There is one area associated with astrology that often inhibits people from considering its use: fate versus free will. It would be pretty scary if an astrologer told you specifically what was going to happen to you, or that rough times lie ahead, or that you have a crummy Natal chart and are destined to a life of misery. Believe it or not, this is the way Western astrology used to be practiced. This does not serve the client, and worse, may lead to a self-fulfilling prophecy.

As Western Astrology evolved over the past several hundred years, its approach has shifted from being predominantly fatalistic to prominently emphasizing free will. In the distant past, Western Astrology readings were conveyed as specific events happening at specific times as well as a person having a blessed or a cursed Natal chart.

For this reason, the Catholic church banned the use of astrology around 1,700 years ago, even though the Bible is littered with references to astrology and Planetary cycles. Because a foundation of Christianity posits that people are born sinners and have their lifetime to redeem themselves through their free will, the former fatalistic use of astrology conflicted with this doctrine.

Now, Western Astrology holds that free will is a significant factor. Thus the concern voiced by the Catholic church has been addressed by virtue of Western astrology having evolved to a free-will focus. Note that Vedic Astrology has a much larger fated component.

Today in Western Astrology, astrologers universally agree that the Natal chart describes the energy within you during your lifetime. It is your choice (free will) to direct your unique energetic make up, sometimes in ways that are constructive and sometimes destructive. You have your lifetime to grow and mature in your choices. Thus, there is NO such thing as a good or a bad Natal chart. What makes the difference is how you exercise your free will in choosing to direct your unique energetic combination.

As an example, suppose you have Mars ♂ in Aries ♈ in the 6th House in your Natal chart. Mars ♂ is the part of you that takes action to get what you want. Aries ♈ gives Mars ♂ an energy that is very adventurous, pioneering, self-sufficient, intense, quick to react, and impulsive. The 6th House represents everyday routines. So if you have Mars ♂ in Aries ♈ in the 6th House and you are evolved in using this energy well, you will respond quickly and effectively in day-to-day situations by rapidly creating and implementing solutions that address your challenges. When you are less evolved in directing this same energy, you may deal with day-to-day situations by routinely making "shoot from the hip" decisions without getting other people involved, and then aggressively pushing your decisions on people without regard to their feelings or needs. Note that you are directing the same energy in different ways depending on your growth and maturity.

The important point in the above example is that you have a unique energetic combination and YOU choose to direct this energy by exercising your free will.

The more unaware and unconscious you are of your unique energetic make-up, the more likely you will resort to autopilot modes that often follow your family patterns. When you are conscious of your unique energetic make up and view it as a gift, your growth in maturely directing your energy will accelerate.

Let's continue this conversation further because it is so important.

10 Growth in Maturity

Let's continue to explore this idea that you have a unique energetic makeup determined at birth AND the free will in deciding how to direct this energy. This implies growth and maturity in choices you make throughout your life.

Earlier in life, you expressed your energy in ways that were sometimes helpful and often not particularly helpful. In either situation, you received a patterned response from your parents (or caregivers). This set up patterns of behavior that you learned early in life.

If you acted out in destructive ways and the response from your parents was to teach you to redirect your energy in more constructive ways, you learned appropriate behaviors that served you well later in life. If, on the other hand, you directed your energy in destructive ways and your parents still gave you what you wanted, a pattern developed that did not serve you well and was often hard to break later in life.

Either way, these are what I call autopilot patterns you learned at an early age. With a favorable upbringing, your growth in constructively directing your unique combination of energy was rapid. In other situations, you had to let go of ineffective ways of directing your energy and replace them with more effective ways. It's still the same energy, just directed differently by you.

One thing that does not work is to suppress or bottle up your energy. This usually results in stress and frustration and then expressing yourself in unhelpful ways at the most inopportune times. A much better approach is to honor your unique combination of energy and learn to channel it in more effective ways.

Understanding your unique energetic combination through your Natal chart and how to direct your energy in constructive ways will accelerate your growth and effectiveness.

Congratulations! You now have an understanding of the fundamentals of astrology. The next section of this book serves as a deeper exploration of the Planets, Aspects, Planet Combinations, Zodiac Signs, and Houses.

Exploration of the Major Components

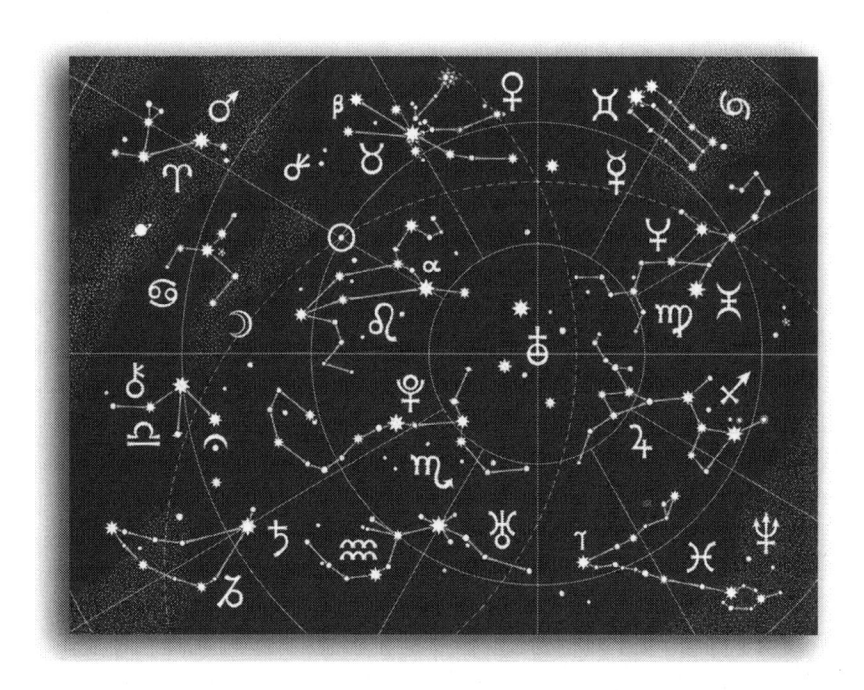

11 Exploration of Planets

The Planets can be thought of as the actors within yourself. Each of these parts of you play a specific role in your life. As with all actors in real life, you develop these parts of yourself over time, resulting in your progression from immaturity to maturity. Some of this development seems to come easily and other development takes significant effort, sometimes by getting hit over the side of the head with a metaphorical 2-by-4.

Below is a brief description of the roles associated with each Planet. Note that the Planets have character traits associated with the Signs of the Zodiac they are in. These Zodiac Sign characteristics are described in more detail in Chapter 15.

Let's take a look at the roles for each Planet.

The **Sun** ☉ can be thought of as the main actor in your life experience. Its role within you is to shine out into the world. The Sun ☉ represents the core of who you are, the source of your creativity, and how you make sense of your world. When your Sun ☉ is less developed, you may have an imbalance between your self-confidence and your actual capabilities (ego challenges), having too much or too little. When your Sun ☉ is well developed, you project yourself into the world in a way that promotes your ideals while honoring the ideals of others.

The **Moon** ☽ actress part of yourself seeks out what you need to nurture yourself and plays a role in how you nurture others. Its language is feelings, moods, and emotions. When your Moon ☽ is out of balance, you may display a range of behaviors from being moody, needy, and demanding to burying your own feelings and needs. When your Moon ☽ is balanced, you find yourself tuning into and caretaking your feelings, emotions, and moods and being conscious that this is an essential part of finding happiness and inner peace. From this grounded and recharged place, you will be better able to nurture others.

Mercury ☿ is the part of you representing your approach toward thinking and communicating. When your Mercury ☿ is less developed, you may find yourself communicating in a way that only fits your autopilot style and not necessarily that of others. With a well-developed Mercury ☿, you think in a way that is clear and concise, and when communicating, you have a powerful influence in shaping the thoughts and feelings of others.

Venus ♀ is the actress within you that has a magnetic personality and attracts relationships, money, possessions, beauty, art, and music. When the Venus ♀ part of you is less developed, you may attract what you desire in imbalanced ways. This can show up as an imbalance in the giving and receiving within your relationships, an imbalance in the earning and spending of money, an imbalance in the possessions you acquire, and an inappropriate use of your physical beauty to manipulate or mislead. When your Venus ♀ is well developed, you are clear about who and what you want to attract, are conscious of the "magnetic" signals you send out, and foster balance in your relationships with people, money, and possessions.

Mars ♂ is the part of you that goes into action when you want something. When your Mars ♂ is less developed, you may find yourself primarily focusing on your wants without regard to others. You may also create unrealistic expectations of others, ranging from ignoring their feelings and desires to expecting them to read your mind. You may show up as a "bull in a china shop" or as passive aggressive. When your Mars ♂ is well developed, you obtain what you want in an assertive, respectful, and collaborative way while honoring your boundaries as well as the boundaries of others. You will also have the patience to collaborate with others before acting.

Jupiter ♃ is the actor within you that is optimistic and expansive. Jupiter's ♃ role is to extend beyond your self-imposed boundaries and venture toward larger endeavors over longer distances as well as to explore higher learning and the meaning and philosophies of life. When your Jupiter ♃ is less developed, you may follow the mantra: "Anything worth doing is worth overdoing." This shows up as indulgence, excess, speculation, and impracticality. When the Jupiter

♃ part of you is well developed, you understand that optimism and expansion, combined with a dose of reality and practicality, is a formula for your success.

Saturn ♄ is the part of you that wants to perform a "sanity check." Saturn's ♄ role is to create boundaries, structures, and limitations for one of two purposes: to get results or to protect you from what you fear. When your Saturn ♄ is less developed, you may find yourself creating self-imposed boundaries that, while well-intentioned, don't serve your intended purpose. This can range from being too controlling of yourself and others at one extreme to unconsciously putting yourself in situations where you are giving up your power to others. When your Saturn ♄ is well developed, boundaries become an art form for you. You construct boundaries that are clear, respectful, and flexible, and feel good when honored. Artful boundaries allow you to feel safe and to get great results while at the same time permitting yourself and others to have plenty of freedom.

Uranus ♅ represents the part of you that wants to "march to the beat of your own drum" and is willing to break free from constraints that prevent you from being who you want to be. Uranus ♅ is also interested in helping to "take the shackles off" and make your world a better place. When your Uranus ♅ is less developed, you may be rebellious, disconnected from the mainstream, and unsympathetic with others who don't believe in your causes. When your Uranus ♅ is well developed, your are on the leading edge of change and innovation, shifting paradigms for the common good, and creating support from others for freedom and liberation.

Neptune ♆ is the actor within you that desires to live beyond the ego, who you really are, your connection with all that exists and beyond, your spirituality, the highest form of love, and higher levels of consciousness. When your Neptune ♆ is less developed, you may find yourself chronically "tuning out" from reality and living in a dream world. This is sometimes accomplished by alcohol, drugs, or spending hours vegetating in front of the television. When your Neptune ♆ is well developed, you discern the difference between true spiritual inner growth and that which is false, misleading, and illusive. You live your life with compassion, understanding, idealism, joy, and peace by consistently coming from the heart.

Pluto ♇ is the part of you that seeks profound growth and transformation as you experience the cycles of death and rebirth in your life. This part of you is there to help you let go of what no longer serves you and make room for new growth, which leads to profound transformation in your life. Pluto ♇ operates at a level deep beneath the surface and often touches those areas Carl G. Jung refers to as the shadow: the parts of you that you don't like, don't want to acknowledge, or want to keep hidden. With a less-developed Pluto ♇, you may use your power in dysfunctional ways to perpetuate the status quo, even when doing that comes at the expense of yourself or others. When your Pluto ♇ is well developed, you display inquisitiveness, openness, deep exploration, acceptance, and surrender to pave the way for profound growth and transformation. Note that the symbol for Pluto is sometimes represented as ♆.

Let's now explore the Aspects.

12 Exploration of Aspects

When two or more Planets are at important angles with each other, their energies interact in unison. These important angles in astrology are referred to as Aspects and are divided into Major Aspects and Minor Aspects. In this chapter, we will explore the major Aspects (Conjunction ☌, Opposition ☍, Trine △, and Square □) as well as the Sextile ✶. The various Aspects provide information on how your Planets (parts of you) will likely interact when you are less evolved. As you mature and become skilled at directing these parts of yourself (Planets), you find the gifts in Aspected Planets, regardless of the specific Aspect.

Let's look at some of these Aspects and how their interactions may manifest in your lifetime evolution.

Conjunction ☌: When two Planets are next to each other (0°), they are likely in the same Sign of the Zodiac, which means they have the same Polarity, same Element, and same Quality. Thus, these parts of you have similar characteristics, approaches, tactics, and behaviors. You are familiar with situations in which a person bothers you and, upon reflection, find out that what bothers you about the other person has to do with facets of yourself you don't like or don't want to acknowledge. It's about you, not the other person. This is what Conjunct ☌ Planets within you are like when you are less evolved in mastering these parts of yourself. Also, because the two Planets are likely to have the same Quality, they will have a tendency to compete for the Quality they mutually possess (e.g. Cardinal) and lack energy for the two they don't possess (e.g. Fixed and Mutable). Your growth path with Conjunct ☌ Planets is to embrace your whole self—the parts you like about yourself and the parts you don't like about yourself.

Opposition ☍: When two Planets are opposite each other (180°), they likely are in their opposite Signs of the Zodiac (e.g. Pisces ♓ and Virgo ♍). Opposite Signs of the Zodiac tend to highlight each other's shortcomings or missing parts. For example, Pisces ♓ has characteristics that are compassionate, connected, and idealistic, while Virgo ♍ has characteristics that are very practical, precise, and analytical. Also, both Planets generally will be in Masculine Zodiac Signs or both will be in Feminine Zodiac Signs. Furthermore, one generally will be in an Air Sign and the other in a Fire Sign (which tend to be compatible), or one will be in a Water Sign while the other will be in an Earth Sign (which also tend to be compatible). Finally, both Planets generally will be in the same Quality (e.g. both Cardinal), so they will both have energy in the same Quality and less so in the other two Qualities (e.g. Fixed and Mutable). This means that they both will have a tendency to compete, say in initiating, while neither has much energy in the other two Qualities, say building, maintaining, and transitioning. In general, these parts of you (Planets) will be compatible while also providing what the other needs, with the exception of the Qualities where they may compete for the Quality they both possess. The growth path is to learn to embrace each Planet's (parts of you) strengths and to support the mutually missing Qualities. When done well, this is a very powerful combination because collectively, the Planets (parts of you) become more whole.

Trine △: Planets that are one-third of a circle (120°) from each other are generally in the same Element (e.g. both in Earth Signs) and in different Qualities (e.g. one Cardinal and one Fixed). Furthermore, both Planets likely will be in Feminine Zodiac Signs or both in Masculine Zodiac Signs. This tends to create an easy, flowing combination because these parts of you are the same in their Element (e.g. in Earth Signs—both grounded and practical) and have different Qualities so they don't need to compete (e.g. one part of you likes to initiate and the other likes to build and maintain). When these Planets within you are less evolved, you can get too comfortable or confident with the winning combination and either walk yourself off a cliff (especially if Mars ♂ or Jupiter ♃ are in the mix) or get complacent (especially if Venus ♀ or Neptune ♆ are in the mix). When done well, you learn to use these compatible Planetary gifts consistently.

Square □: Planets that are one-quarter of a circle (90°) from each other are very different, almost like two foreigners from different cultures. They most likely will be in different and less compatible Elements (e.g. Fire and Water, Fire and Earth, Air and Water, or Air and Earth), and have the same Qualities (e.g. Mutable) so there may be competition for their mutually-preferred Quality. Furthermore, one Planet will likely be in a Feminine Sign and the other in a Masculine Sign. In less-evolved states, these parts of you (Planets) can be like oil and water. They have very different characteristics, approaches, and tactics. Furthermore, these parts of you have energy surrounding the same Quality, which can show up as internal competition. In general, Planets that are Square □ take the most time and experience for you to evolve into a well-developed state. However, once you mature in these energies, your strengths tend to become towering.

Sextile ✶: Planets that are one-sixth of a circle (60°) from each other are usually either both Masculine in Sign or both Feminine in Sign. Furthermore, they have different Qualities (e.g. Cardinal and Fixed), so there is little competition. While they are in different Elements, the Elements are likely to be compatible (i.e. either in Fire and Air, or in Water and Earth). While this is not quite as compatible a combination as the Trine △ (where both Planets are in the same Element), it's not far from it. In less-developed stages, this combination within you, like the Trines △, can either become too complacent or too confident. With a bit of maturity, this combination can work harmoniously together.

The Aspects reveal which Planets (parts of you playing specific roles) are active in unison and how they will interact when at less-evolved stages. You often learn to master your Trine △ and Sextile ✶ Planetary combinations earlier in life than you master those that are Conjunct ☌, Opposition ☍, or especially Square □.

When your Planets within you are evolved, you will direct these parts of you well, regardless of the type of Aspect linking your Planets.

13 Two Planet Combinations

The interactions between Planets (parts of yourself) create interesting and unique challenges and gifts, depending on your maturity in their combined use. When two or more of your Planets are Aspected, these parts of you want to be heard at the same time.

As described in Chapter 5, these important Aspects include the Major Aspects: Conjunction (0° ☌), Opposition (180° ☍), Trine (120° △), and Square (90° □) as well as numerous Minor Aspects including the Sextile (60° ✶), Semisquare (45° ∠), Inconjunct (150° ⚻), and Sesquiquadrate (135° ⚼).

Aspects affect the method of growth between your Planets (parts of yourself) but not the desired end state. The paths toward growth and maturity are just different.

I have discovered that people gain more insight by simply understanding how the energies of their Planet combinations can manifest, ranging from the less evolved to the more evolved. Telling the client that a particular combination is going to be easy or hard to handle does not serve him well. In practice, I primarily use the Major

Aspects plus the Sextile ✶, as they seem to consistently foster insightful dialog and there are more than enough of them to handle in a single consultation.

This chapter only includes combinations of two Planets. Developing meaning from combinations of three or more Planets is very useful, but because there are hundreds of such combinations, I did not include them in this book.

The descriptions of the Planet combinations below are generic in the sense that their energies are also ultimately colored by the Zodiac Signs and their emphasis in Houses.

With that being said, here is a succinct description of how you can grow in various two-Planet combinations.

Sun ☉ Combinations

Sun - Moon (☉ ☽): Growth in the ability to move on a positive path using your innate creativity and desires in combination with a sensitivity to your basic needs.

Sun - Mercury (☉ ☿): Growth in the ability to be a genuine authority as an independent thinker and communicator while still being open to the thoughts and ideas of others.

Sun - Venus (☉ ♀): Growth in the ability to love and be loved in a way that is mutually balanced and from the heart.

Sun - Mars (☉ ♂): Growth in the ability to attain accomplishments by taking action in a way that is assertive and respectful.

Sun - Jupiter (☉ ♃): Growth in the ability to inspire with confidence and optimism in the pursuit of far-reaching yet realistic endeavors.

Sun - Saturn (☉ ♄): Growth in the ability to get results through time, patience, and significant effort in a way that is structured yet flexible enough to allow room for creativity.

Sun - Uranus (☉ ♅): Growth in the ability to gracefully make changes that are more closely aligned with who you really are while respecting that you are entangled in a system that naturally resists change.

Sun - Neptune (☉ ♆): Growth in the ability to transcend the ego and move to deeper forms of spirituality and love while maintaining a healthy respect for your own individuality.

Sun - Pluto (☉ ♇): Growth in the ability to recognize and act on the need for profound transformation through surrender, acceptance, respectful use of power, and support from others.

Remaining Moon ☽ Combinations

Moon - Mercury (☽ ☿): Growth in the ability to respect and reconcile instinct and feelings with rational thought, and to powerfully communicate from both the head and the heart.

Moon - Venus (☽ ♀): Growth in the ability and willingness to have relationships that are balanced and mutually support each other's needs.

Moon - Mars (☽ ♂): Growth in the ability to respond to situations in a way that involves mutual sharing of feelings and needs before taking action.

Moon - Jupiter (☽ ♃): Growth in the ability to be caring, good-natured, and generous with others as well as with yourself.

Moon - Saturn (☽ ♄): Growth in the ability to be emotionally connected with others while simultaneously focusing on desired accomplishments.

Moon - Uranus (☽ ♅): Growth in the ability to create an environment where you and others have the freedom to express your common interests in an emotionally-connected manner.

Moon - Neptune (☽ ♆): Growth in the ability to be compassionate and empathetic while still maintaining clear boundaries between yourself and others.

Moon - Pluto (☽ ♇): Growth in the ability to dive deeply into emotions and feelings while respecting your power and motives.

Remaining Mercury ☿ Combinations

Mercury - Venus (☿ ♀): Growth in the ability to be diplomatic, charming, and graceful in your communication while still being clear about your needs.

Mercury - Mars (☿ ♂): Growth in the ability to assertively share ideas with others, communicate with powerful influence, and effectively solicit action.

Mercury - Jupiter (☿ ♃): Growth in the ability to optimistically and confidently think and communicate big ideas, concepts, aspirations, and philosophies in a way that is realistic and can achieve practical results.

Mercury - Saturn (☿ ♄): Growth in the ability to become a voice of authority through hard work, achievement of results, flexible control, and awareness of the needs of others.

Mercury - Uranus (☿ ♅): Growth in the ability to think radically and freely in order to create and communicate beneficial solutions that work alongside of or within existing systems.

Mercury - Neptune (☿ ♆): Growth in the ability to conceptualize and practically communicate that which is spiritual, mystical, mysterious, and nebulous.

Mercury - Pluto (☿ ♇): Growth in the ability to be a powerful and transformative communicator using positive influence and respectful participation with others.

Remaining Venus ♀ Combinations

Venus - Mars (♀ ♂): Growth in the ability to have romantic adventures, immerse oneself in the arts, and acquire resources with respectful, sincere, and genuine intent.

Venus - Jupiter (♀ ♃): Growth in the ability to have positive and expansive energy in relationships while being present to the effort it takes to continually nurture and enhance those close to you.

Venus - Saturn (♀ ♄): Growth in the ability to develop lasting relationships through artful boundaries and safety, which allow the opening up of heart-to-heart exploration.

Venus - Uranus (♀ ♅): Growth in the ability to continually explore and experiment with and within relationships in ways that are liberating, original, and emotionally connected.

Venus - Neptune (♀ ♆): Growth in the ability to have wonderful, romantic, made-in-heaven relationships by carefully selecting partners who are compassionate, idealistic, and spiritually evolved.

Venus - Pluto (♀ ♇): Growth in the ability to develop deep, intense, and transformational relationships by creating a safe space for the relationships to flourish.

Remaining Mars ♂ Combinations

Mars - Jupiter (♂ ♃): Growth in the ability to pursue and effectively participate in causes that have larger life purposes and wide-ranging involvement, and accomplishing this through assertiveness, positive influence skills, and a dose of realism.

Mars - Saturn (♂ ♄): Growth in the ability to direct strong ambition and energy in a way that is participatory, efficient, effective, and flexibly structured.

Mars - Uranus (♂ ♅): Growth in the ability to create novel and liberating change through assertiveness, initiative, and patience.

Mars - Neptune (♂ ♆): Growth in the ability to act on visions, dreams, and ideals in a way that respects your boundaries and the boundaries of others.

Mars - Pluto (♂ ♇): Growth in the ability to guide strong energy and desire in fruitful and productive directions using approaches that get to the root of situations.

Remaining Jupiter ♃ Combinations

Jupiter - Saturn (♃ ♄): Growth in the ability to realize big dreams through patience, hard work, and a willingness to be inclusive of the perspective and ideas of others.

Jupiter - Uranus (♃ ♅): Growth in the ability to engage in radical and original pursuits that improve the lives of yourself and others in a way that considers existing norms.

Jupiter - Neptune (♃ ♆): Growth in the desire and ability to expand one's consciousness and relationships with higher forms of love, compassion, understanding, and empathy and to develop higher meaning from these pursuits.

Jupiter - Pluto (♃ ♇): Growth in the ability to explore the depths of the unseen and the unconscious in order to increase awareness and insight that lead to profound transformation.

Remaining Saturn ♄ Combinations

Saturn - Uranus (♄ ♅): Growth in the ability to realize radical and beneficial change using effective structure, discipline, and patience.

Saturn - Neptune (♄ ♆): Growth in the ability to enter the realms of the unseen in pragmatic and methodical ways in order to open yourself to empathy, compassion, idealism, and an exploration of deeper meaning.

Saturn - Pluto (♄ ♇): Ability to guide and channel tremendous power and intensive effort to achieve positive change that involves fundamental structural changes.

Remaining Uranus ♅ Combinations

Uranus - Neptune (♅ ♆): Ability to explore the higher meaning of life using original and radical ideas and approaches.

Uranus - Pluto (♅ ♇): Growth in the ability to foster radical transformation of existing systems using a grass roots approach.

Remaining Neptune ♆ Combination

Neptune - Pluto (♆ ♇): Growth in the ability to effectively transform society and civilization to higher ideals.

Next, we will explore the Personal Points.

14 Exploration of Personal Points

Personal Points are not Planets but, rather, conceptual places on your Natal chart that serve to provide significant additional information. Let's take a look at each of the four Personal Points.

The **Ascendant** A^s is the point at the eastern horizon intercepted by the Ecliptic (see Chapter 27) at the time and location of birth. It is also referred to as the Rising Sign. For example, if a person has a Scorpio ♏ Ascendant A^s at the time of birth, the backdrop stars behind the Ecliptic on the eastern horizon at the time and location of birth was in the portion of the sky represented by Scorpio ♏. The Ascendant A^s represents the mask you wear, how you portray yourself to others, and how others see you at the surface level and as a first impression. Once others get to know you better, they gradually see the other parts of you represented by your Planets, Zodiac Signs, Houses, and Aspects. Note that Planets in your 1st House, and that Rule your 1st House (Chapter 26 on advanced House activity), will also influence how you portray yourself to others.

The **Midheaven (Medium Coeli)** M^c is the point on the Ecliptic that is intersected by an arc formed by pointing straight up at the place of birth and sweeping your arm toward the south (Chapter 27). The Midheaven M^c, which is at the Cusp of your 10th House (in most House systems), represents your career, the reputation you develop for yourself, your positions of power, and what you are known for. Note that Planets in your 10th House and that Rule your 10th House (Chapter 26) will also add additional information about your career and reputation.

The **North Node** ☊ is the north side of the line created by the intersection of the plane formed by the Moon ☽ circling the Earth ⊕ and the plane formed by the Earth ⊕ revolving around the Sun ☉. The North Node ☊ represents the area of life you innately desire to grow and develop in order to gain new experience and make fresh new progress. This area feels like virgin territory and thus, your learning is often guided more by trial and error than by instinct.

The **South Node** ☋ is the south side of the line created by the intersection of the plane formed by the Moon ☽ circling the Earth ⊕ and the plane formed by the Earth ⊕ circling the Sun ☉. Like the North Node ☊, the South Node ☋ also represents areas of your life in which you innately want to further develop. In the case of the South Node ☋, these are areas for lifetime growth where you already have well-developed instincts—almost like you've been there before, but don't remember when.

The Zodiac Signs are up next for exploration.

15 Exploration of Zodiac Signs

The 12 Signs of the Zodiac give character and personality to each of the Planets (actors) that represent specific roles you direct in your life. The Zodiac Signs are determined by viewing the backdrop of stars behind each Planet at the time of your birth. The backdrop of the stars is divided into 12 segments, with each segment corresponding to a Zodiac Sign. As an example, the Moon ☽ in Aries ♈ indicates that the portion of the background stars behind the Moon ☽ is located in the segment of the backdrop of stars represented by Aries ♈. Below is a description of the characteristics associated with each Sign of the Zodiac.

Aries ♈: A Planet (part of you) in Aries ♈ will have a tendency to be independent, quick to act, fiercely protective, and energetic in approach. A Planet with less-developed Aries ♈ characteristics may appear as moving forward without taking the time to create acceptance with others, being aggressive, displaying impatience, overwhelming others with forceful energy, and acting alone because it feels easier than waiting for others to finally take action. A Planet with well-developed Aries ♈ characteristics is assertive, inspiring, energizing to others, fast paced, encouraging, and patient with those who are not as quick to make decisions and take action.

Taurus ♉: A Planet in Taurus ♉ will have a tendency to be practical, predictable, pragmatic, grounded, slower moving, and realistic. A Planet with less-developed Taurus ♉ characteristics may appear as stubborn, possessive, boring, too slow to act, and too predictable. With well-developed Taurus ♉ characteristics, the affected Planet will tend to be at peace, practical, predictable, deliberate, quietly confident, grounding, and dependable.

Gemini ♊: A Planet in Gemini ♊ will be quicker, come more from the head and have a tendency to learn everything about everything and to be a distributor of this knowledge. Planets with less-developed Gemini ♊ characteristics are more scattered, less focused, unorganized, overwhelmed due to a lack of priorities, and possess a lack of conciseness in communication. A Planet with well-developed Gemini ♊ characteristics is well-informed, willing to explore all sides of issues, an artful communicator, has clear priorities, and is quick on its feet and flexible.

Cancer ♋: A Planet in Cancer ♋ will be sensitive to moods, emotions, and feelings. Planets with less-developed Cancer ♋ characteristics may find their judgement clouded by wallowing in their own emotions, which can feel overwhelming. The tendency may be to bury feelings, only to have them come out in inappropriate ways at the most inopportune times. A Planet with well-developed Cancer ♋ characteristics is able to tap into its instincts, be sensitive to the feelings of others, communicate from the heart, have a well-developed sense of timing, and provide and receive nurturing.

Leo ♌: A Planet in Leo ♌ will convey a strong sense of self that desires to shine out and be seen as unique and creative. Planets with less-developed Leo ♌ characteristics may appear to others as self serving and wanting to be the center of attention. Planets with well-developed Leo ♌ characteristics come across as warm, magnanimous, fun, creative, and a catalyst for getting others out of their comfort zone and joining in the fun and creativity. In this mature stage, the ego is the servant and not the master.

Virgo ♍: A Planet in Virgo ♍ tends to be discriminating, attentive to detail, desiring to improve oneself and others, and wanting to be of service. A Planet with less-developed Virgo ♍ characteristics has a focus on perfection, fixing flaws and imperfections. Often this perfectionism comes across as being too critical and dissatisfied. A Planet with well-developed Virgo ♍ characteristics has a focus on excellence, seeking out strengths and gifts, and helping oneself and others transform these strengths and gifts into towering abilities.

Libra ♎: A Planet in Libra ♎ reaches out to others in order to create harmony, balance, beauty, and connectedness. A Planet with less-developed Libra ♎ characteristics often finds the extreme edges of imbalance in relationships before coming to a balanced place. There is also a tendency to not include oneself in the balance equation, resulting in stress and dissatisfaction. One other interesting tendency is to avoid making decisions that will upset the existing balance. A Planet with well-developed Libra ♎ characteristics is a natural diplomat, has finely tuned interpersonal skills, enjoys the finer things in life, and is adept at finding ways to simultaneously preserve relationships, get what one wants, and retain one's self respect.

Scorpio ♏: A Planet in Scorpio ♏ has a tendency to dig beneath the surface to get to the root of issues, even if it involves exploring taboo areas and uncomfortable subjects. This deep exploration is necessary for true transformation to take place. A Planet with less-developed Scorpio ♏ characteristics may drag others into deep places when they either don't want to go there or aren't ready to go there yet. This less-developed state may display the ability to throw "darts" at others' "soft spots" when upset. A Planet with well-developed Scorpio ♏ characteristics is able to create a safe climate and invite others to probe deeply. This requires having healthy boundaries for oneself, a respect for the boundaries of others, and a magnetism that attracts others to safely explore at a deeper level.

Sagittarius ♐: A Planet in Sagittarius ♐ wants to look down upon the forest instead of running through the trees. This manifests as putting situations into perspective by viewing the big picture, by exploring the big questions in life, and by venturing on wide-ranging quests—either physically, mentally, or spiritually—in order to explore the unknown. A Planet with less-developed Sagittarius ♐ characteristics may appear as having its head in the clouds and not converting ideas and ideals into practical results. There is also a tendency to blurt out the obvious without regard to the feelings of others. A Planet with well-developed Sagittarius ♐ characteristics has high ideals, keeps things in perspective, explores widely, and communicates big ideas that are inspiring and grounded.

Capricorn ♑: A Planet in Capricorn ♑ is ambitious and wants results. The key to getting these results lies within the approach toward structure, discipline, and boundaries. A Planet with less-developed Capricorn ♑ characteristics may over control and micromanage or just the opposite, have sparse or vague boundaries. When the Planet in Capricorn ♑ is less confident, the tendency is to build a fortress of boundaries for protection and to keep as much as possible under control. The opposite can also happen, which is to unconsciously attract another to provide the stifling boundaries on oneself. A Planet with well-developed Capricorn ♑ characteristics possesses realism about the present, clarity surrounding a better future, and clear communication about the "boundaries of the reservation." This offers oneself as well as others considerable freedom while still maintaining appropriate direction and risk, and ultimately achieving the desired result.

Aquarius ♒: A Planet in Aquarius ♒ will have a desire for liberation as well as a willingness to follow its passions, even if it means that accepted conventions and expectations of others are ignored. This liberation involves pursuing endeavors that advance the world to a better place. Quite often, use of the latest technology is evident. A Planet with less-developed Aquarius ♒ characteristics may display rebelliousness, unpredictable changes, and a lack of empathy for others. A Planet with well-developed Aquarius ♒ characteristics has sudden insights, ingenious and profoundly different ideas, and an ability to inspire and prepare others for a collective effort that will lead to disruptive improvements for the betterment of all.

Pisces ♓: A Planet in Pisces ♓ will be more perceptive, less judgmental, have more empathy and compassion, and advance the ideals of who we as human beings really are. This is an ultimate recognition that we are not our body, nor are we our thoughts, nor are we our emotions. We are ultimately a manifestation of our spirit, and our spirit is part of a oneness. Practically, this often shows up as compassion, dreaminess, transcendence of the material world at times, and a recognition that when we help others we are also helping ourselves and the collective. A Planet with less-developed Pisces ♓ characteristics will have a disproportionate balance of time "tuning out" and will not focus enough attention on keeping one foot in the material world in order to accomplish practical results. A Planet with well-developed Pisces ♓ characteristics finds the right balance between navigating the world as it currently is and visualizing and creating the idealistic world it imagines. There is a tendency to have pursuits with a higher personal and collective meaning.

Last, but not least, let's explore the Houses.

16 Exploration of Houses

The Houses indicate the areas of life in which the Planets emphasize their roles. To clarify, a Planet exerts its influence in ALL areas of life AND has additional emphasis in the particular House (area of life) it is in or that it Rules (Chapter 26). Here is a summary of the Houses (areas of life).

1st House: This is the area of first impressions: how you initially appear to other people. Once people get to know you better, they will see more of your other facets, i.e. your Planets in action. This is like the mask you wear to either consciously or unconsciously portray yourself. Expressing your personality to the world in a way that allows your inner self to shine is the fulfillment of the 1st House.

2nd House: This is the area in which you collect your possessions whether they be money or the objects you surround yourself with. To some extent, the possessions you surround yourself with reflect your self-image and self-worth. As a result, this House also represents the development of your self-confidence. Being at peace with yourself, your relationship to money, and your possessions is the fulfillment of the 2nd House.

3rd House: This is the area of your day-to-day thinking and communicating. Included is your daily, short-term travel. Clarity in thinking and exchanging information, ideas, and concepts with others is the fulfillment of the 3rd House.

4th House: This is the area that represents the safe place you retreat to, often at the end of each day. For most people, this is their home. Since the home is where you originally absorbed your ancestral patterns and autopilot behaviors, this House also represents your psychological roots. Creating a safe environment where you can meaningfully connect with family is the fulfillment of the 4th House.

5th House: This is the House that represents your arena for pleasure, play, creativity, fun, and your favorite activities. When you are in this arena, you are often less inhibited, more creative, take more risks, and explore your desires. Life is much easier to navigate when you take the time for fun, creativity, and pleasure, which is the fulfillment of the 5th House.

6th House: This is the area of your daily habits and routines, including how you take care of your health, how you approach your activities to achieve your goals, how you approach problem solving, and the service you provide for others. Having and using meaningful skills that are of value to others fulfills the needs of the 6th House.

7th House: This is the area of your very close relationships, whether they be spouses, close friends, business partners, and yes, even your personal enemies. The ability to truly empathize with another, display curiosity, and have a balanced interdependent and growing relationship fulfills the needs of the 7th House.

8th House: This is the area of transformation, including personal transformations as well as transformations resulting from outside events and circumstances. Fundamentally, transformation is about having one facet of your life die, which then makes room for a new facet to be born. Because parts of your life include the actual death of people close to you as well as the birth of lifetime relationships (such as. marriage), this House also includes inheritances and sharing of resources with others. Surrendering and embracing change in order to make room for new understanding and growth fulfills the needs of the 8th House.

9th House: This is the area of your life that encompasses endeavors that are expansive and growth-oriented. This includes expansion that is physical (long trips), mental (higher learning and education), and philosophical (morality, ethics, religion). Experiencing the wider territories in life to make room for higher understanding is the fulfillment of the 9th House.

10th House: This is the area of your reputation and accomplishments. It is also associated with your career and your status in the world. Achieving results that are consistent with your true aspirations and your energetic flow is the fulfillment of the 10th House.

11th House: This is the area where you collaborate with others who share your dreams and aspirations, where together you create something bigger than yourself through mutual support and giving back in meaningful ways. Making progress toward your ideals through support from like-minded people is the fulfillment of the 11th House.

12th House: This is your inner sanctuary where you connect with who you really are and what you are here to do, where you appreciate life's gifts, and where you find solace from the craziness of the world. When this area of life is explored, you gravitate toward compassion, forgiveness, surrender, and acceptance. When you block out this area, you lose your spiritual bearings and often numb yourself through alcohol and drugs, resulting in anxiety, depression, maintaining hidden secrets, and dissatisfaction. Fulfillment of this House requires that you periodically visit your inner sanctuary and nurture a place of peace, empathy, love, appreciation, joy, and oneness.

Now that we have covered the basics of astrology as well as a deeper exploration of the major components, we are ready to delineate a Natal chart. We will do this in the next section.

Exploration of Houses

Delineating Natal Charts

17 Delineating Individual Components

Now it's time to put it all together and interpret Natal charts. At this stage, we will ignore the big picture and dissect Karen's Natal chart into its individual components. While this is a very useful and necessary part of the interpretation process, it is not sufficient because we are missing the overall "look" of the chart. In the following chapter, we will look at a variety of Natal charts and observe the larger themes and patterns so we can find some simplicity in the details. Two chapters from now, we will look at the methodology for interpreting Natal charts so you will have ideas for an overall procedure depending on your experience level.

Let's now interpret Karen's Natal chart into its myriad of components. To keep this chapter at a reasonable length, I will be brief in my comments, much more brief than I would in an actual consultation. I did this to give you a feel for how to quickly garner information from a Natal chart.

Throughout this chapter, you may find it helpful to refer to the keyword charts for the Planets, Personal Points, Zodiac Signs, and

Houses from the earlier chapters. I have duplicated these charts on pages 108-110. If you want to explore more deeply, you can use sticky notes or tabs to mark the pages for the Planets (Chapter 11, page 71), Planet Combinations (Chapter 13, page 81), Personal Points (Chapter 14, page 89), Zodiac Signs (Chapter 15, page 91), and Houses (Chapter 16, page 97). While it will take you a while to flip back and forth between these chapters, it is a great way to learn to interpret a Natal chart.

We will interpret Karen's Natal chart in four steps: (1) individual Planets and Personal Points, (2) two Planet combinations, (3) multiple Planet combinations, and (4) a tour of the Houses. For easy reference, I have repeated Karen's Natal chart on the next page.

You can have a variety of interpretations for a specific Planet, Zodiac Sign, House, or Planet combination, and each of these interpretations requires a dialogue with the client about how it may show up in less-evolved and fully-evolved ways.

This is a part of astrology that takes a long time to learn. You need to not only understand the details of Planets, Zodiac Signs, Aspects, Houses, and Planet combinations, but also be able to synthesize this information and communicate it in a meaningful way. You will naturally evolve using your own style as you interpret charts.

Let's begin by delineating Karen's individual Planets and Personal Points in their Zodiac Signs and Houses. We will explore how Karen may express her energy in less- and more-evolved ways.

107

Karen Raven
March 17, 1955
10:37 PM
New Haven, Connecticut
Standard Time
Time Zone: 5 hours West
Tropical Krusinski

NATAL CHART

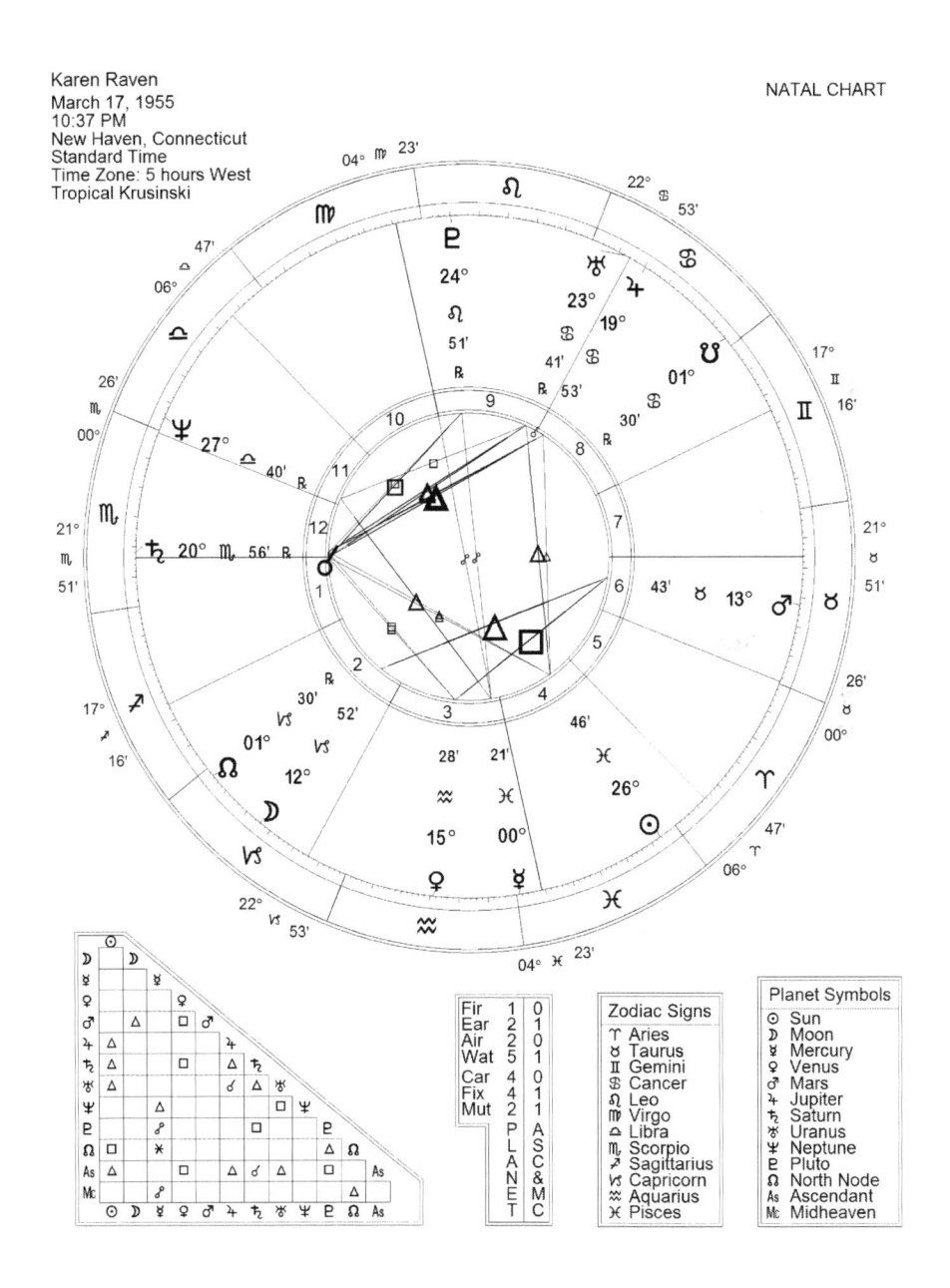

Zodiac Signs	Planet Symbols
♈ Aries	☉ Sun
♉ Taurus	☽ Moon
♊ Gemini	☿ Mercury
♋ Cancer	♀ Venus
♌ Leo	♂ Mars
♍ Virgo	♃ Jupiter
♎ Libra	♄ Saturn
♏ Scorpio	♅ Uranus
♐ Sagittarius	♆ Neptune
♑ Capricorn	♇ Pluto
♒ Aquarius	☊ North Node
♓ Pisces	As Ascendant
	Mc Midheaven

Fir	1 0
Ear	2 1
Air	2 0
Wat	5 1
Car	4 0
Fix	4 1
Mut	2 1
PLANET	ASC & MC

Delineating Individual Components

Key Words for Planets and Personal Points

Planet or Personal Point	Glyph	Key Words
Sun	☉	Your main actor, coming out in the world
Moon	☽	Nurturing, receiving, feeling
Mercury	☿	Thinking and communicating
Venus	♀	Attracting and relating, sensuality
Mars	♂	Initiating, getting what you want, passion
Jupiter	♃	Expanding, projecting optimism
Saturn	♄	Structuring, controlling, promoting realism
Uranus	♅	Breaking free, being unique, social change, rebel
Neptune	♆	Growing spiritually, transcending the ego
Pluto	♇	Transformation, using power, sexuality
Ascendant	A^s	Personality you portray to others
Midheaven	M^c	Characteristics of your career and reputation
North Node	☊	Areas for lifetime growth that are not instinctual
South Node	☋	Areas for lifetime growth that are instinctual

Zodiac Sign Characteristics		
Zodiac Sign	**Glyph**	**Characteristics**
Aries	♈	Pathfinder, action-oriented, spirited
Taurus	♉	Predictable, pragmatic, sensual, practical
Gemini	♊	Quick, communicative, collector of knowledge
Cancer	♋	Feeling, intuitive, nurturing, giving & receiving
Leo	♌	Creative, fun, ego balance, magnanimous
Virgo	♍	Improvement-focused, discriminating, service
Libra	♎	Harmony, balance, relationship-oriented
Scorpio	♏	Exploring the hidden depths, use of power
Sagittarius	♐	Wide-ranging, philosophical, distant ventures
Capricorn	♑	Structured, ambitious, achiever, disciplined
Aquarius	♒	Innovative, altering social paradigms, original
Pisces	♓	Spiritual connectedness, idealistic, visionary

Areas of Life for each House	
House	**Areas of Life**
1st	How you convey yourself to other people
2nd	Possessions, how you earn money, self-confidence
3rd	Your thinking and communicating, short-term travel
4th	Home, psychological roots, family patterns
5th	Creativity, recreation, hobbies, pleasure, fun, romance
6th	Daily routines and habits, health attitudes
7th	Close relationships, influence, diplomacy, intimacy
8th	Cycles of death and rebirth, resource sharing, sexuality
9th	Long-distance travel, philosophy, higher education, ethics
10th	Career, reputation, status, achievement
11th	Your dreams and aspirations, friends and associations
12th	Your inner sanctuary and how you care for it

1. Individual Planets and Personal Points

Sun ☉ in Pisces ♓ in the 4th House:

Less evolved: Karen may spend considerable time in her own internal world, often at home, disconnecting from the outer world through alcohol, drugs, or unproductive daydreaming. Because she is so compassionate and understanding, she may be easy prey for others to take advantage of her generosity.

More evolved: Karen is evolving toward higher levels of consciousness that invoke compassion, empathy, understanding, love, and peace. She uses her ability to tune out of her surroundings at times (especially at home) in order to visualize ideas, concepts, and scenarios that serve her well. She empathizes with others to find better solutions.

Moon ☽ in Capricorn ♑ in the 2nd House:

Less evolved: Karen takes herself a bit too seriously. She puts enormous effort into controlling her surroundings so she can achieve her goals, regardless of the effects on others. She is task-oriented to a fault. Her self worth is tied to how much money she earns.

More evolved: Karen has a need to get results in terms of assets (money and belongings) through hard work, discipline, and structure. Her self-confidence has grown as she accrued accomplishments. She has learned to detach her self-worth from her accomplishments and has developed strong skills in guiding, coaching, and directing others.

Mercury ☿ in Pisces ♓ in the 3rd House:

Less evolved: Karen is a daydreamer at heart, to the point where it gets in the way of her ability to complete her daily tasks. Her communication comes across to others as ungrounded and nebulous.

More evolved: Karen's thinking and communicating is often visionary, idealistic, and compassionate. Because she is so adept at visualizing, she often thinks strategically and imagines outcomes of scenarios. This helps her to anticipate and prepare for probable surprises and turn of events.

Venus ♀ in Aquarius ♒ in the 3rd House:

Less evolved: In close relationships, Karen is attracted to the outliers of society. She often communicates thoughts that, while well-intentioned and unique, don't consider how other people may receive her messages. At times, she is tuned into others and at other times, she is very distant, captured in her own thoughts and ideas.

More evolved: Karen attracts and is attracted to people who are unconventional and inspirational. She develops relationships through communication in areas that are often outside the box and altruistic. She builds her ideas and approaches through input and feedback from others.

Mars ♂ in Taurus ♉ in the 6th House:

Less evolved: While very practical, Karen can be quite stubborn and rigid in her daily routines and work life. When conditions necessitate change, Karen often puts up resistance and is hard to convince.

More evolved: Karen has a long-lasting and steady energy as she navigates through her daily activities. Her approach to getting tasks accomplished is generally planned and pragmatic. In relationships, her calm, predictable, and steady energy is grounding for others. She is attuned to the needs of others and offers accommodating flexibility.

Jupiter ♃ in Cancer ♋ in the 8th and near the 9th House:

Less evolved: Karen can be overwhelmed with feelings and emotions. At times, she finds herself jumping into unrealistic changes in her life with too much optimism and feeling and not enough consideration of the practical challenges and the associated details.

More evolved: Karen is present to feelings and emotions, whether they be with individuals or organizations. Her focus is on the human side of change: how people need to be nurtured during shifting times.

Saturn ♄ in Scorpio ♏ in the 12th and near the 1st House:

Less evolved: Karen can be controlling to the point of being too intense. It often feels that she is pushing others into areas that are too touchy or sensitive. She sometimes gets so dedicated to her goals that she works long and hard hours to the point of burnout.

More evolved: Karen is a structured and disciplined person who thinks deeply and is not overly emotional. She has the ability and tenacity to transform ideas into results. Over time, she has learned to develop boundaries that keep progress on track while allowing room for creativity and inevitable surprises. She prefers to solve problems by getting to the root of issues.

Uranus ♅ in Cancer ♋ in 9th and near the 8th House:

Less evolved: Karen has a reputation for being disruptive, constantly challenging the system and disconnecting from what she views as uncaring dogma. She doesn't do much to develop relationships with others if she senses they are too task-oriented.

More evolved: Karen has a desire to explore subjects outside the conventionally-accepted norms, especially in areas connected to human emotions, psychology, and coaching. She also enjoys traveling to exotic places.

Neptune ♆ in Libra ♎ in the 11th and near the 12th House:

Less evolved: Karen often hangs out in groups to tune out of day-to-day life, sometimes through alcohol and drugs in a party atmosphere.

More evolved: Karen enjoys being with groups that share a common compassion, understanding, and desire for peace. She uses her learning for her own internal growth and development.

Pluto ♇ in Leo ♌ in the 9th House:

Less evolved: Karen has a way of dominating the space as she shares her rigid beliefs and philosophies with others. She often comes across as trying to force her beliefs on others.

More evolved: Karen has a keen interest in transformation and power with a focus on guiding others and organizations through significant change by radiating her unique personality.

Scorpio ♏ on the Ascendant A^s:

Less evolved: Karen instinctively knows the soft spots of other people. When irritated or off balance, she throws verbal darts at these soft spots.

More evolved: Karen likes to go beneath the surface in her interactions with others. This includes deeper motivations and aspirations as well as those parts of others which are hidden. She has an interest in understanding the "story behind the story."

Virgo ♍ at the Midheaven M^c:

Less evolved: Karen is obsessed with perfection in the work place.

She constantly points out flaws and mistakes made by those around her.

More evolved: Karen finds herself gravitating toward careers that help others make improvements. Over time, she is learning to shift her focus from fixing what is wrong to further strengthening that which is already great.

North Node ☊ in Capricorn ♑ in the 2nd House: An important part of Karen's growth in her lifetime involves hard work and discipline to achieve her desires. A key piece of this growth will be to inspire others and tend to their needs while simultaneously getting the tasks completed.

South Node ☋ in Cancer ♋ in the 8th House: Karen has very good instincts and strong feelings. A significant part of her growth will be to incorporate her feelings and instincts in her life transitions.

2. Two Planet Combinations

When two of your Planets are Aspected, these parts of you will express their roles simultaneously. The grid on the lower left side of Karen's Natal chart identifies the two Planet combinations. You can also view the same information by looking at the Aspect lines in the center of Karen's Natal chart. The table on page 117 offers a summary of Karen's Planetary Aspects. Referring back to Chapter 13 (page 81) on Planet combinations will be helpful. Note that we are substantially ignoring the Houses as they will be covered in Part 4 of this chapter. The descriptions below summarize how Karen may express her Planetary combinations when less and more evolved.

Sun ☉ in Pisces ♓ Trine △ Jupiter ♃ in Cancer ♋:

Less evolved: Karen spends excessive time daydreaming unproductively. She often comes across to others as living on another planet. She is idealistic to a fault and ignores concrete information that contradicts her dreams, instincts, and feelings.

More evolved: Karen projects confidence and has an optimistic attitude toward life. She develops high aspirations that are realistic in nature.

Sun ☉ in Pisces ♓ Trine △ Saturn ♄ in Scorpio ♏:

Less evolved: Karen develops idealistic endeavors and then attempts to tightly control every step of the way. She becomes frustrated when events don't go as planned.

More evolved: A significant contributor to Karen's successes has come from focus, discipline, and patience. She likes to explore and gain understanding of the deeper meaning and motivations within herself and of others.

Sun ☉ in Pisces ♓ Trine △ Uranus ♅ in Cancer ♋:

Less evolved: Karen recognizes ways the world could be more compassionate and understanding and then joins numerous protests and activist groups with a mindset of rebellion.

More evolved: Karen is very good at creating original and unique ideas that help improve life and work conditions in meaningful ways for others.

Aspected Planets for Karen's Natal Chart	
Planet	**Planet Aspects**
Sun ☉	Sun ☉ Trine △ Jupiter ♃ Sun ☉ Trine △ Saturn ♄ Sun ☉ Trine △ Uranus ♅
Moon ☽	Moon ☽ Trine △ Mars ♂
Mercury ☿	Mercury ☿ Trine △ Neptune ♆ Mercury ☿ Opposition ☍ Pluto ♇
Venus ♀	Venus ♀ Square □ Mars ♂ Venus ♀ Square □ Saturn ♄
Mars ♂	Mars ♂ Trine △ Moon ☽ Mars ♂ Square □ Venus ♀
Jupiter ♃	Jupiter ♃ Trine △ Sun ☉ Jupiter ♃ Trine △ Saturn ♄ Jupiter ♃ Conjunct ☌ Uranus ♅
Saturn ♄	Saturn ♄ Trine △ Sun ☉ Saturn ♄ Square □ Venus ♀ Saturn ♄ Trine △ Jupiter ♃ Saturn ♄ Trine △ Uranus ♅ Saturn ♄ Square □ Pluto ♇
Uranus ♅	Uranus ♅ Trine △ Sun ☉ Uranus ♅ Conjunct ☌ Jupiter ♃ Uranus ♅ Trine △ Saturn ♄ Uranus ♅ Square □ Neptune ♆
Neptune ♆	Neptune ♆ Trine △ Mercury ☿ Neptune ♆ Square □ Uranus ♅
Pluto ♇	Pluto ♇ Opposition ☍ Mercury ☿ Pluto ♇ Square □ Saturn ♄

Delineating Individual Components

Moon ☽ in Capricorn ♑ Trine △ Mars ♂ in Taurus ♉:

Less evolved: Karen is the ultimate taskmaster. She demands results, even when those involved attempt to provide her feedback on her unrealistic expectations. She is a workaholic and expects the same of others.

More evolved: Karen has a need to get results and an approach that is steady, practical, and pragmatic. While her natural tendency is to focus on tasks and outcomes, she ensures that she attends to people's ideas, emotions, and feelings.

Mercury ☿ in Pisces ♓ Trine △ Neptune ♆ in Libra ♎:

Less evolved: Karen's thinking is often nebulous and uncertain. She communicates in ways that appear ungrounded and overly idealistic.

More evolved: Karen has spent many years exploring the connections between consciousness and science (quantum mechanics and cosmology). She enjoys conversations about these topics through her clear communication focused on these nebulous areas. This allows her to find higher meaning in her endeavors and help others to do the same.

Mercury ☿ in Pisces ♓ Opposition ☍ Pluto ♇ in Leo ♌:

Less evolved: Karen can become dominant in her communication with others, often by choosing to take advantage of her status and position of authority.

More evolved: Karen enjoys exploring transformation at both the individual and the organizational levels. She has developed frameworks for helping others recognize the need for change and communicates these in powerful and meaningful ways.

Venus ♀ in Aquarius ♒ Square □ Mars ♂ in Taurus ♉:

Less evolved: Karen often sends mixed signals in relationships. She seeks connections with people who are eclectic and unique and then expresses disappointment when they don't behave in practical and pragmatic ways.

More evolved: Karen enjoys exploring the practical aspects of people who live their lives outside the mainstream of conventional norms. While she is pragmatic herself, she has learned to support the uniqueness of others.

Venus ♀ in Aquarius ♒ Square □ Saturn ♄ in Scorpio ♏:

Less evolved: While Karen enjoys being with others who are very different than the norm, she frustrates these individuals by being too controlling and inflexible.

More evolved: Karen enjoys working closely with others to turn unconventional ideas and approaches into practical results. She creates structure that gets the job done while allowing creativity and flexibility for others.

Jupiter ♃ in Cancer ♋ Trine △ Saturn ♄ in Scorpio ♏:

Less evolved: Karen comes up with unrealistic ideas and attempts to implement these ideas through a rigid and inflexible approach.

More evolved: Karen has the ability to take big ideas and build structure around them to create concrete results.

Jupiter ♃ in Cancer ♋ Conjunct ☌ Uranus ♅ in Cancer ♋:

Less evolved: Karen openly rebels against rules and regulations when she feels they don't serve a purpose. She often is delinquent in following through on commitments that involve what she considers bureaucracy.

More evolved: Karen is prolific at generating ideas that are out of the box and uses her enthusiasm and trust in herself to create acceptance of these ideas with others.

Saturn ♄ in Scorpio ♏ Trine △ Uranus ♅ in Cancer ♋:

Less evolved: Karen works hard to ensure that she has plenty of room for creativity, yet does just the opposite with those who work with her, demanding structure and discipline at the expense of their creativity and freedom.

More evolved: Karen uses her discipline, structure, and organization to create the atmosphere for transforming novel ideas into practical results.

Saturn ♄ in Scorpio ♏ Square □ Pluto ♇ in Leo ♌:

Less evolved: Karen seems like she is only willing to reveal so much in her interactions with others. This creates a lack of trust and rumors about her hidden agendas.

More evolved: Karen develops a structured and disciplined approach for helping organizations navigate significant transformations by tapping into the emotions and feelings of those affected.

Uranus ♅ in Cancer ♋ Square □ Neptune ♆ in Libra ♎:

Less evolved: Karen has a habit of jumping into the latest New Age fad, often attaching herself to the popular guru of the moment. She is easily led into joining activities with hype and glitter.

More evolved: Karen enjoys exploring unconventional ideas and approaches that have the potential to make this world a better place. She is careful to investigate areas that she finds interesting before participating.

3. Three or More Planet Combinations

The multiple combinations of Aspected Planets will form unique blends of energy within a person. The more evolved you are in getting each of your individual Planets to express their gifts, the more effective you will be in directing the combinations of your Planets to serve you well. Let's take a look at selected Planet combinations in Karen's Natal chart to illustrate how Karen may express these energetic combinations in ways that are more evolved. I'm going to skip the less-evolved interpretation, since it will get repetitious with the previous section. You may find it useful to refer to Chapter 13 on Planet combinations.

Mars ♂ in Taurus ♉ Trine △ Moon ☽ in Capricorn ♑, and Square ☐ Venus ♀ in Aquarius ♒: Karen has the patience, discipline, and stamina to deliver concrete results through cooperation with people who are altruistic and express themselves in ways that allow their uniqueness to flourish.

Pluto ♇ in Leo ♌ Square ☐ Saturn ♄ in Scorpio ♏, and Opposition ☍ Mercury ☿ in Pisces ♓: Karen has the ability to generate ideas that people find personally inspiring and creates structure allowing this transformation to unfold.

Saturn ♄ in Scorpio ♏ Trine △ Sun ☉ in Pisces ♓, Square ☐ Venus ♀ in Aquarius ♒, Trine △ Jupiter ♃ in Cancer ♋, Trine △ Uranus ♅ in Cancer ♋, Square ☐ Pluto ♇ in Leo ♌, Conjunct ☌ the Ascendant As: Karen has a desire to generate ideas that are out of the box and based on compassion and idealism, and then convert these ideas into reality. Much of her approach is instinctual and guided by what feels good in her heart. She exudes optimism in these transformative endeavors.

Neptune ♆ in Libra ♎ Square □ Uranus ♅ in Cancer ♋, and Trine △ Mercury ☿ in Pisces ♓: Karen is able to visualize and communicate idealistic and unconventional ideas that benefit the collective.

4. Houses

Now we will look at the Houses. The table on the next page is a summary of the House activity. This is the same chart you viewed in Chapter 8 on House activity. Obviously, there is a lot going on in each House.

1st House: Karen has Saturn ♄ in Scorpio ♏ very close to her Ascendant A^s and her Ascendant (Rising Sign) in Scorpio ♏. Her general way of showing herself to others will convey a sense that she is reserved, a deep thinker with structured discipline. When less evolved, she may appear to be secretive, inflexible, and a bit too deep for comfort.

2nd House: Karen has Sagittarius ♐ on the Cusp of her 2nd House as well as her North Node ☊ in Capricorn ♑ and her Moon ☽ in Capricorn ♑. When it comes to earning money, Karen has two sides to her. She may find herself earning money through activities involving travel and higher education. Yet, she also has a strong need to earn money the old-fashioned way: through structure, discipline, and hard work. When less evolved, she may be a speculator looking for the quick win or a workaholic.

House Activity for Karen's Natal Chart

House	Planets & Personal Points in House	Planets near the House borders	Zodiac Sign at Cusp
1st		Saturn ♄	Scorpio ♏
2nd	Moon ☽ N. Node ☊		Sagittarius ♐
3rd	Venus ♀ Mercury ☿		Capricorn ♑
4th	Sun ☉		Pisces ♓
5th			Aries ♈
6th	Mars ♂		Taurus ♉
7th			Taurus ♉
8th	Jupiter ♃ S. Node ☋	Uranus ♅	Gemini ♊
9th	Uranus ♅ Pluto ♇	Jupiter ♃	Cancer ♋
10th			Virgo ♍
11th	Neptune ♆		Libra ♎
12th	Saturn ♄	Neptune ♆	Scorpio ♏

Delineating Individual Components

3rd House: Karen has Capricorn ♑ at the Cusp of her 3rd House as well as her Venus ♀ in Aquarius ♒ and Mercury ☿ in Pisces ♓ in her 3rd House. While her thinking is very idealistic and visionary, she also can be very organized in structuring her communication. She is attracted to creative ideas and finds herself drawn into conversations with people who are original, altruistic, and out of the norm. When less evolved, her communication may appear disjointed, with too many mixed energies. She will probably be shy about presenting in front of groups.

4th House: Karen has Pisces ♓ at the Cusp of her 4th House as well as the Sun ☉ in Pisces ♓ in her 4th House. She has a desire to put a lot of her energy into her home life. In fact, her home is her spiritual sanctuary where she finds respite from the outside world. When less evolved, she may use her home as a place to vegetate and tune out from the world, perhaps through illegal or addictive substances.

5th House: Karen has Aries ♈ at the Cusp of her 5th House. She enjoys adventurous endeavors for fun and recreation. Karen may express her energy through ardent activities such as hiking, camping, river rafting, flying, and motorcycle riding. When less evolved, she may be so impulsive that she puts herself in dangerous situations such as jumping off cliffs into a lake (true story).

6th House: Karen has Taurus ♉ at the Cusp of her 6th House as well as Mars ♂ in Taurus ♉ in her 6th House. Note that with a different House system or a birth time a few minutes earlier, Karen would have Aries ♈ on the Cusp of her 6th House. In these situations, we need to explore Karen's 6th House daily routines and habits to determine whether Aries ♈ or Taurus ♉ is on the Cusp. It turns out that Karen's typical behaviors in daily patterns and routines indicate that Taurus ♉ is on the Cusp. With that, Karen's daily work habits and routines are pragmatic, practical, and steady. With Mars ♂ in Taurus ♉ in her 6th House, she will be like the "energizer bunny" in the commercials: she just keeps going and going and going. When less evolved, she will be a slave to routines, hard to inspire, and difficult to change.

7th House: Karen has Taurus ♉ on the Cusp of her 7th House. When viewing the 7th House of relationships, we also include her two Planets associated with relationships: Venus ♀ in Aquarius ♒ and Mars ♂ in Taurus ♉. Venus ♀ is associated with giving and Mars ♂ with receiving. For many people, the more challenging of the two to develop is the ability to receive by being clear about what you want and then opening up yourself to what is offered (Mars ♂). It's important in healthy relationships to have not only a balance between giving (Venus ♀) and receiving (Mars ♂), but an ability to have clear communication about each other's desires. Karen is attracted to people who are very different from the norm (Venus ♀) while at the same time promoting practicality and steadiness in her relationships (Mars ♂). When less evolved, she may get too set in her ways and become boring, while expecting those close to her to provide inspiration.

8th House: Karen has Gemini ♊ at the Cusp of the 8th House. She also has her South Node ☋ in Cancer ♋ and Jupiter ♃ in Cancer ♋ in her 8th House. Furthermore, Uranus ♅ in Cancer ♋ is in the 9th House, but also very close to the end of her 8th House. Karen finds herself in numerous transformations and changes, as this is an instinctual pattern for her. She is also adept at navigating sudden changes and surprises. She has had a wide variety of experiences in her life, mastering one and then moving on to another. When less evolved, she may chronically jump from one endeavor to another. She also may try to juggle so many activities and interests that she is unable to make progress on any.

9th House: Karen has Cancer ♋ on the Cusp of her 9th House. She also has Uranus ♅ in Cancer ♋ and Pluto ♇ in Leo ♌ in her 9th House as well as Jupiter ♃ in Cancer ♋ in the 8th House near the Cusp of her 9th House. When it comes to higher education and distant travels, Karen has a curiosity toward other cultures and ways of life, especially those that are very different from her own. It wouldn't be surprising for her to attain an advanced degree or certification as well as travel the world. When less evolved, she may be a literate wanderer: brilliant, but unable to connect big ideas and philosophies to practical reality.

10th House: Karen has Virgo ♍ on the Cusp of her 10th House. Karen's career and reputation involve helping individuals and organizations make improvements by both fixing what is broken and enhancing unique strengths. When less evolved, she may be the nightmare boss, constantly catching others doing something wrong and rarely being satisfied.

11th House: Karen has Libra ♎ on the Cusp of her 11th House. She also has Neptune ♆ in Libra ♎ in her 11th House. Karen's ideals and aspirations include helping groups of people work better together through her skills at facilitating and coaching. Her approach conveys that we are all in the same boat and can work better together when we have more compassion and understanding. When less evolved, she may be lured into groups, associations, or ventures that look idealistic on the surface, but are significantly flawed in reality.

12th House: Karen has Scorpio ♏ on the Cusp of her 12th House. She also has Saturn ♄ in Scorpio ♏ in her 12th House as well as Neptune ♆ in Libra ♎ very close to her 12th House. This is another situation where Karen may have Libra ♎ at the Cusp of her 12th House instead of Scorpio ♏ because Libra ♎ is so close to the Cusp. In these situations, we need to explore both possibilities. Knowing Karen well, it appears she has Scorpio ♏ on the Cusp of her 12th House. The key to Karen's inner growth is in her exploration of what C.G. Jung calls the shadow: the parts of her that she would like to disown and not reveal to others. By embracing these parts of herself, she is on the path toward becoming more whole, which allows her to become more effective in her life. When less evolved, she may wallow in her own deep muck for long periods of time before coming out of her funk. She also will probably be very hard on herself, expecting to behave like the perfect role model.

Hopefully you are now getting a feel for how to dismantle the pieces of a Natal chart and translate these pieces into useful information.

Next we will view the Natal chart as a whole to find the larger themes and patterns.

18 Approaching Natal Charts

In the previous chapter, delineating individual components showed that you learned the mechanics of breaking the Natal chart into pieces by viewing individual Planets in Zodiac Signs, Planet combinations, and House activity. This will keep you busy all by itself. After interpreting a few dozen Natal charts, you will naturally find yourself stepping back and looking at Natal charts as a whole before diving into the details. Every Natal chart is truly unique. Having the ability to briefly view Natal charts and see larger themes will serve you well and will occur naturally over time. Let's look at a few Natal charts, step back, and see what stands out. I have changed the names of each person to a fictitious name.

Patty Franco: On page 131 is the Natal chart for Patty Franco. Look at the chart for a few seconds and see what stands out for you. You probably observed six of her 10 Planets are in the Zodiac Sign of Virgo ♍, and all are in her 9th House or within 3° of her 9th House. These six Planets are the Sun ☉, Moon ☽, Mercury ☿, Venus ♀, Uranus ♅, and Pluto ♇. With this considerable 9th House emphasis, Patty will find herself drawn to higher education, long-distance travel, and wider philosophical exploration. She will have a strong desire for self improvement and to help others improve themselves (Virgo ♍). Also notice that nine out of 10 of her Planets are in Feminine Signs (six in Earth and three in Water). Furthermore, seven out of 10 of her Planets are in Mutable Signs. Patty has plenty of energy for transitions through nebulous times (Mutable). Her strength will come from drawing from within (Feminine Signs) through her feelings, emotions, and practicality. Notice that if her birth time were about one minute later, her Ascendant A^s would be in Capricorn ♑. This will need to be explored with her.

Britney Smith: Let's next see what stands out for the Natal chart of Britney Smith, which is depicted on page 132. Most obvious in her chart is an abundance of Capricorn ♑ where she has six Planets (Mercury ☿, Venus ♀, Mars ♂, Saturn ♄, Uranus ♅, and Neptune ♆), mostly in her 3rd House of thinking and communicating. This will convey strong characteristics related to structure, discipline, and ambition. Her growth in life will include effective structure in her communication (Capricorn ♑ in her 3rd House). Britney has the potential to be a voice of authority in some areas of life. She has nine out of 10 Planets in Feminine Signs (six in Earth and three in Water). Thus, Britney also will have a desire to spend considerable time and energy exploring her feelings, emotions, and the practical side of herself. What makes all this even more interesting is that her main actor (Sun ☉) is in Aquarius ♒ next to her North Node ☊. While she will have plenty of structure (Capricorn ♑), she desires to take the shackles off, freeing herself to be who she wants to be, which will be an important part of her growth (North Node ☊).

Fast Track Astrologer

Patty Franco
September 13, 1966
2:53 PM
Brooklyn, N.Y.C., NY
Daylight Saving Time
Time Zone: 5 hours West
Tropical Krusinski

NATAL CHART

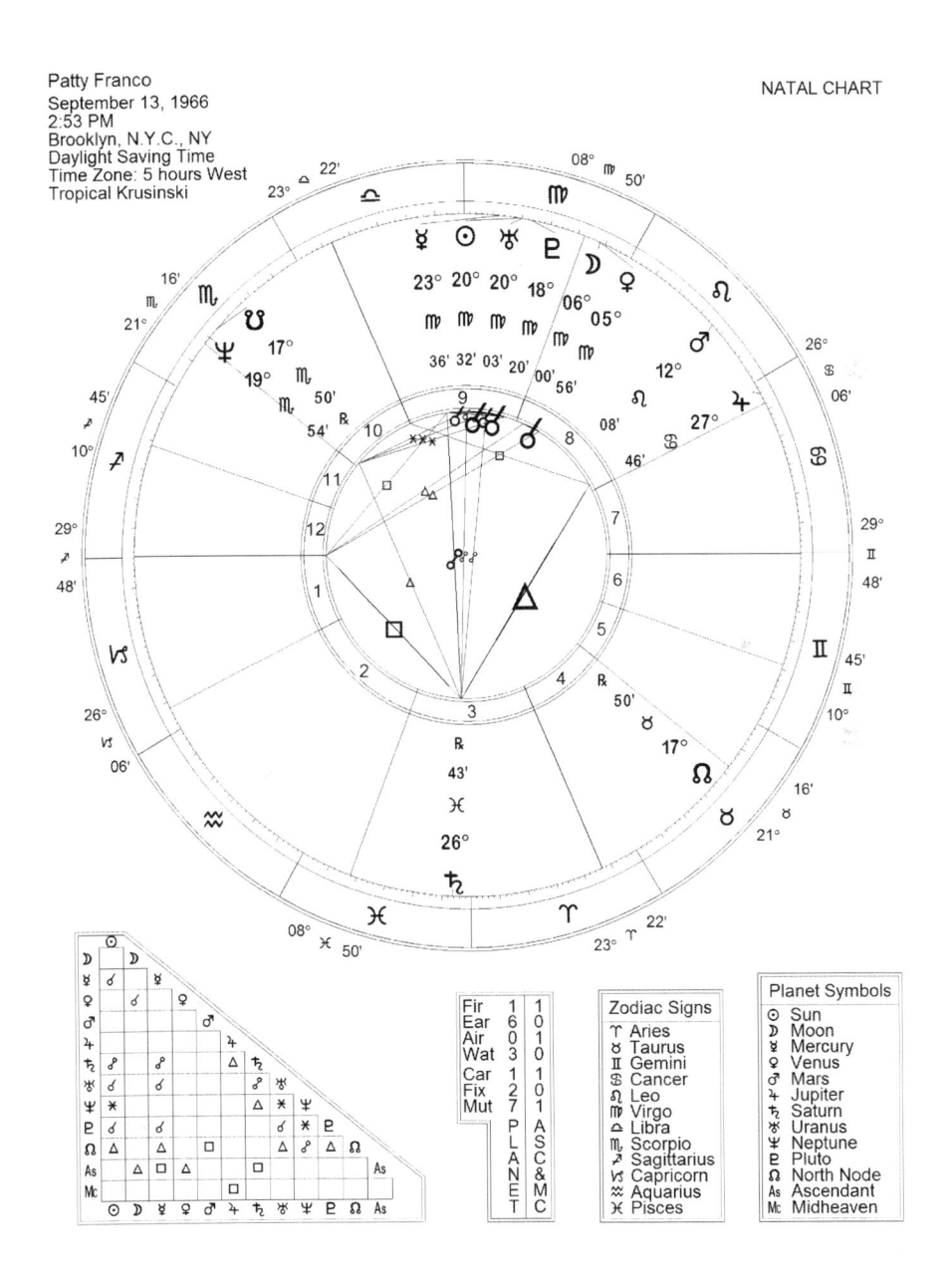

Zodiac Signs	Planet Symbols
♈ Aries	☉ Sun
♉ Taurus	☽ Moon
♊ Gemini	☿ Mercury
♋ Cancer	♀ Venus
♌ Leo	♂ Mars
♍ Virgo	♃ Jupiter
♎ Libra	♄ Saturn
♏ Scorpio	♅ Uranus
♐ Sagittarius	♆ Neptune
♑ Capricorn	♇ Pluto
♒ Aquarius	☊ North Node
♓ Pisces	As Ascendant
	Mc Midheaven

Fir	1	1
Ear	6	0
Air	0	1
Wat	3	0
Car	1	1
Fix	2	0
Mut	7	1
	PLANET	ASC&MC

Approaching Natal Charts

132

Britney Smith
February 9, 1990
10:15 PM
Scranton, Pennsylvania
Standard Time
Time Zone: 5 hours West
Tropical Krusinski

NATAL CHART

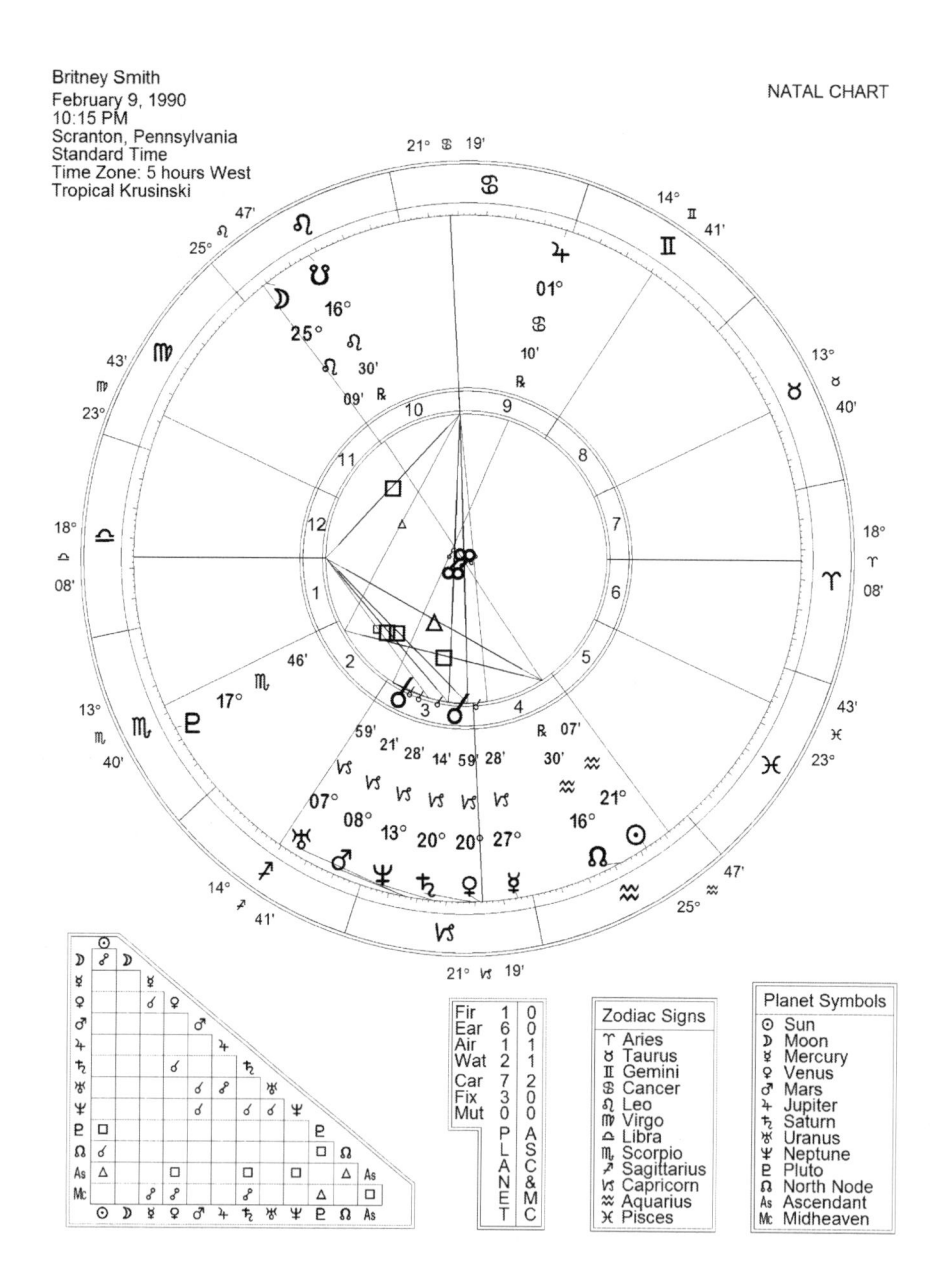

Fast Track Astrologer

Alice Jain: Next, let's see what is prominent in Alice Jain's Natal chart on page 134. Alice has seven out of 10 of her Planets in Masculine Signs (Fire, Air). Furthermore, both her Ascendant A^s and Midheaven M^c are in Fire Signs (Leo ♌ and Aries ♈, respectively), five out of 10 of her Planets are in her 10th House (Sun ☉, Moon ☽, Mercury ☿, Venus ♀, and Mars ♂), and her North Node ☊ is within 3° of her 10th House. Alice puts a lot of energy into shining out (Sun ☉ in 10th House in Aries ♈ and Leo ♌ Ascendant A^s) in her career and the reputation she develops (five Planets in the 10th House). Her Saturn ♄ (structure, discipline) interacts strongly (Square □) with her Moon ☽, which will add structure (Saturn ♄) to her adventurous and ardent approach (Aries ♈) in her career.

Hans Bjorn: Now this is an interesting Natal Chart on page 135. All Planets are in Hans' 8th, 9th, and 11th Houses (transformation, higher exploration, and community, respectively). Five out of his 10 Planets are in Air Signs and none in Earth Signs. Furthermore, his Moon ☽, Neptune ♆, and Saturn ♄, all in Libra ♎ in the 11th House, are very strongly Conjunct ☌, and these three Planets are very strongly Square □ with Mars ♂ in Cancer ♋. Hans will most likely put a lot of energy into exploring the bigger picture in order to keep everything in perspective (9th House). In his wide-ranging exploratory ways (9th House), he will be attuned to the higher aspirational needs (Moon ☽ and Neptune ♆) of the collective (11th House) and ensure they are represented (Saturn ♄).

With time and enough exposure to Natal charts, you will find yourself gradually spotting larger themes in every chart.

134

Alice Jain
May 18, 1947
10:30 AM
Hazleton, Pennsylvania
Daylight Saving Time
Time Zone: 5 hours West
Tropical Krusinski

NATAL CHART

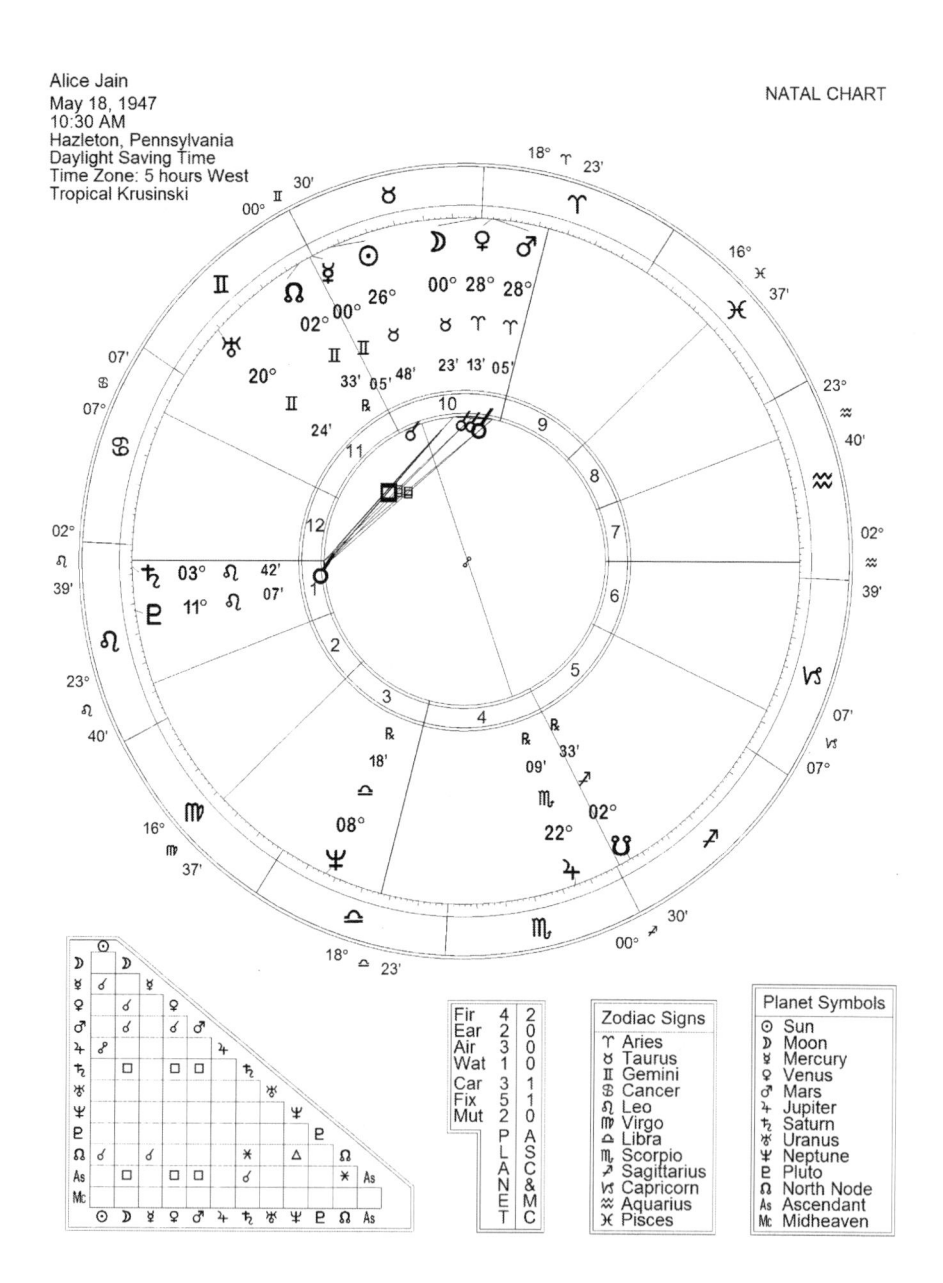

Fast Track Astrologer

Hans Bjorn
July 18, 1953
3:30 PM
Erie, Pennsylvania
Daylight Saving Time
Time Zone: 5 hours West
Tropical Krusinski

NATAL CHART

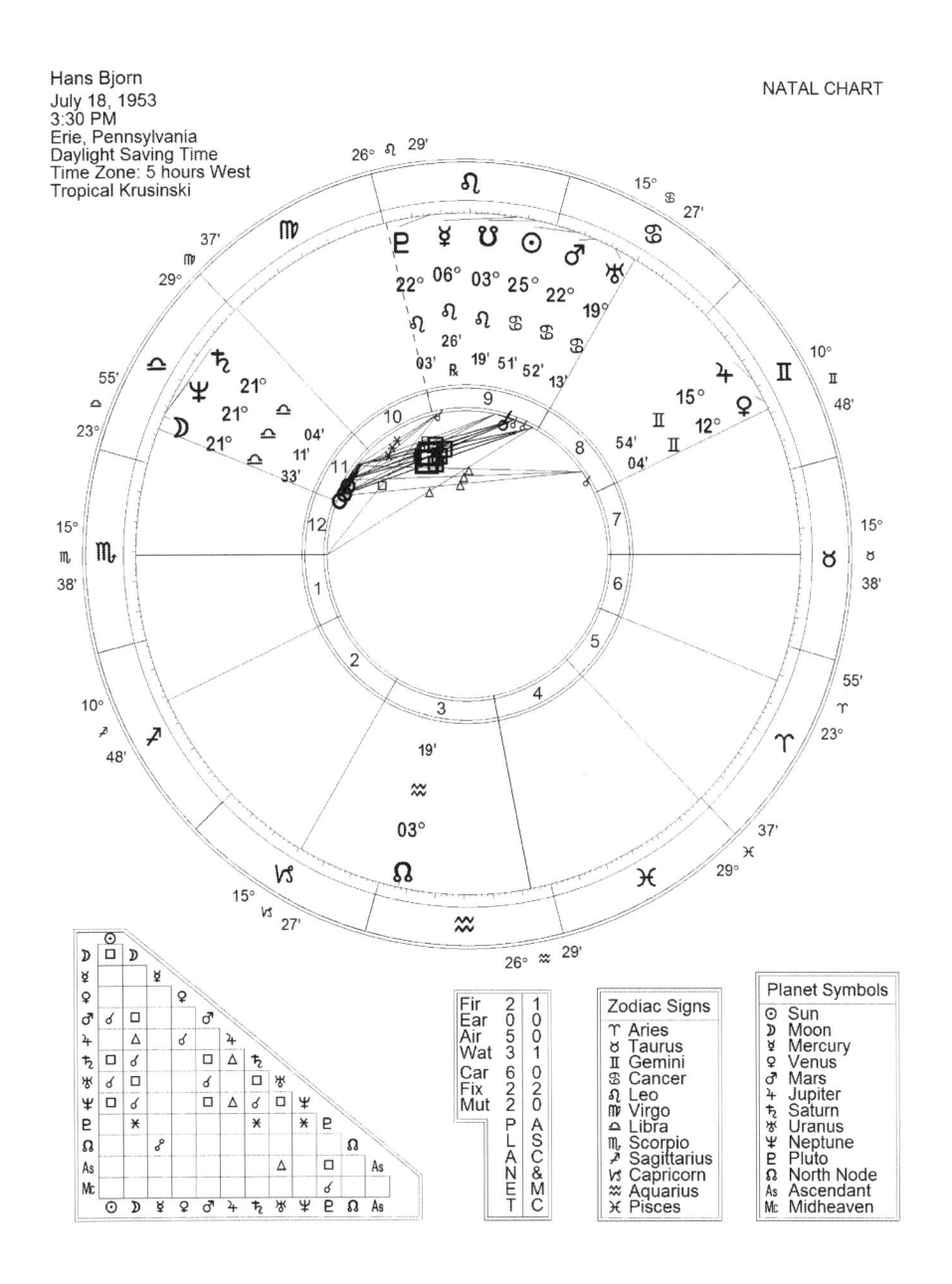

Approaching Natal Charts

19 Delineation Methodology

You've probably figured out by now that a Natal chart contains enough information to spend many hours in a conversation with a person. Generally, astrologers spend one to two hours in a consultation, not only to interpret the Natal chart but also to have a forecasting conversation (next chapter), and sometimes a relocation discussion (Chapter 21). This means that you will have only enough time for a conversation about the most important and relevant information.

Figuring out the gems in a Natal chart takes practice and experience. So you will need to have patience with yourself when you are first learning astrology.

Below, I have outlined suggestions for getting started and gradually evolving and expanding your methodology as you become more proficient in astrology.

Beginner

If you've never delineated astrology charts before, I suggest you start by only delineating each Planet and Personal Point in its Zodiac Sign and House. You experienced this in part 1 of Chapter 17 on delineating components. As you prepare, visualize how the Planetary roles may play out in less-evolved and more-evolved ways.

Novice

Once you get comfortable with the individual Planets and Personal Points in their Zodiac Signs and Houses, I suggest you discuss Planet combinations, which I've summarized in Chapter 13 and you've studied in parts 2 and 3 of Chapter 17 on delineating components. This will add a richness to your conversations. You can also begin to look at House activity, especially for the 1st (initial impressions), 7th (relationships), 10th (career), and 2nd (possessions and self-confidence) Houses. You viewed an example of this in part 4 of Chapter 17 on delineating components.

Experienced

This is a good time to be using all four parts of delineating Natal chart components, which you studied in Chapter 17. At this point, you are probably getting a good feel for finding the larger themes and patterns in a Natal chart, which we covered in the previous chapter on approaching Natal charts. In your conversations with people, you probably will find yourself providing a short overview of the major components of astrology (Chapter 2), so the person can orient your conversation to the configuration of the Natal chart. It's also a good time to use a Transit chart (next chapter) for forecasting the parts of the Natal chart that will be prominent over the next 12 months. When it makes sense, you also can have a conversation on relocation to other areas (Chapter 21).

Professional

At this point, you have been experimenting with all the delineation methods in this book, including the additional three sources of House activity described in Chapter 26 under advanced House activity. You have done enough experiments that you will discover a preferred approach and methodology. All professional astrologers have a basic methodology they prefer and inevitably find better ways and make adjustments as they continue to gain experience. Most professional astrologers become more flexible in their approach so they can have an enhanced focus on the interest of their clients to maximize two-way conversation and take the necessary time to delve deeply into important areas.

I've noticed that experienced astrologers often go back to the basics and delve much more deeply with the client in their conversations. It's a natural evolution from mastering all the details to finding the simplicity and essence in the complexity. I know several prominent astrologers who substantially ignore the Houses because they have found that they can have deep and profound conversations using only the Planets in their Zodiac Signs and the combinations of Planets in unison (Aspects).

There are many useful methodologies, and no single right one. You will discover what works best for you by leveraging the unique gifts you already possess.

In the next section, we will explore other methods including Transits, Relocation, Compatibility and Mundane (World) astrology.

Other Astrology Methods

20 Transits

Up to this point, we have focused on understanding the Natal chart, which is a depiction of your life path toward growth and maturity using the unique combination of energy (Planets, Zodiac Signs, Aspects, and Houses) you are gifted with. We will next turn our attention to Transits, which provide information on the parts of your Natal chart that will be more alive and active during a specific period of time. The concept for Transits is that the Planets in the sky over a period of time (Transiting Planets) will shine their energy on your Natal Planets in situations where Transiting and Natal Planets are Aspecting each other.

BiWheel Chart

To illustrate how Transits work, it will be helpful to first look at BiWheel charts. A BiWheel chart is an overlay of two charts, in this case your Natal chart (i.e. where the Planets were when you were born) and the location of the Planets at a different point in time such as the present. Let's illustrate this by creating a BiWheel chart for Karen. In her BiWheel chart on the next page, the inner ring is her Natal chart. The outer ring is where the Planets were at a specific date, in this case Nov. 30, 2011 at 3:57 pm MST in Santa Fe, New Mexico.

If we simulate the motion of the Transiting Planets within the Zodiac Signs in the outer ring of the BiWheel chart, the Moon ☽ moves counterclockwise and takes approximately 27 days to go full circle around all the Zodiac Signs. The Transiting Sun ☉ takes one year, again in the counterclockwise direction. Note that all the Transiting Planets eventually go full circle in the counterclockwise direction. At the other extreme, Transiting Pluto ♇ takes 248 years to go completely around the 12 Signs of the Zodiac.

Except for the Sun ☉ and Moon ☽, the Transiting Planets periodically move backwards relative to the backdrop of stars (position in the Zodiac) and then, after a few weeks to a few months, resume their forward motion. This effect of Transiting Planets moving backward relative to the Zodiac is referred to as Retrograde ℞ motion. It occurs because we are viewing the Planets from the perspective of the Earth ⊕ relative to the backdrop of stars (Zodiac).

145

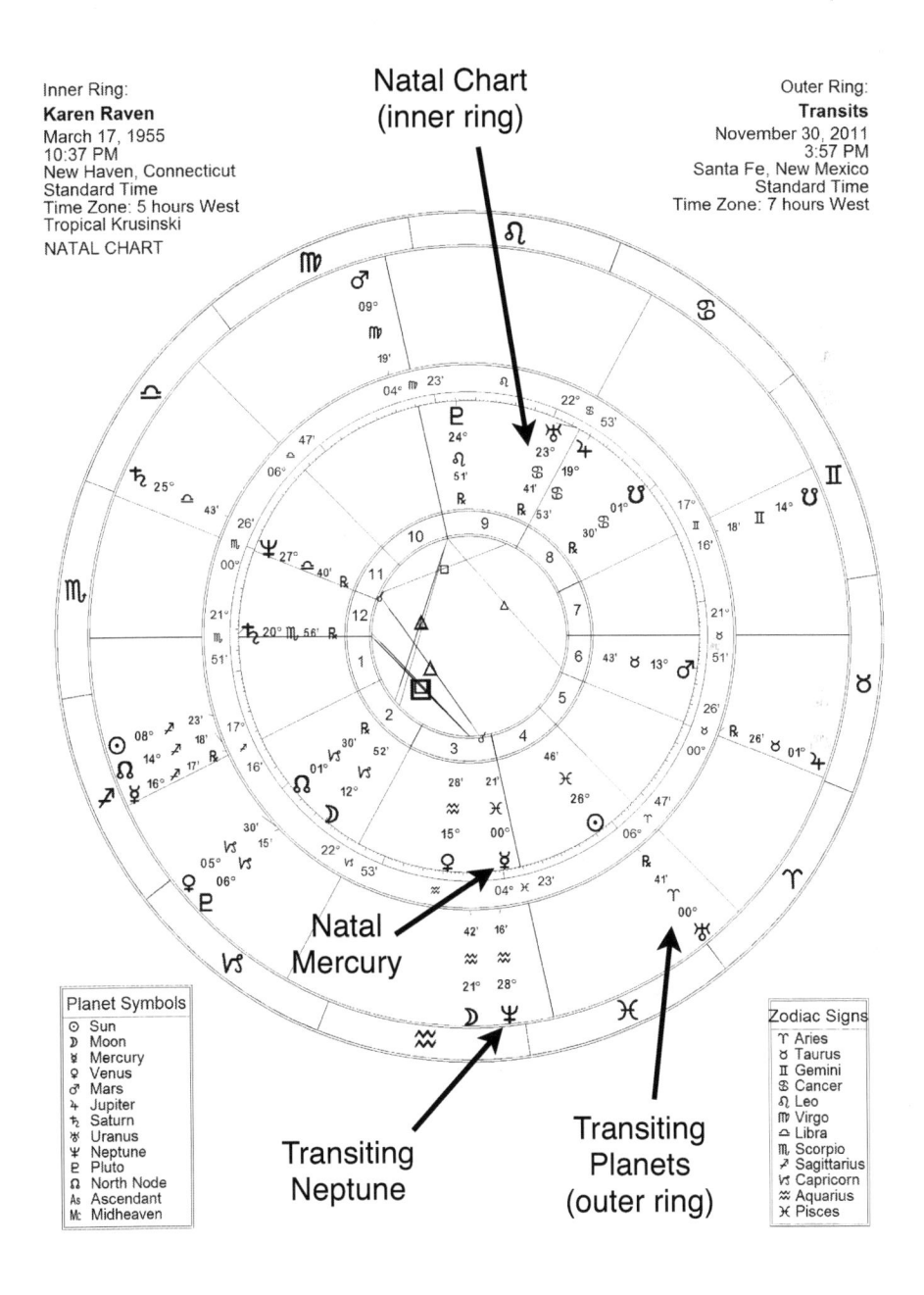

Inner Ring:
Karen Raven
March 17, 1955
10:37 PM
New Haven, Connecticut
Standard Time
Time Zone: 5 hours West
Tropical Krusinski
NATAL CHART

Natal Chart (inner ring)

Outer Ring:
Transits
November 30, 2011
3:57 PM
Santa Fe, New Mexico
Standard Time
Time Zone: 7 hours West

Natal Mercury

Transiting Neptune

Transiting Planets (outer ring)

Planet Symbols	
☉	Sun
☽	Moon
☿	Mercury
♀	Venus
♂	Mars
♃	Jupiter
♄	Saturn
♅	Uranus
♆	Neptune
♇	Pluto
☊	North Node
As	Ascendant
Mc	Midheaven

Zodiac Signs	
♈	Aries
♉	Taurus
♊	Gemini
♋	Cancer
♌	Leo
♍	Virgo
♎	Libra
♏	Scorpio
♐	Sagittarius
♑	Capricorn
♒	Aquarius
♓	Pisces

Transits

In the Biwheel chart on the previous page, notice that Transiting Uranus ♅ (outside ring) in the 4th House has the Retrograde ℞ symbol to indicate that at the particular time of the Transit (November 30, 2011 at 3:57 PM MST), Uranus ♅ was Retrograde ℞. For very slow-moving Transiting Planets such as Pluto ♇, this motion may occur such that Pluto ♇ appears to pass back and forth in front of a particular background star (point in the Zodiac) two or three times before progressing forward in its circular (actually elliptical) motion around the BiWheel.

Let's go back to Karen's BiWheel chart. When one of the Transiting Planets at the present (outer ring) lines up with a Natal Planet (inner ring), the Transiting Planet shines its energy on the Natal Planet. When I say lines up with, I am referring to situations where the two Planets (one Transiting and the other Natal) are Conjunct ☌, Opposition ☍, Trine △, or Square □. Note that some astrologers also include the Minor Aspects.

Let's take a quick example to illustrate this. Viewing Karen's BiWheel chart, we see that Transiting Neptune ♆ (outer ring) in Aquarius ♒ in the 3rd House is lining up (Conjunct ☌) with Natal Mercury ☿ (inner ring) in Pisces ♓ in the 3rd House. Thus, Mercury ☿ in Karen's Natal chart is being energized by Transiting Neptune ♆. During this Transit, Karen's thinking and communication ☿ will have an extra dose of idealism, compassion, and empathy with the collective provided by Transiting Neptune ♆. Since Transiting Neptune ♆ moves slowly (approximately 2° per year on average), this will affect Karen for almost three years before fading out. Note that I use an orb of 3° which means that Karen will have this Planetary effect while

Neptune ♆ and Mercury ☿ are within 3° of each other. Some astrologers use greater or smaller Orbs in their Transit analysis.

A practice with astrologers is to focus only on the slow-moving Transiting Planets, typically Jupiter ♃, Saturn ♄, Uranus ♅, Neptune ♆, and Pluto ♇. I jokingly refer to these slow-moving Transiting Planets as the Chinese water torture Planets because their affect when energizing a Natal Planet can range from several weeks (Transiting Jupiter ♃) to more than three years in the case of Transiting Pluto ♇. When a slow-moving Transiting Planet Aspects a Natal Planet, the effect is very powerful because it is sustained for a long period of time. In contrast, the affect of a Transiting Moon ☽ typically lasts less than half a day.

Looking at a BiWheel chart and trying to figure out all the Transits and their timing over a period of a year (which is pretty typical) is too complicated for most astrologers since Transiting Planets are moving at different speeds and periodically going Retrograde ℞. It turns out there is a better way: Transit charts.

Transit Chart

A Transit chart is a timeline of the Transiting Planets relative to the Natal Planets. An example of a Transit chart for Karen is shown on the next page. This chart is for November 2011 through October 2012. It depicts not only the Transits, but also provides information on the Zodiac Signs and Houses for the Transiting Plants.

Let's first look at the Zodiac Signs and Houses for the Transiting Planets.

148

Transiting Neptune
Conjunct
Natal Mercury

Fast Track Astrologer

The first 10 rows in the Transit chart on the previous page depict Zodiac Sign and House information for the five slowest-moving Transiting Planets (Jupiter ♃, Saturn ♄, Uranus ♅, Neptune ♆, and Pluto ♇). For example, the first row indicates that Jupiter ♃ is in the Zodiac Sign of Taurus ♉ until June 2012 at which time it moves into Gemini ♊. Notice the thin, darker line at the bottom of the bar from November through most of December and again for October 2012. This indicates that Jupiter ♃ is Retrograde ℞ during these times.

The second row focuses on Jupiter's ♃ position relative to Karen's Houses in her Natal chart. We see that from November through most of December, Jupiter ♃ is Retrograde ℞ (the thin, dark line at the bottom of the bar) and in the 6th House. For a short period in December, Jupiter ♃ Retrogrades ℞ far enough backwards that it goes back into Karen's 5th House, and when Direct, moves back into her 6th House. In May of 2012, Jupiter ♃ moves into Karen's 7th House. This Transit chart provides similar Zodiac Sign and House information for each of the remaining four Transiting Planets (third through the tenth rows). Note that the first 10 rows are for the Transiting Planets only. Natal Planets are fixed for life.

Next, let's look at the Transiting Planets affecting Karen's Natal Planets. These are listed from the 11th row to the bottom of Karen's Transit chart. It's time for another example. In Karen's Transit chart, there is a bar about half-way down the chart that goes all the way across the 12 months. That is the same Transiting Neptune ♆ Conjunct ☌ Natal Mercury ☿ example we explored in the Biwheel chart section. The effect lasts a long time (the entire year plus some) because Transiting Neptune ♆ moves slowly. Transiting Neptune ♆ Conjunct ☌ Natal Mercury ☿ indicates that Karen's thinking and communicating will have a strong dose of Neptune ♆ energy: increased compassion and exploring the bigger questions in life.

There is one other facet to consider in this example. Scanning across the same bar, you'll see the number 13 in the middle of February. This indicates that the two Planets (Transiting Neptune ♆ and Natal Mercury ☿) are exactly Conjunct ☌ on February 13, when the effect will be at its peak.

Note that in this Transit chart design, the first Planet is always the Transiting Planet and the second is always the Natal Planet or Personal Point.

Let's look at one other set of Transits. Referring back to Karen's Transit chart above, we see in the bottom four rows that her Natal Midheaven M^c (career) is being Transited by Jupiter ♃ (expansion), Neptune ♆ (higher meaning), and Pluto ♇ (transformation) on and off over the next 12 months. This would indicate that Karen most likely will be looking forward to transforming her career so that she finds higher meaning in her profession.

While you can delineate every Transit in the chart above, it would take too long. What makes more sense is to look for the bigger themes and patterns in the Transit chart based on the areas the client would like to explore.

Those are the basics of Transit charts. In terms of Forecasting, astrologers also use what are known as Progressions and Solar Returns. I find that the Transits are consistently reliable and provide more information than I can cover in a single consultation.

Next, we look at relocating to a new place of residence.

Fast Track Astrologer

21 Relocation

From the perspective of astrology, what is the effect if you move to a place different from your birth location? To explore this, astrologers create a Relocation chart. This is your Natal chart, but with the birth location changed to the new place of residence.

As an example, if you were born at 4:00 PM in Boston and moved to Los Angeles, your Relocation chart would have your same birth date, but your birth time and location would be changed to 1:00 PM in Los Angeles (4:00 PM in Boston is 1:00 PM in Los Angeles).

In this chapter, we will compare the Natal chart with Relocated charts and explore the effects.

Let's start by examining three Relocated charts for Karen, along with her Natal chart. In all four situations, she was born at the exact same time: 10:37 pm EST.

The three new locations we will explore are Honolulu, Hawaii (birth time of 5:37 PM HAST on March 17), Santa Fe, New Mexico (birth time of 8:37 PM MST on March 17) and Milan, Italy (birth time of 4:37 AM CET on March 18).

You can view the three Relocated charts and the one Natal chart on the next four pages. Note that the Natal chart for New Haven, Connecticut is the same Natal chart we have been previously using for Karen.

Observations

Let's make some observations. Comparing any particular Planet in all four charts, we see that the locations for this selected Planet relative to the Zodiac are identical. For example, the Sun ☉ is 26° 46' in Pisces ♓ in all four charts. This makes sense, because the birth times are identical for all four charts. The calculation of a Planet's position in the Zodiac is time-dependent and not location- (on the Earth ⊕) dependent.

What does change in all four charts is the position of the Planets within the Houses. This makes sense as the 1st House begins, by definition, at the eastern horizon at the location and time of birth. While all the times are the same, the eastern horizon will point to a different backdrop of stars (Zodiac) as the location on Earth ⊕ varies (due to the curvature of the Earth ⊕).

153

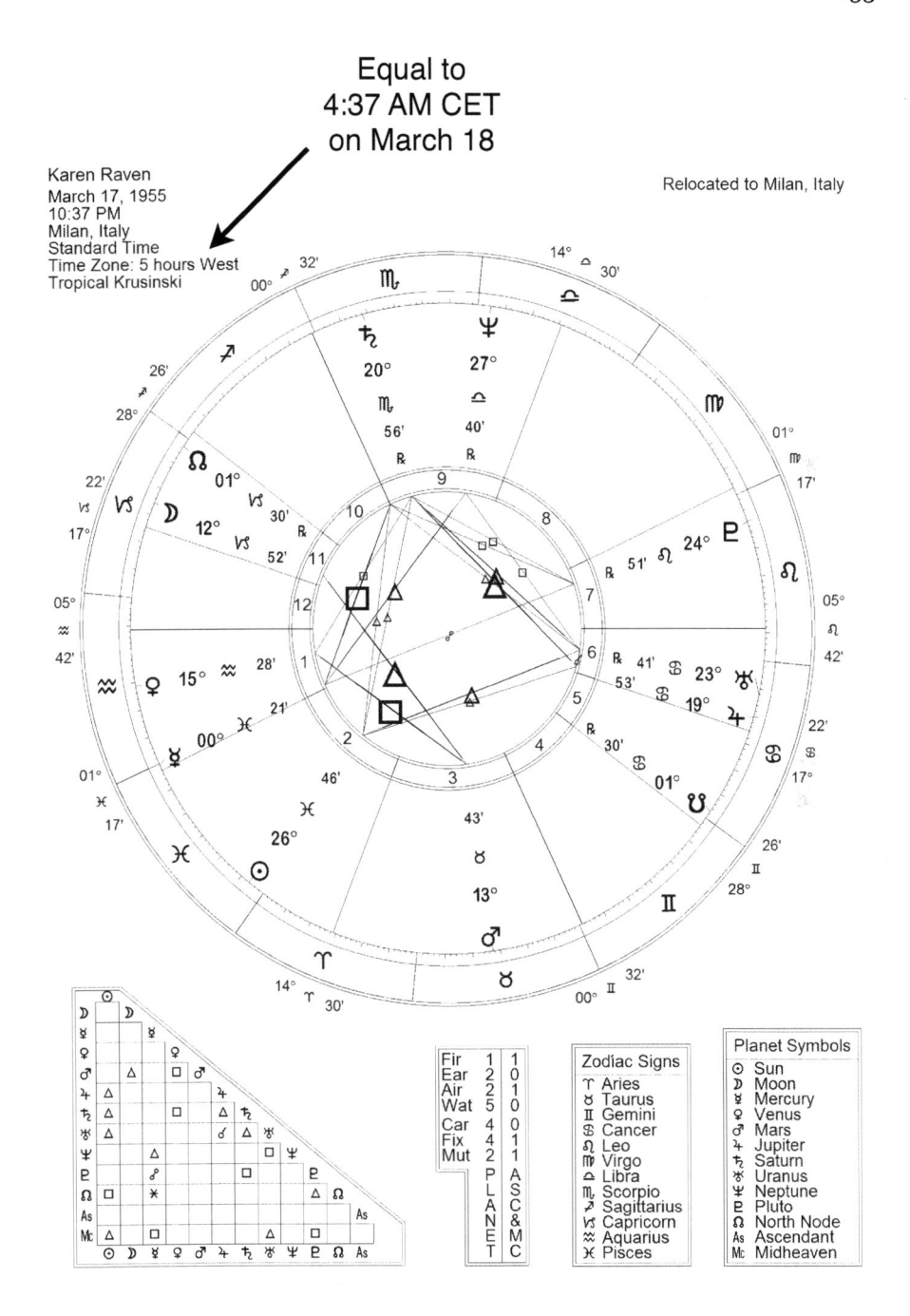

Equal to
4:37 AM CET
on March 18

Karen Raven
March 17, 1955
10:37 PM
Milan, Italy
Standard Time
Time Zone: 5 hours West
Tropical Krusinski

Relocated to Milan, Italy

Relocation

154

Karen Raven
March 17, 1955
10:37 PM
New Haven, Connecticut
Standard Time
Time Zone: 5 hours West
Tropical Krusinski

NATAL CHART

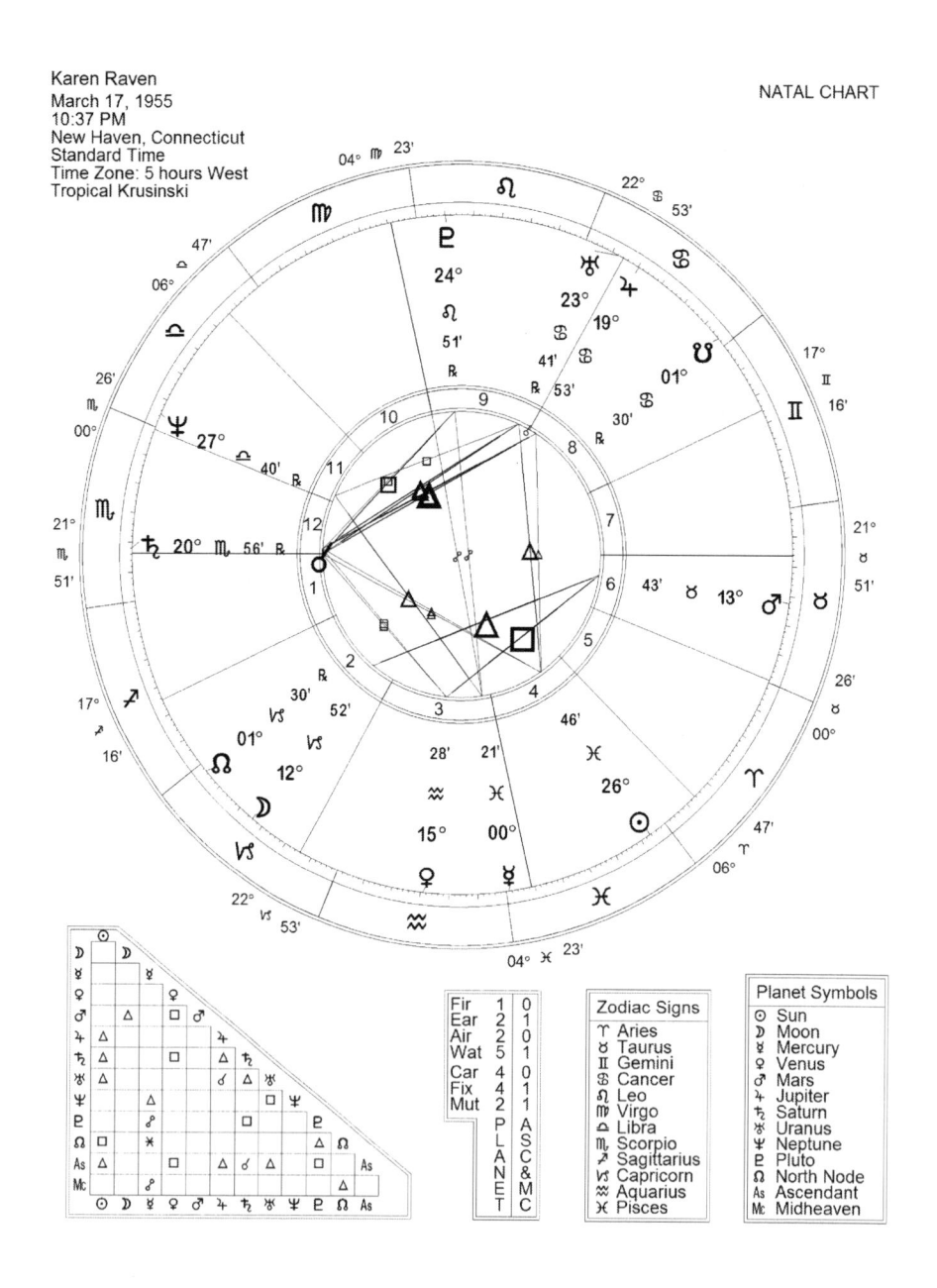

Fast Track Astrologer

155

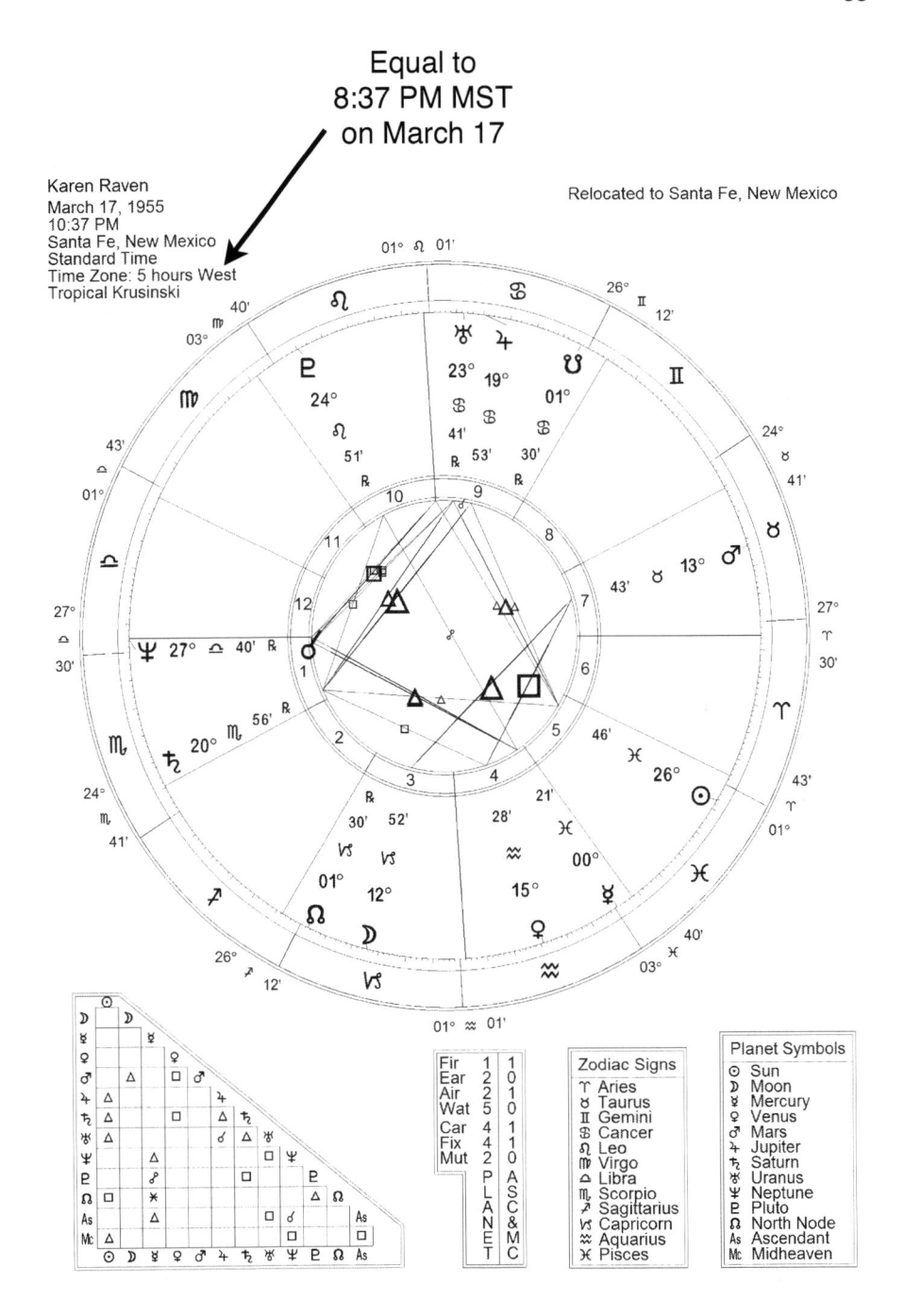

Equal to
8:37 PM MST
on March 17

Karen Raven
March 17, 1955
10:37 PM
Santa Fe, New Mexico
Standard Time
Time Zone: 5 hours West
Tropical Krusinski

Relocated to Santa Fe, New Mexico

Relocation

156

**Equal to
5:37 PM HAST
on March 17**

Karen Raven
March 17, 1955
10:37 PM
Honolulu, Hawaii
Standard Time
Time Zone: 5 hours West
Tropical Krusinski

Relocated to Honolulu, Hawaii

Fast Track Astrologer

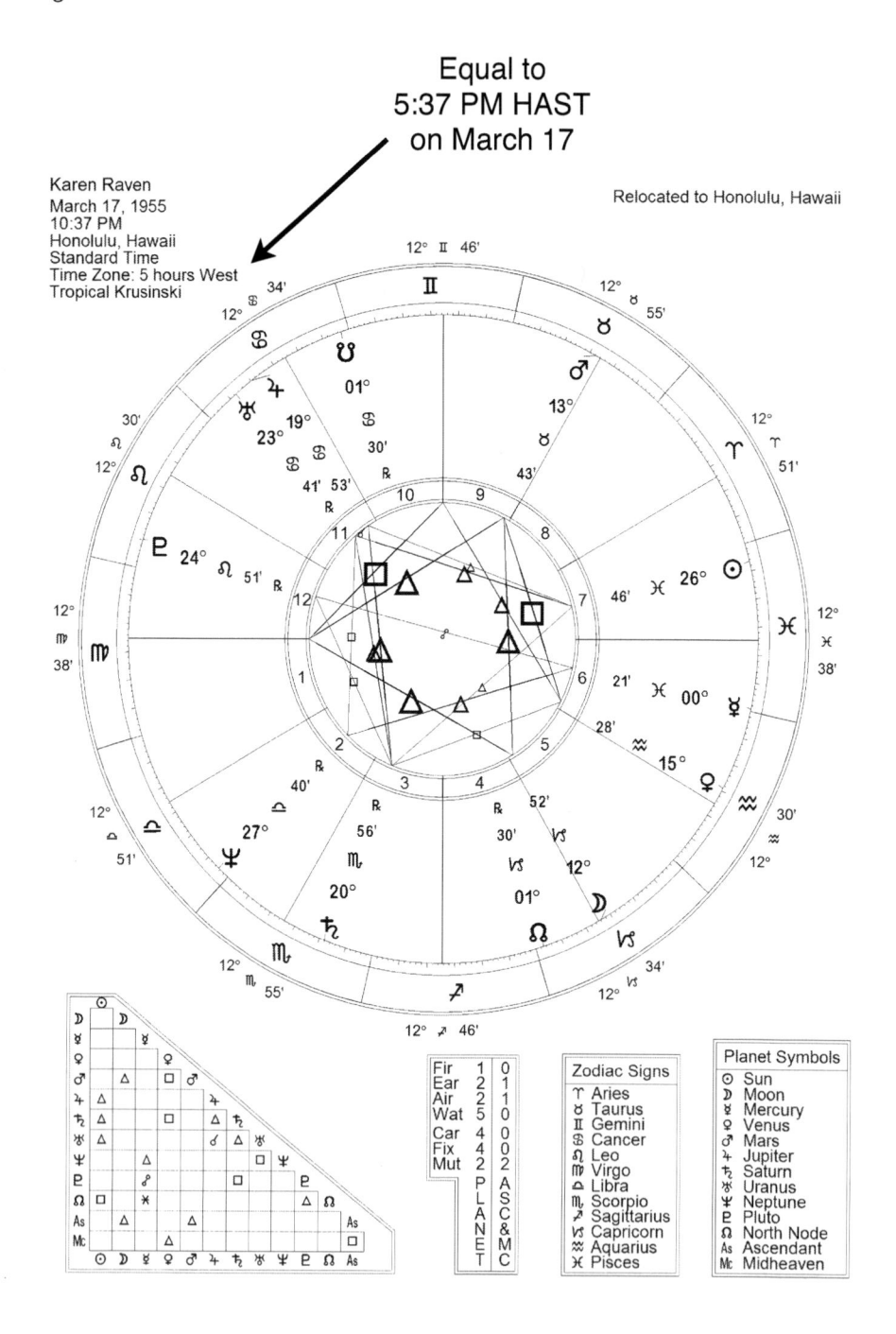

As we move the birth location from east to west (Milan to Honolulu), the Planets and Zodiac Signs rotate counterclockwise (relative to the Houses), while the Houses stay essentially the same, with the 1st House always beginning at the eastern horizon at the particular location.

As we move the birth location from west to east (Honolulu to Milan), the Planets and Zodiac Signs rotate clockwise while the Houses stay essentially the same. The Houses will not be the same sizes as their calculations are affected by the latitude of the location, time of day, and time of year. This will become clearer for you in Chapter 27 on celestial geometry.

Effect on Delineation of the Charts

What is the effect on the delineation of a Natal chart compared to a Relocated chart?

First of all, what doesn't change are the Planet positions relative to the Zodiac (backdrop of stars) as well as the Planet Aspects. Thus, all Planets (parts of you) have the same characteristics in both charts and they play out in the same cliques (Aspects).

What does change are the Positions of the Planets within the Houses as well as the Aspects of the Planets relative to the Ascendant A^s and the Midheaven M^c. The effect on the delineation of the Natal chart is to change the emphasis Planets have in the various areas of life (Houses).

For example, in Karen's Natal chart, her Sun ☉ is in the 4th House, so she has an emphasis in shining out in her home. In Honolulu, Karen's Sun ☉ is in her 7th House, so she may have more emphasis on developing close relationships. In Milan, her Sun ☉ is in her 2nd House, which will emphasize her possessions, money, and development of self-confidence. Again, the change that occurs is the emphasis the Planets have in the different areas of life (Houses) as well as the characteristics the person portrays (1st House Cusp) and the characteristics of the person's career (10th House Cusp).

As another example, Mars ♂ is in Taurus ♉ in the 6th House in Karen's Natal chart. At her birth place, she will have additional steady energy in her day-to-day activities (6th House). In Milan, Mars ♂ is in her 3rd House, so she will have increased energy in her thinking and communicating. If Karen wants to write a book, Milan might be a good place because of the extra emphasis in her House of thinking and communicating. Santa Fe also would be a good location for Karen to write a book as her Moon ☽ in Capricorn ♑ (need to get results) moves to her 3rd House of thinking and communicating.

Astrologers use this technique, called Relocation, to help clients gain insights about the effect of living in locations that differ from their birth place. When you move to a new location, the influence of your Natal chart (at your birth location) is still dominant. In other words, moving to another location does not change the unique combination of gifts you were born with, but rather the areas of life where you emphasize these gifts.

Thanks to the advancement of computers and graphic displays, there is another approach for determining possibilities for relocating to another area. It is referred to as astrocartography. This technique involves viewing a map of the world, or parts of the world, and looking at computer-generated lines on the map depicting locations that will emphasize certain features in your Relocation chart. For example, you may want to emphasize the career aspects of your life. In this case, an approach is to look at the areas of the world where your Relocated chart will have multiple Planets (or specific Planets) in your 10th House of your career. Astrocartography is a quick and crude way to narrow down possibilities for relocation. Many, but not all astrology software programs have this astrocartography feature.

Let's next look at compatibility. As you will see, I have a view on this topic that differs from the views of many other astrologers.

22   Compatibility

There are a number of books written about Natal chart compatibility with numerous guidelines on good and bad combinations. Here's the problem: I have delineated many charts for couples who have an astrological combination made in heaven, according to the classic textbooks on compatibility. Many of these couples are now divorced. I also have delineated charts for many couples who, according to the classic texts, are like oil and water and will not work. Many of these couples are still together and have flourishing relationships that are a model for all.

What's Going On Here?

As emphasized earlier in this book, there is no such thing as a good or a bad Natal chart. A Natal chart is a depiction of the unique combination of energy possessed by an individual. It is up to the individual to grow and mature in directing her energies in ways that work well for her. It's a lifetime commitment to grow and learn through experience, observation, and experimentation.

The same is true for couples. Two people in a relationship possess their own unique combination of energetic gifts and have their lifetimes to learn to grow and mature in using these gifts.

After hundreds of consultations, I am absolutely convinced that the key factor in a couple staying together and enjoying a growing and fruitful relationship has to do with two elements:

- Each person's level of maturity and desire to grow in directing their own unique combination of energetic gifts; and
- The willingness of each person to learn about the other with the intent of nurturing and supporting the other's growth.

What Does This Mean?

If two people are together as a couple and one or both are directing their energies in ways that are less mature with no interest in individually growing, the relationship will be limited and perhaps short-lived.

If both people in a relationship are committed to consciously striving for self-improvement and seeking to understand and support the other person, the relationship will likely grow and blossom.

Where Does Astrology Fit In?

When a couple asks me for a compatibility consultation, I let them know that there is no such thing as a good or a bad combination. The foundation for a blossoming relationship requires that both people (1) understand themselves and commit to self-growth, and (2) understand their partner and commit to supporting the partner's growth.

My approach is to have a Natal chart discussion with each person separately, followed by a discussion with both people present for the purpose of helping them understand each other better and learning how to support each other.

The question for the couple then becomes: "Do you want to continue this relationship and, if so, what will you do differently?"

If the couple decides not to take on the commitment with each other, a celebration is in order because they made the decision to alter their relationship before getting much deeper into a partnership that eventually may not have worked.

If the couple decides to make the commitment to stay together, they will be much more likely to have a blossoming relationship because they have a better understanding of themselves and each other and a conscious commitment to support each other's growth.

23 Mundane (World) Astrology

Mundane astrology is devoted to the exploration of worldwide events over a period of time. This is currently a fun area to explore as we are experiencing unusual events at the time of this writing (beginning of 2012).

A Mundane analysis is done by generating a Transit chart for the Planets as they move through the sky over a period of time. This is a bit different from the Transit chart described earlier, which compared the Planets moving over a period of time to a set of fixed Natal Planets.

In the case of a Mundane Transit chart, we are generating a timeline of the Planets moving through a period of time and viewing their

Aspects (angles) with each other. This is like generating a series of Natal charts, say one per day for 100 days in a row. For each chart, we record the Planet Aspects. We then plot these changing Aspects over time (e.g. 100 days in a row) to see how they change. The technical name for this is a Transit to Transit chart. In Chapter 20, the Transit chart generated is technically referred to as a Transit to Natal chart.

On pages 168 and 169, you'll find Transit to Transit charts for 2012 through 2015, each chart covering one year. Take a few minutes to explore these Transit charts.

As you scan these four charts, we can make several observations:

- **Pluto ♇ is in Capricorn ♑** during the entire five-year period (and will be until 2023).
- **Uranus ♅ is in Aries ♈** during the entire five-year period (and will remain there until 2018).
- **Neptune ♆ is in Pisces ♓** (and will remain there until 2025).
- **Pluto ♇ will Square ☐ Uranus ♅ on an off** until the spring of 2015. This Square ☐ will be exact seven times on the following dates: **June 24 and September 18, 2012; May 20 and November 1, 2013; April 21 and December 14, 2014; and March 16, 2015.**

Finally, we see combinations of Transits occurring simultaneously:

- **June 24/25, 2012** Uranus ♅ Squares ☐ Pluto ♇, and Jupiter ♃ Squares ☐ Neptune ♆.
- **July 17/19, 2013** Jupiter ♃ Trines △ Saturn ♄, Jupiter ♃ Trines △ Neptune ♆, and Saturn ♄ Trines △ Neptune ♆. This

configuration is known as a Grand Trine because all three Planets are approximately one-third of a circle from each other, which looks like a large triangle in a Natal chart. Note that all three Planets are in Water Signs: Jupiter ♃ in Cancer ♋, Saturn ♄ in Scorpio ♏, and Neptune ♆ in Pisces ♓. Planets in a Grand Trine have a very easy flow of energy with each other. It's like "greasing the skids."

- **April 20/21, 2014** Jupiter ♃ Squares □ Uranus ♅, Jupiter ♃ Opposes ☍ Pluto ♇, and Uranus ♅ Squares □ Pluto ♇. This is known as a T-Square, which occurs when two Planets are in Opposition ☍ and a third Planet is Squaring □ the first two. Note that all three Planets are in Cardinal Signs: Jupiter ♃ in Cancer ♋, Uranus ♅ in Aries ♈, and Pluto ♇ in Capricorn ♑. Planets in a T-Square in Cardinal Signs tend to be very powerful because Cardinal Signs have characteristics of initiating action.

- **March 3/16, 2015** Jupiter ♃ Trines △ Uranus ♅, and Uranus ♅ Squares □ Pluto ♇.

I've summarized these key dates in the table on page 170.

In the remainder of this chapter, we will look at the three outer Planets, Pluto ♇, Neptune ♆, and Uranus ♅, individually followed by an analysis of the Transits depicted in the table on page 170.

168

Transits

Transit to Transit:

2012	Jan	Feb	Mar	Apr	May	Jun	Jul	Aug	Sep	Oct	Nov	Dec
♃ in sign			♉						♊			
♄ in sign					♎						♏	
♅ in sign	♒											
♆ in sign							♓					
♇ in sign							♑					
♃ ☍ ♄ (♉, ♎)						25						
♃ □ ♆ (♊, ♓)												
♄ △ ♆ (♎, ♓)			12			24						
♄ △ ♇ (♉, ♑)									18	10		
♅ □ ♇ (♈, ♑)												
2012	Jan	Feb	Mar	Apr	May	Jun	Jul	Aug	Sep	Oct	Nov	Dec

Transits

Transit to Transit:

2013	Jan	Feb	Mar	Apr	May	Jun	Jul	Aug	Sep	Oct	Nov	Dec
♃ in sign			♊						♋			
♄ in sign							♏					
♅ in sign							♈					
♆ in sign							♓					
♇ in sign							♑					
♃ △ ♄ (♋, ♏)								21				
♃ □ ♅ (♋, ♈)							17					
♃ △ ♆ (♋, ♓)							17					
♄ ☍ ♆ (♏, ♓)						11	19	7				
♄ △ ♇ (♏, ♑)					20							12
♅ □ ♇ (♈, ♑)												
2013	Jan	Feb	Mar	Apr	May	Jun	Jul	Aug	Sep	Oct	Nov	Dec

Fast Track Astrologer

169

Transits

Transit to Transit:

2014	Jan	Feb	Mar	Apr	May	Jun	Jul	Aug	Sep	Oct	Nov	Dec
♃ in sign				♋			♏			♌		♐
♄ in sign							♈					
⛢ in sign							♓					
♆ in sign							♑					
♇ in sign									25			
♃△♄ (♋, ♏)		26		20	24							
♃△⛢ (♋, ♈)				20								
♃□⛢ (♋, ♈)				21								
♃☍♇ (♋, ♑)	31											14
⛢□♇ (♈, ♑)												
2014	Jan	Feb	Mar	Apr	May	Jun	Jul	Aug	Sep	Oct	Nov	Dec

Transits

Transit to Transit:

2015	Jan	Feb	Mar	Apr	May	Jun	Jul	Aug	Sep	Oct	Nov	Dec
♃ in sign				♌						♍		
♄ in sign			♐					♏				
⛢ in sign						♈						
♆ in sign						♓						
♇ in sign						♑						
♃□♄ (♌, ♏)		3						3				
♃△⛢ (♌, ♈)						22						
♃☍♆ (♍, ♓)												
♄□♆ (♐, ♓)			16								26	
♃△♇ (♍, ♑)										11		
⛢□♇ (♈, ♑)									16			
2015	Jan	Feb	Mar	Apr	May	Jun	Jul	Aug	Sep	Oct	Nov	Dec

Mundane (World) Astrology

Key Transit Dates: 2012 - 2015	
Key Date	**Transit(s)**
June 24/25, 2012	Uranus ♅ Square □ Pluto ♇ Jupiter ♃ Square □ Neptune ♆
September 18, 2012	Uranus ♅ Square □ Pluto ♇
May 20, 2013	Uranus ♅ Square □ Pluto ♇
July 17/19, 2013	Jupiter ♃ Trine △ Saturn ♄ Jupiter ♃ Trine △ Neptune ♆ Saturn ♄ Trine △ Neptune ♆
November 1, 2013	Uranus ♅ Square □ Pluto ♇
April 20/21, 2014	Uranus ♅ Square □ Pluto ♇ Jupiter ♃ Square □ Uranus ♅ Jupiter ♃ Oppose ☍ Pluto ♇
December 14, 2014	Uranus ♅ Square □ Pluto ♇
March 3/16, 2015	Uranus ♅ Square □ Pluto ♇ Jupiter ♃ Trine △ Uranus ♅

Outer Planets

Pluto ♇ in Capricorn ♑: Pluto ♇ represents fundamental transformation as well as the use of power. When Pluto ♇ is in play, there is attention to that which is secret, hidden, and not wanting to be revealed. Because Pluto ♇ is in Capricorn ♑, the focus will be on worldwide structures such as institutions, governments, financial industry, big businesses, and all other structures that exert power and control.

The last time Pluto ♇ was in Capricorn ♑ was from 1762 until 1778. In the United States of America (USA), this period coincided with the English government gradually increasing its power and control over the American colonies until the situation became intolerable for the colonists. This led to the Declaration of Independence and the American Revolution, resulting in the birth of the USA.

Pluto ♇ entered Capricorn ♑ in 2008 and will remain there until 2023. In 2008, the world saw the near collapse of the financial institutions. Secretly, the USA Federal Reserve lent more than $7 trillion dollars (equivalent to half of the USA gross domestic product) to the major banking institutions to keep them afloat. The near collapse of the financial institutions led to a severe recession, which was still in play at the beginning of 2012. From 2008 to 2012, governments, big businesses, and financial institutions have been secretly working together to increase surveillance on citizens, promote sweetheart deals that benefit large institutions and government, and override the compelling evidence that shows the world's environment is significantly degrading.

Neptune ♆ in Pisces ♓: Neptune ♆ represents the collective consciousness of the world. It is an energy that strives to create a more beautiful place emphasizing compassion, fairness, understanding, and coming from the heart. When Neptune ♆ is in Pisces ♓, which it Rules (Rulers are covered in Chapter 26), its emphasis is at its strongest.

The last time Neptune ♆ was in Pisces ♓ was from 1847 until 1862. During this time in USA history, slavery became unconscionable for a critical mass of Americans, resulting in the American Civil War in the early 1860s and the freeing of the slaves.

Neptune ♆ crossed the Cusp of Pisces ♓ in early 2011 and then Retrograded ℞ back into Aquarius ♒. Early in 2012, it went back into Pisces ♓, where it will remain until 2025. Over the next 13 years, we can expect the collective consciousness of the people of the world to express a theme of fairness, understanding, and compassion by imagining what the world can be like when we see each other as one. The Occupy Wall Street movement, Arab Spring, and increasing protests throughout the world beginning in 2011 are examples of how Neptune ♆ in Pisces ♓ energy can manifest.

Uranus ♅ in Aries ♈: Uranus ♅ represents the part of humanity that wants to be liberated. Where tensions occur between the status quo of structures and people desiring to be liberated, Uranus ♅ is there as the catalyst for sudden change to help make the world a better place. With Uranus ♅ in Aries ♈, the energy of Uranus ♅ will be more ardent and impulsive and display less patience.

The last time Uranus ♅ was in Aries ♈ occurred between 1927 and 1935. In world history, this was when the excesses of businesses and speculation led to the sudden collapse of the world stock markets in 1929, followed by the Great Depression, which lasted throughout the 1930s. During this time, substantial reforms were enacted to reign in financial institutions and the New Deal was created in the USA to help support those in need, significantly enhancing the social support network for the people.

In the present cycle, Uranus ♅ entered Aries ♈ in 2010, where it will remain until 2018, when Uranus ♅ moves into Taurus ♉. Up to this point in 2012, we have seen a groundswell of dissension for the status quo. People have been protesting the oppression they feel from high unemployment, the housing downturn, the special treatment given by governments to the banking industry and other big businesses, the erosion of environmental legislation, and the gradual decline of our rights. With Uranus ♅ in Aries ♈, we can expect disruptive changes to occur where tension exists.

Major Transits from 2012 through 2015

While I have provided exact dates for the most significant Transits in the table on page 170, you should view these energies playing out in force from a month or two before the exact dates to a month or two after the exact dates. When Uranus ♅ is in play as it is here, the tensions build until a sudden change occurs. It is impossible to say exactly when this will occur. It's like trying to predict when an earthquake will occur.

Uranus ♅ in Aries ♈ Square ☐ Pluto ♇ in Capricorn ♑ on June 24, 2012, September 18, 2012, May 20, 2013, November 1, 2013, April 21, 2014, December 14, 2014, and March 16, 2015: Because of the Retrograde ℞ motion of Uranus ♅ and Pluto ♇, these two Planets are exactly Square ☐ seven times between 2012 and 2015. Uranus ♅ in Aries ♈ can be thought of as representing the people of the world wanting to liberate themselves in areas of their lives where they feel oppressed or that they're getting a raw deal. Pluto ♇ in Capricorn ♑ represents the institutions, big businesses, major associations, and governments wanting to protect and expand their power, often through secret dealings. In a sense, this is a squaring off of the collective wanting to change the status quo with the major institutions wanting to protect and enhance their position of power and influence.

Jupiter ♃ Square ☐ Neptune ♆ (June 25, 2012), Jupiter ♃ Trine △ Saturn ♄ (July 17, 2013), Jupiter ♃ Trine △ Neptune ♆ (July 17, 2013), Jupiter ♃ Square ☐ Uranus ♅ (April 20, 2014), Jupiter ♃ Oppose ☍ Pluto ♇ (April 20, 2014), and Jupiter ♃ Trine △ Uranus ♅ (March 3, 2015): When Jupiter ♃ Aspects another Planet, it adds expansion, optimism, faith, and a positive, "can do" attitude to the Planet it Aspects. When Aspecting Pluto ♇ in Capricorn ♑, this expansion is focused on the power of institutions; when Aspecting Neptune ♆ in Pisces ♓, the expansion is focused on the betterment of humanity; when Aspecting Uranus ♅ in Aries ♈, the expansion is focused on sudden change, which creates liberation and freedom; and when Aspecting Saturn ♄, the expansion is focused on expanding institutional structures.

June 24/25, 2012: Uranus ♅ Square □ Pluto ♇, and Jupiter ♃ Square □ Neptune ♆: This is a time when the collective energy of the people (Uranus ♅) squares off with the institutions in power (Pluto ♇ in Capricorn ♑), and both have an added emphasis (Jupiter ♃) on compassion, understanding, and visualizing a better place for all (Neptune ♆).

July 17/19, 2013: Grand Trine with Neptune ♆, Jupiter ♃ and Saturn ♄: This is a time when there is an expansive (Jupiter ♃) and fluid movement of energy (Grand Trine) to elevate mankind to a better place (Neptune ♆) by making changes to the major institutional structures (Saturn ♄).

April 20/21, 2014: T-Square with Jupiter ♃, Uranus ♅ and Pluto ♇: This is similar to the seven times when Uranus ♅ Squares □ Pluto ♇, but magnified by the expansionary energy of Jupiter ♃. The energy for both liberation and control will be high.

March 3/16, 2015: Uranus ♅ Square □ Pluto ♇, and Jupiter ♃ Trine △ Uranus ♅: This is similar to the seven times Uranus ♅ Squares □ Pluto ♇, but with the Uranus ♅ energy magnified by Jupiter ♃. This will provide a strong desire by the collective to make sudden changes for the benefit of all.

The period we are going through from 2012 through 2015 will, from an astrological perspective, bring profound change. The end result of this time period will be interesting to see.

On a Lighter Note

I'd like to conclude this chapter on a lighter note and have some fun doing it. We will move forward in time to the ancient city of João Pessoa in Brazil. The date is October 17, 2015 and the chart is shown on the next page.

Let's see if you can find the famous song in this chart. I'll give you a hint. This is a time "when the Moon ☽ is in the 7th House." If you still can't figure it out, relax and let your "hair" down. If that still doesn't work for you, go to an Internet search engine and type the phrase: "when the moon is in the seventh house."

While the Moon ☽ is in the 7th House and Jupiter ♃ aligns ☌ with Mars ♂ about every 27 months, the rest of this Natal configuration is interesting. Pluto ♇ is shining its strong transformational energy on Mars ♂, the Planet of action, and this combination is magnified by Jupiter's ♃ expansive energy (Pluto ♇ Trine △ both Mars ♂ and Jupiter ♃). Furthermore, Uranus ♅ is opposing ☍ the Sun ☉ and Trine △ with the Moon ☽, which is an inward and outward energy for liberation and freedom. Finally, Venus ♀, the Planet of relationship, is opposing ☍ Neptune ♆, the Planet associated with the higher form of love, which emphasizes relationships at the individual and collective level. So, this could be a very interesting point in time in 2015.

Hopefully, you now have a feel for Mundane astrology, which involves an analysis of worldwide Transits.

NATAL CHART

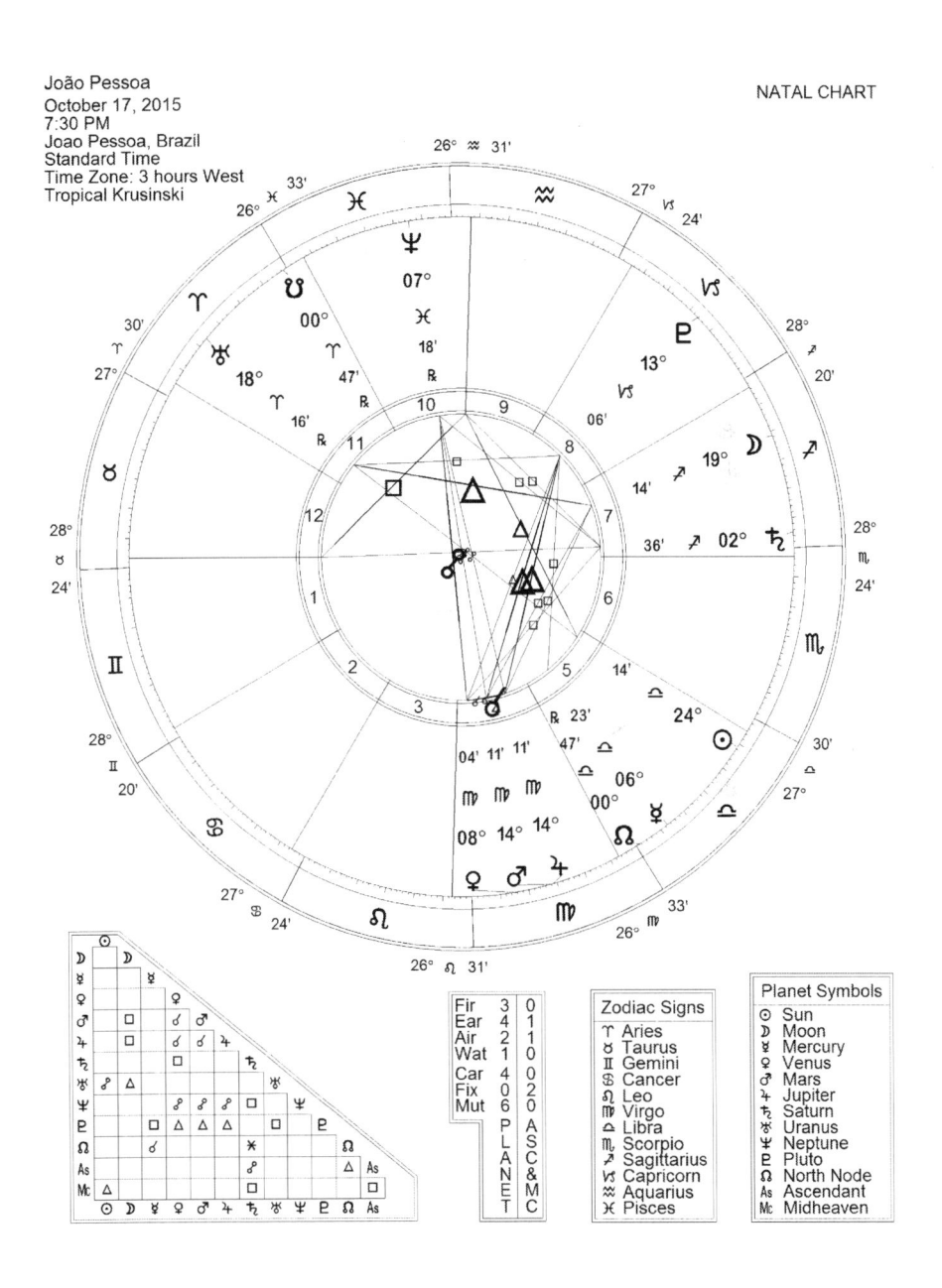

João Pessoa
October 17, 2015
7:30 PM
Joao Pessoa, Brazil
Standard Time
Time Zone: 3 hours West
Tropical Krusinski

Mundane (World) Astrology

Finale

Finale

Fast Track Astrologer

24 Now It's Your Turn

As you can tell from reading this book, astrology is methodical and straight-forward. It is also very robust in that it conveys a unique energetic combination that is abundant in meaning and reveals enormous potential for growth.

There are four basic components of astrology that add a richness to the unique energetic combinations within each individual. These include the Planets, the actors within you and a part of you; the Zodiac Signs, conveying personality to each Planet; the Aspects, indicating the combinations of Planets that interact in unison; and the Houses, depicting the areas of life in which the Planets have emphasis.

Now that you have an understanding of how astrology works, I invite you, if you haven't done so already, to create and delineate your own Natal chart.

There are a number of sites on the web where you can create and print out your Natal chart for free. One very useful web location is Astrodienst (www.astro.com). Another is Astrolabe (www.alabe.com/freechart/). While these free Natal charts will not have the same look as the charts in this book, you will be able to easily draw the parallels.

Another option is to go to my Astrology web site at www.usefulastrology.com and click on the "Purchase a Service" button. For $19.00 USD I will create the charts you will need for this book in high-resolution color graphics in pdf format. These charts include your Natal chart, BiWheel chart, Transit chart, and Relocation chart. You'll receive these charts in the same format as used throughout this book. NOTE: In the final PayPal page before submitting your payment, select the "note to seller" option. Please include the following information: your name, birth date, birth time, birth location (town, state, country), current location (town, state, country), and your email. When I create your charts, I will email you the pdf files for you to print out.

Give it a go. Once you have printed out your charts, you can make a list of each Planet, its Sign of the Zodiac, and House. Then go to chapters 11, 15, and 16 and put together short descriptions about the different parts of yourself you learned in Chapter 17. You can even try identifying larger themes in your chart, which we explored in Chapter 18. I'm convinced you will be impressed with the results.

If you want to use an astrology computer software program to generate your own charts, you have plenty of options. I am not familiar with all the software available, but I can share with you the programs I use.

If you are using a PC or have an Apple computer with Bootcamp, then Sirius (Cosmic Patterns Software, Inc.) is a great choice. While expensive, it allows you to generate a wide variety of chart types with a wealth of customization options. All the charts in this book were created using Sirius. The one feature I like most about Sirius is the Transit chart capability. No other program can generate such easy-to-visualize graphical displays. Most programs just give you a listing of the Transits and you have to use your imagination to visualize how they fade in and out over time.

If you have an Apple computer, a terrific choice is IO Edition and its companion program, IO Sprite, both created by Time Cycles Research. IO Edition and IO Sprite are invaluable programs for me, as I can quickly find dates when slow-moving Planets enter or leave Houses or Transit each other. I also use IO Sprite exclusively for my research on Mundane astrology. It is amazing in its flexibility. Like Sirius, both IO Edition and IO Sprite have the capability to use the Krusiński House system (chapters 27 and 28)

Astrology offers you a better understanding of your unique energetic makeup as well as insights into using your uniqueness in ways that can assist you in your quest to manifest your intentions. It also will help you understand other people close to you so you can support and nurture them toward their amazing potential.

As you continue to explore astrology, I invite you to be patient with your progress. While it is quite straightforward, learning by memory all the meanings of the Planets, Zodiac Signs, Houses, and combinations takes a while. When I first started learning astrology, I had this idea that I would be proficient within three months of full-time effort. In actuality, it took about three years before I felt confident using it with clients. I have no doubt that if I had this book when I first started out, I could have dramatically shortened my learning curve. I also recognize that astrology will be a lifetime of learning for me, because it is so rich in its application.

The remainder of this book consists of special topics to assist you in deepening your knowledge of astrology. Included is an understanding of the effects of birth time uncertainty, advanced House activity, celestial geometry, and an an exploration of House systems.

Now It's Your Turn

Bonus Section

25 Birth Time Uncertainty

As an astrologer, it is important to have an understanding of how the Natal chart would change if the birth time were a bit sooner or later than the time the person has provided. Having this understanding is helpful in situations where a House Cusp is very close to the beginning or end of a Zodiac Sign.

In Karen's Natal chart on the next page, we see that the Cusp of her 6th House is at 0° 26' in Taurus ♉, and the Cusp of her 12th House is at 0° 26' in Scorpio ♏. Because the Planets and Zodiac Signs rotate through the Houses at about 1° every four minutes, Karen only needed a birth time error of about two minutes to have the Cusp of her 6th House in Aries ♈ and the Cusp of her 12th House in Libra ♎. What direction in time (forward or backward) will give this result?"

To figure this out, I created two variations of Karen's Natal chart. One variation has her birth time 10 minutes earlier (10:27 pm) and the other has her born 10 minutes later (10:47 pm). These two charts are shown on pages 191 (birth time 10:27 pm) and 192 (birth time 10:47). Let's examine the effects and see what we can learn.

190

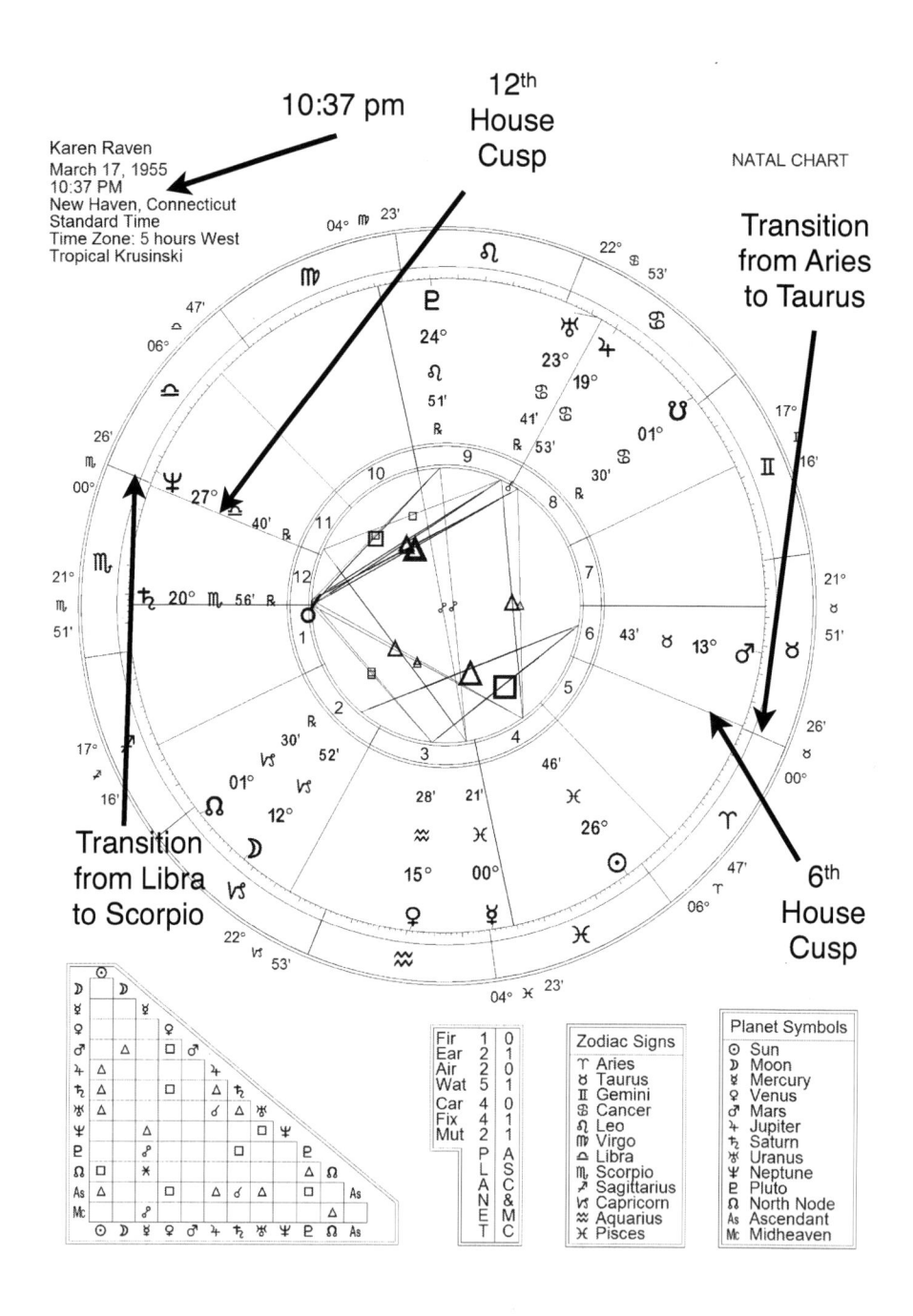

10:37 pm

12th House Cusp

Karen Raven
March 17, 1955
10:37 PM
New Haven, Connecticut
Standard Time
Time Zone: 5 hours West
Tropical Krusinski

NATAL CHART

Transition from Aries to Taurus

Transition from Libra to Scorpio

6th House Cusp

Fir	1	0
Ear	2	1
Air	2	0
Wat	5	1
Car	4	0
Fix	4	1
Mut	2	1
	P	A
	L	S
	A	C
	N	&
	E	M
	T	C

Zodiac Signs	
♈	Aries
♉	Taurus
♊	Gemini
♋	Cancer
♌	Leo
♍	Virgo
♎	Libra
♏	Scorpio
♐	Sagittarius
♑	Capricorn
♒	Aquarius
♓	Pisces

Planet Symbols	
☉	Sun
☽	Moon
☿	Mercury
♀	Venus
♂	Mars
♃	Jupiter
♄	Saturn
♅	Uranus
♆	Neptune
♇	Pluto
☊	North Node
As	Ascendant
Mc	Midheaven

Fast Track Astrologer

191

10:27 pm

Karen Raven
March 17, 1955
10:27 PM
New Haven, Connecticut
Standard Time
Time Zone: 5 hours West
Tropical Krusinski

NATAL CHART

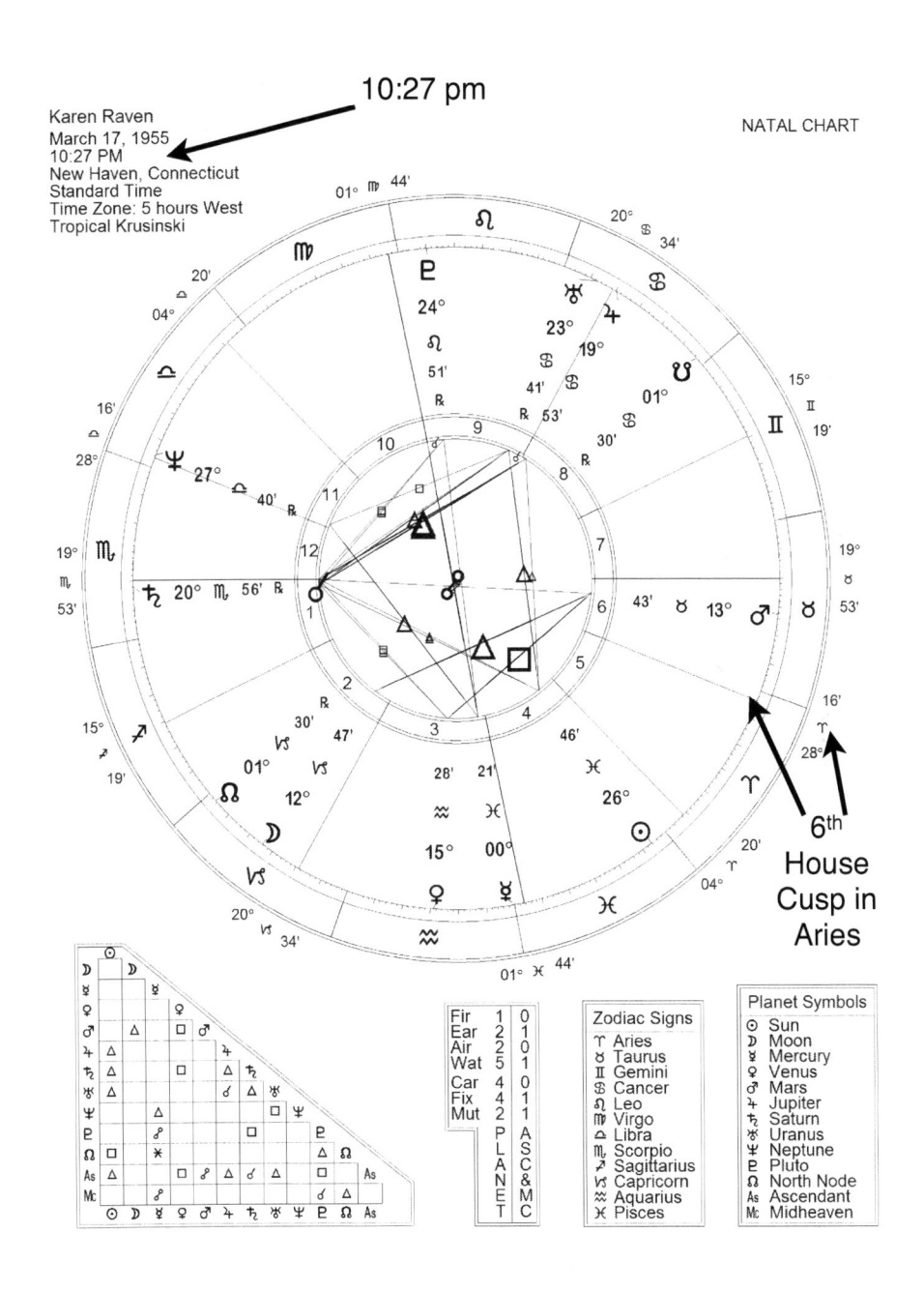

6th House Cusp in Aries

	Zodiac Signs	Planet Symbols
Fir 1 0	♈ Aries	☉ Sun
Ear 2 1	♉ Taurus	☽ Moon
Air 2 0	♊ Gemini	☿ Mercury
Wat 5 1	♋ Cancer	♀ Venus
Car 4 0	♌ Leo	♂ Mars
Fix 4 1	♍ Virgo	♃ Jupiter
Mut 2 1	♎ Libra	♄ Saturn
PLANET ASC&MC	♏ Scorpio	♅ Uranus
	♐ Sagittarius	♆ Neptune
	♑ Capricorn	♇ Pluto
	♒ Aquarius	☊ North Node
	♓ Pisces	As Ascendant
		Mc Midheaven

Birth Time Uncertainty

192

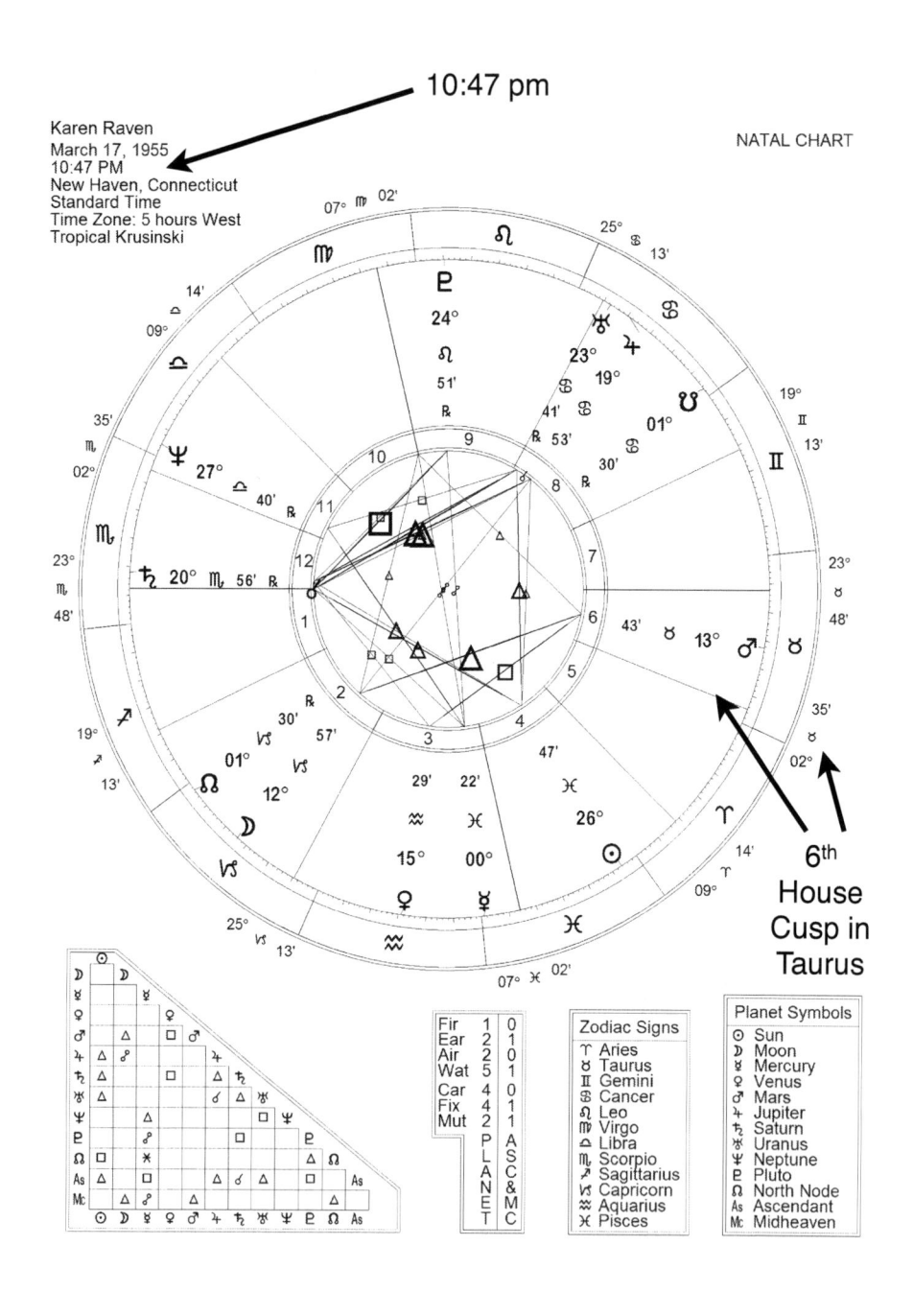

Karen Raven
March 17, 1955
10:47 PM
New Haven, Connecticut
Standard Time
Time Zone: 5 hours West
Tropical Krusinski

10:47 pm

NATAL CHART

6th House Cusp in Taurus

Fast Track Astrologer

Comparing the two Natal charts on pages 191 and 192, it is obvious that moving Karen's birth time backwards changed her 6th and 12th House Cusps to Aries ♈ and Libra ♎, respectively.

As we think about this, it makes sense. As time moves forward, the Sun ☉, along with the other Planets, moves clockwise from sunrise (Cusp of 1st House) to midday (Cusp of 10th House) to sunset (Cusp of 7th House) to midnight (Cusp of 4th House). The effect of moving forward in time is to rotate the Planets and Zodiac Signs clockwise relative to the Houses. The effect of moving backward in time is to rotate the Planets and Zodiac Signs counterclockwise.

While Karen's Cusps of her 6th and 12th Houses were at the very beginning of the Zodiac Signs of Taurus ♉ and Scorpio ♏, respectively, moving time backwards will have the effect of moving her Planets and Zodiac Signs backwards (counterclockwise) into the previous Zodiac signs of Aries ♈ and Libra ♎, respectively.

Understanding this is very useful when you view a Natal chart that has House Cusps very close to the beginning or the end of Zodiac Signs. This situation happens fairly frequently. Just remember that the rotation rate of the Planets and Zodiac Signs through the Houses is about 1° every four minutes.

26 Advanced House Activity

In Chapter 8 on House activity, we covered the first four of the seven sources of House activity. We will now cover the remaining three sources. In order to keep this chapter self-contained, I have also repeated the first four sources (with different examples), and then continued on to cover the remaining three sources.

This chapter might feel a bit complicated for you. There is so much going on in each House that it can be overwhelming.

As a review, there are 10 Planets representing our internal actors and each has a unique role to play, 12 Zodiac Signs providing characteristics to each of the Planets, and 12 Houses signifying the areas of life emphasized by the Planets. Since there are 10 Planets and 12 Houses, at least two Houses will be empty, and usually more. In Karen's Natal chart on the next page, notice that there are no Planets in the 1st, 5th, 7th, and 10th Houses.

196

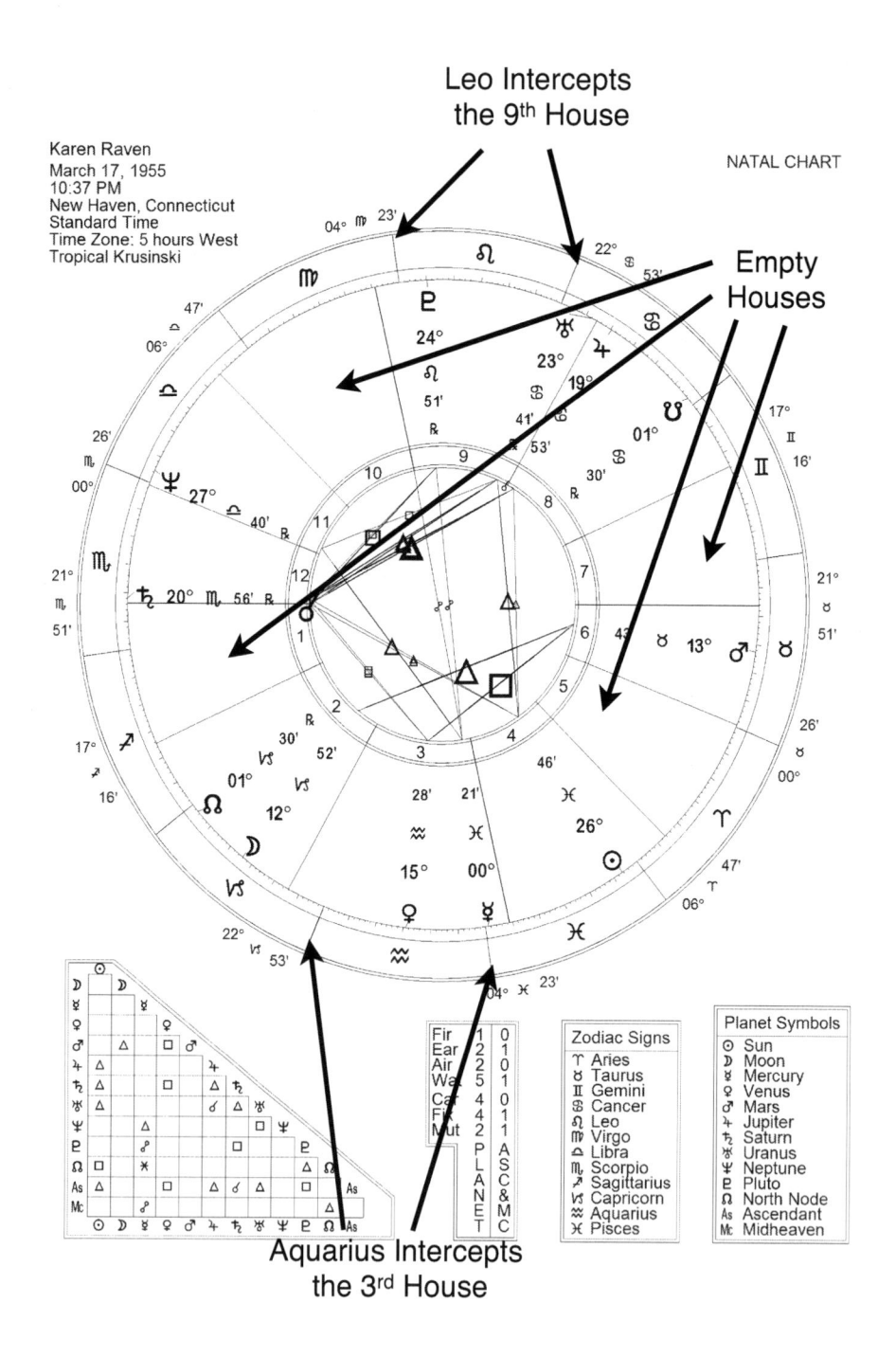

Fast Track Astrologer

The House activity comes from seven sources: (1) All Planets, (2) Planets within a House, (3) Planets near the borders of a House, (4) the Zodiac Sign at the Cusp of the House, (5) Planets that Rule the House, (6) Natural Rulers of Houses, and (7) Intercepted Houses. Let's take a closer look at each of these seven sources including the first four which were covered in Chapter 8.

1. All Planets

It is important to recognize that all your Planets (parts of you) play their roles in all Houses (areas of life). While a particular Planet emphasizes its role in particular Houses, that same Planet is also active in all other Houses, though with less emphasis.

2. Planets within a House

A Planet in a particular House has an emphasis in that area of life. For example, Karen's Natal chart has her Venus ♀ in Aquarius ♒ in her 3rd House. While her Venus ♀ is active in all Houses, it has an emphasized role in her 3rd House of communication.

3. Planets near the borders of a Houses

Planets in the neighboring two houses (on either side) and close to the border of the House will emphasize their role in both Houses. In Karen's Natal chart, her Neptune ♆ in Libra ♎ is in her 11th House and also very close to her 12th House. In this situation, Neptune ♆ will also be emphasized in Karen's 12th House as well as her 11th House. I generally consider a Planet within 3° from a House border to emphasize its role in both Houses.

4. Zodiac Sign at the Cusp of a House

The Zodiac Sign at the Cusp of a House will indicate the characteristics for that House (area of life). For example, in Karen's Natal chart above, Virgo ♍ is at the Cusp (beginning of) of her 10th House (career). Viewing the characteristics of Virgo ♍ in the appendix, Karen will, in part, desire careers (10th House) in which there is an element of organizational or individual improvement such as change management or individual coaching.

5. Planets that Rule the House

Here's where it gets more complicated. Another source of Planetary energy comes from the Ruling Planet(s) of the Zodiac Sign at the Cusp of a particular House.

Each Sign of the Zodiac is Ruled by either one or two Planets. For example, the Moon ☽ Rules Cancer ♋. As another example, Scorpio ♏ is Ruled by both Mars ♂ and Pluto ♇.

The table on the next page depicts which Planets Rule each Zodiac Sign.

So, here's how we figure out the Ruler(s) of a House. The Planet that Rules a House is determined by looking at the Zodiac Sign at the Cusp of the House and figuring out which Planet(s) Rules that Zodiac Sign. Then that is the Planet(s) Ruling the House. I know, this can be confusing. So let's take a couple of examples.

Rulers of Zodiac Signs

Zodiac Sign	Ruling Planet(s)
Aries ♈	Mars ♂
Taurus ♉	Venus ♀
Gemini ♊	Mercury ☿
Cancer ♋	Moon ☽
Leo ♌	Sun ☉
Virgo ♍	Mercury ☿
Libra ♎	Venus ♀
Scorpio ♏	Pluto ♇, Mars ♂*
Sagittarius ♐	Jupiter ♃
Capricorn ♑	Saturn ♄
Aquarius ♒	Uranus ♅, Saturn ♄*
Pisces ♓	Neptune ♆, Jupiter ♃*

* Before the outer Planets were discovered, Mars ♂, Saturn ♄, and Jupiter ♃ were the Rulers of Scorpio ♏, Aquarius ♒, and Pisces ♓, respectively. These three Planets are now referred to as the Traditional Rulers.

Advanced House Activity

In Karen's Natal chart, Taurus ♉ is at the Cusp of her 7th House (Descendant Ds). From the table on the previous page, we see that Taurus ♉ is Ruled by Venus ♀. Venus ♀ is in Karen's 3rd House. So, Venus ♀ Rules the 7th House and thus carries its 3rd House role into the 7th House as well as having its role in the 3rd House.

Let's delineate this. Karen has Venus ♀ in Aquarius ♒ in the 3rd House. Considering the role of Venus ♀, her Aquarius ♒ characteristics, and the 3rd House area of life (see appendix), Karen is attracted to and attracts (Venus ♀) people who are unconventional and altruistic (Aquarius ♒), in part, through her way of thinking and communicating (3rd House). Since Karen has Taurus ♉ on the Cusp of her 7th House and Taurus ♉ is Ruled by Venus ♀, her Venus ♀ will not only emphasize its role in the 3rd House, but also in the 7th House.

Let's take one last example and just figure out the Ruling Planet(s) of her 1st House. Viewing Karen's Natal chart, we see that Scorpio ♏ is on the Cusp of her 1st House (Ascendant As). From the table on the previous page, we note that both Mars ♂ and Pluto ♇ Rule Scorpio ♏. Thus Mars ♂ and Pluto ♇ Rule Karen's 1st House. This means that Mars ♂ in Taurus ♉ in the 6th House will carry its energy into the 1st House and also have an emphasis in the 6th House. Furthermore, Pluto ♇ in Leo ♌ in the 9th House will carry its energy into Karen's 1st House and also have an emphasis in the 9th House.

6. Natural Rulers of Houses

There is one other variation of Rulers used by astrologers called Natural Rulers of Houses. These are determined by identifying the 1st House with the 1st Zodiac Sign (Aries ♈), the 2nd House with the 2nd Zodiac Sign (Taurus ♉), and so on to the 12th House with the 12th

Zodiac Sign (Pisces ♓). We then attribute the Planetary Ruler of the particular Zodiac Sign to that particular House.

For example, Aries ♈ is identified with the 1st House, and Aries ♈ from the table on page 199 is Ruled by Mars ♂. So we say that Mars ♂ is the Natural Ruler of the 1st House. Continuing this method, we have Venus ♀ as the Natural Ruler of the 2nd House because Taurus ♉, which is identified with the 2nd House, is Ruled by Venus ♀. Continuing on, Mercury ☿ is the Natural Ruler of the 3rd House because the 3rd House is identified with the 3rd Zodiac Sign (Gemini ♊), and Gemini ♊ is Ruled by Mercury ☿. This process continues on through the 12th House which is identified with the 12th Zodiac Sign of Pisces ♓. Since Pisces ♓ is Ruled by Neptune ♆ and Jupiter ♃, then Neptune ♆ and Jupiter ♃ are the Natural Rulers of the 12th House. The table on the next page depicts the Natural Rulers for each of the 12 Houses. This table is also included in the appendix at the end of this book.

With the Natural Rulers methodology, the Planet(s) that is the Natural Ruler of the House emphasizes its role in that House. In Karen's Natal chart, you can see that Mercury ☿ is in the 3rd House, and from the table on the next page, Mercury ☿ is also the Natural Ruler of the 3rd House. This would give Mercury ☿ extra emphasis in the 3rd House because it is in the House it Naturally Rules. As another example using Karen's Natal chart, the Sun ☉ is in her 4th House. Since the Sun ☉ is the Natural Ruler of the 5th House, the Sun ☉ also will emphasize its role in the 5th House.

Advanced House Activity

Natural Rulers of Houses	
House	**Natural Ruler(s)**
1st	Mars ♂
2nd	Venus ♀
3rd	Mercury ☿
4th	Moon ☽
5th	Sun ☉
6th	Mercury ☿
7th	Venus ♀
8th	Pluto ♇, Mars ♂*
9th	Jupiter ♃
10th	Saturn ♄
11th	Uranus ♅, Saturn ♄*
12th	Neptune ♆, Jupiter ♃*

* Before the outer Planets were discovered, Mars ♂, Saturn ♄, and Jupiter ♃ were the Natural Rulers of the 8th, 11th, and 12th Houses, respectively. These three Planets are now referred to as the Traditional Natural Rulers.

7. Intercepted Houses

Had enough? Hang in there as we only have one source left. One configuration that often occurs in a Natal chart is that a House is Intercepted by a Zodiac Sign. This occurs when a Zodiac Sign is completely encompassed within a House. In Karen's Natal chart on page 196, notice that Leo ♌ is entirely encompassed within the 9th House. Also, Aquarius ♒ is entirely encompassed within the 3rd House.

In these cases, the Intercepted Zodiac Sign and its Planetary Ruler(s) have similar but weaker effects than the Zodiac Sign on the Cusp of the House and its Planetary Ruler(s).

For the 9th House in Karen's Natal chart where Leo ♌ is Intercepted, this would mean that the influence of Leo ♌ and the Sun ☉ (which Rules Leo ♌, see page 199) will be less than Cancer ♋ (which is at the Cusp of the 9th House) and the Moon ☽ (which Rules Cancer ♋, see page 199).

Likewise in the 3rd House, which is Intercepted by Aquarius ♒, the influence of Aquarius ♒ and its Rulers, Uranus ♅ and Saturn ♄ (see page 199), will be less than Capricorn ♑ (which is at the Cusp of the 3rd House) and Saturn ♄ (which Rules Capricorn ♑, see page 199). This situation is interesting because Saturn ♄ is the Ruler of both Capricorn ♑ (at the Cusp of the 3rd House) and Aquarius ♒ (which Intercepts the 3rd House), so Saturn ♄ (ambition, structure, discipline) will have a strong influence in the 3rd House of thinking and communicating.

Advanced House Activity

Example

Let's look at Karen's 9th House of wider exploration to see how all seven sources of energy play into that House.

1. **All Planets:** All Planets play their roles in Karen's 9th House.

2. **Planets Within a House:** Uranus ♅ is in Karen's 9th House so the Uranus ♅ role within Karen (unique, original, altruistic) will be emphasized in her 9th House.

3. **Planets Near the Borders of a House:** Jupiter ♃ is in Karen's 8th House, 3° from the beginning of her 9th House. So the Jupiter ♃ role played out by Karen (expansion, optimism) will also have an emphasis in her 9th House.

4. **Zodiac Sign at the Cusp of a House:** Cancer ♋ is at the Cusp of Karen's 9th House, so her approach toward higher exploration (9th House) will have Cancer ♋ characteristics (instinctual, feeling).

5. **Planets That Rule the House:** Cancer ♋ is at the Cusp of Karen's 9th House. From the table on page 199, Cancer ♋ is Ruled by the Moon ☽. So the Moon ☽ in Capricorn ♑ in the 2nd House also will emphasize its role in Karen's 9th House.

6. **Natural Rulers of Houses:** The 9th Zodiac Sign (Sagittarius ♐) is associated with the 9th House. Since Sagittarius ♐, from the table on page 199, is Ruled by Jupiter ♃, then Jupiter ♃ is the Natural Ruler of the 9th House (see table on page 202). Thus Jupiter ♃ in Cancer ♋ in the 8th House will emphasize its role in Karen's 9th House. Since Jupiter ♃ is already close to the 9th House (part 3

above) and Jupiter ♃ is the Natural Ruler of the 9th House, it will have extra emphasis there.

7. **Intercepted Houses:** Because Karen's 9th House is Intercepted by Leo ♌, the Sun ☉ (which Rules Leo ♌) in Pisces ♓ in the 4th House will also emphasize its role in the 9th House, but to a lesser extent than the Moon ☽ which is the Ruler of the 9th House.

I've summarized all the House activity for Karen's Natal chart in the table on the next page. While it is a bit complicated, it will be worth it for you to examine this chart and ensure that you can make sense of all the entries. If you can, congratulations, you just successfully learned the hardest part of astrology.

I often use the last three sources of House activity to round out the picture for Houses with no Planets. For example, in Karen's Natal chart, she has no Planets in the 10th House of her career. Referring to the table on the next page, she has Virgo ♍ on the Cusp of her 10th House. Furthermore, the 10th House is Ruled by Mercury ☿ in Pisces ♓ and has a Natural Ruler of Saturn ♄ in Scorpio ♏. Thus, Karen's career will not only involve organizational and individual improvement ♍, but also have elements of communication with higher meaning (☿ in ♓) and structured approaches, which help people and teams probe beneath the surface for deeper motivations surrounding change and improvement (♄ in ♏).

Becoming fluent in all facets of House activity allows you to deeply explore areas important to you and with others.

House Activity for Karen's Natal Chart

House	Planets in House	Zodiac Sign at Cusp	House Ruler(s)	Natural Ruler(s)
1st	Saturn ♄ ✝	Scorpio ♏	Pluto ♇ 9th Mars ♂ 6th	Mars ♂ 6th
2nd	Moon ☽ N. Node ☊	Sagittarius ♐	Jupiter ♃ 8th	Venus ♀ 3rd
3rd	Venus ♀ Mercury ☿	Capricorn ♑ Aquarius ♒ *	Saturn ♄ 12th Uranus ♅ 9th ❖ Saturn ♄ 12th ❖	Mercury ☿ 3rd
4th	Sun ☉	Pisces ♓	Neptune ♆ 11th Jupiter ♃ 8th	Moon ☽ 2nd
5th		Aries ♈	Mars ♂ 6th	Sun ☉ 4th
6th	Mars ♂	Taurus ♉	Venus ♀ 3rd	Mercury ☿ 3rd
7th		Taurus ♉	Venus ♀ 3rd	Venus ♀ 3rd
8th	Jupiter ♃ S. Node ☋ Uranus ♅ ✝	Gemini ♊	Mercury ☿ 3rd	Pluto ♇ 9th Mars ♂ 6th
9th	Uranus ♅ Pluto ♇ Jupiter ♃ ✝	Cancer ♋ Leo ♌ *	Moon ☽ 2nd Sun ☉ 4th ❖	Jupiter ♃ 8th
10th		Virgo ♍	Mercury ☿ 3rd	Saturn ♄ 12th
11th	Neptune ♆	Libra ♎	Venus ♀ 3rd	Uranus ♅ 9th Saturn ♄ 12th
12th	Neptune ♆ ✝ Saturn ♄	Scorpio ♏	Pluto ♇ 9th Mars ♂ 6th	Neptune ♆ 11th Jupiter ♃ 8th

✝ Planet is in next or previous House and near the border of the House
* House is Intercepted by this Zodiac Sign
❖ Considered a Minor Ruler as House was Intercepted by Ruler of Zodiac Sign

Fast Track Astrologer

27 Celestial Geometry

When you enter birth information into an astrology software program, a Natal chart magically appears. The Natal chart is a two-dimensional (2-D) picture of a particular configuration in the three-dimensional (3-D) cosmos. It's useful to understand the 3-D cosmological picture and to draw connections with the 2-D Natal chart. I know many of you cringe at the thought of geometry, so we will proceed slowly, step by step.

In this chapter, we will determine all the House Cusps. First we will find the Cardinal House Cusps, which are the 1st House Cusp (Ascendant A^s), 4th House Cusp (Imum Coeli I^c), 7th House Cusp (Descendant D^s), and 10th House Cusp (Midheaven, Medium Coeli M^c). There is agreement with all House systems for determining all four of these Cardinal House Cusps. The variety of House systems in use employ various methods to determine the intermediate House Cusps: 2nd, 3rd, 5th, 6th, 8th, 9th, 11th, and 12th. We'll use the Krusiński House system to determine the intermediate House Cusps.

Four Seasons

Let's begin by viewing the Earth ⊕ revolving around the Sun ☉. In the diagram below, we can see positions of the Earth ⊕ during the equinoxes and solstices. The plane formed by the Earth ⊕ revolving around the Sun ☉ is called the Ecliptic plane. Notice that it slices the Earth ⊕ into two equal hemispheres. The circle formed around the Earth's ⊕ surface by the Ecliptic plane is called the Ecliptic.

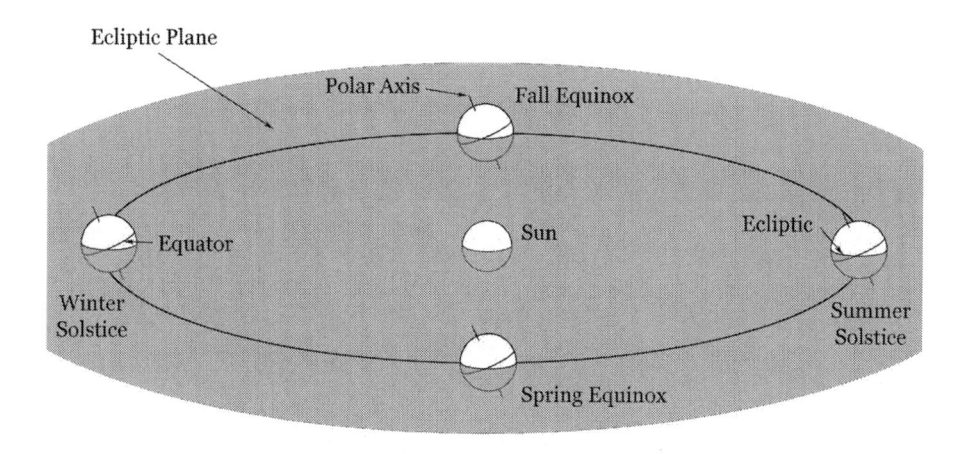

Next we will move our vantage point to the center of the Sun ☉ and see what the Earth ⊕ looks like during the solstices and equinoxes. This is shown in the diagram on the next page. Because we are viewing the Earth ⊕ from the Sun ☉, the portions of the Earth ⊕ you can see on the next page are receiving daylight while the back sides of the Earth ⊕ are in darkness. During the winter solstice, the North Pole is in darkness and the South Pole receives sunlight all day. During the summer solstice, the North Pole receives sunlight all day while the South Pole remains in darkness.

Spring Equinox

Ecliptic

Polar Axis Equator

Winter Solstice

Equator

Ecliptic

Polar Axis

Summer Solstice

North Pole Polar Axis

Equator Ecliptic

Polar Axis

Fall Equinox

Ecliptic

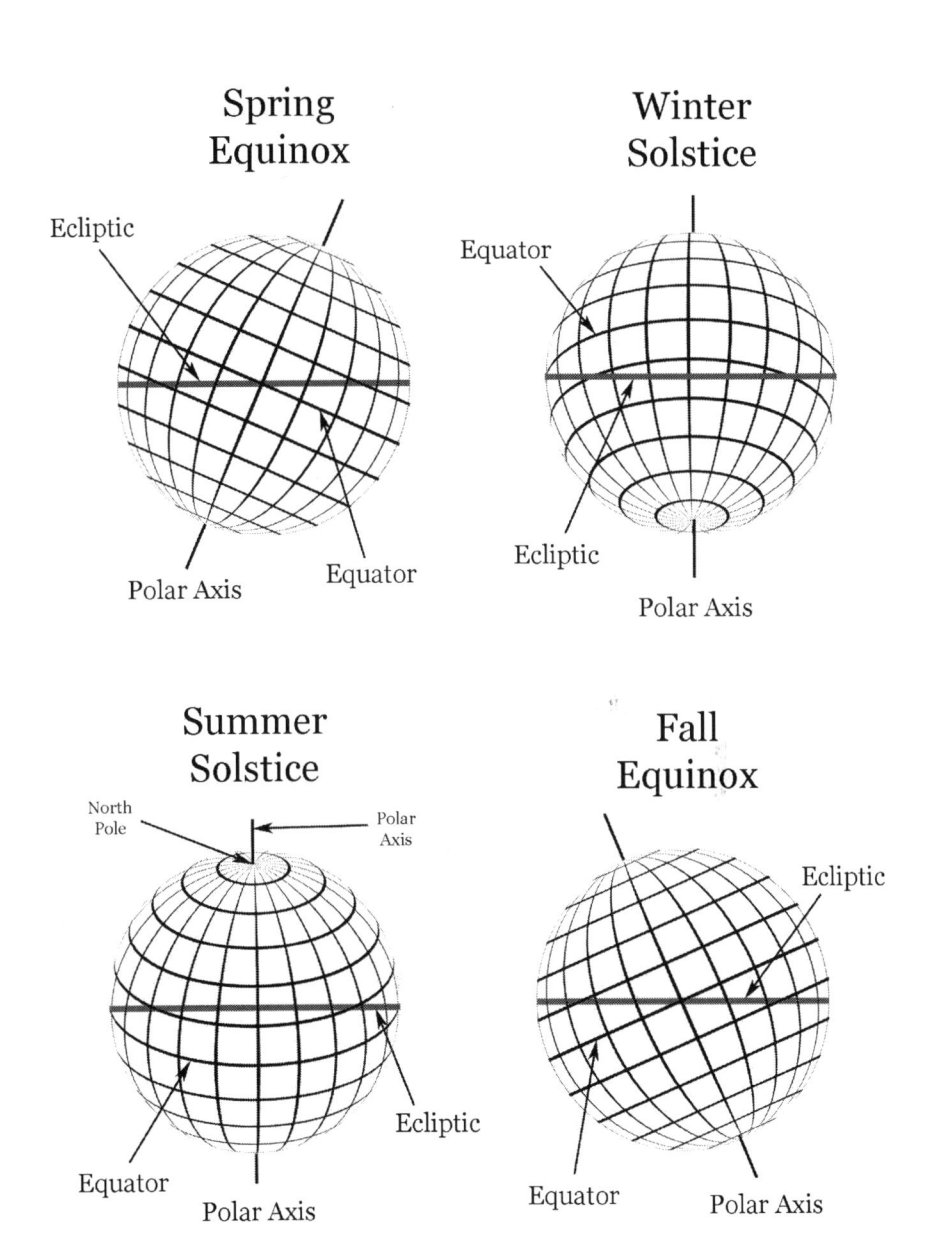

Equator Polar Axis

Earth's Polar axis is tilted
23.5° relative to the Ecliptic

Celestial Geometry

View of the Earth from the Center of the Sun

We will gradually construct a celestial diagram of the Earth ⊕ when viewed from the center of the Sun ☉. The birth will be on May 5, 1990 at 10:45 am in Washington, DC, U.S.A.

We will begin by viewing the Earth ⊕ from the perspective of the Sun ☉ on May 5, 1990. This is shown in the figure on the next page.

Because we are viewing the Earth ⊕ from the center of the Sun ☉, the entire front side of the Earth ⊕ is receiving sunlight while the back side is experiencing night time. May 5th is past the spring equinox, so we would expect the North Pole to be lit 24 hours a day as the Earth ⊕ spins around its polar axis. You can see this is the case as the North Pole is visible in the diagram on the next page.

Viewing the polar axis from above the North Pole, the Earth ⊕ rotates counterclockwise. Over a period of 24 hours, the Earth ⊕ will rotate completely around its polar axis.

I'd like to also point out the meridians (lines of longitude), which run north-south, and the parallels (lines of latitude), which run east-west.

Finally, we see that the equatorial plane slices the Earth ⊕ into two equal-sized hemispheres that form the equator at the earth's surface.

Celestial Geometry

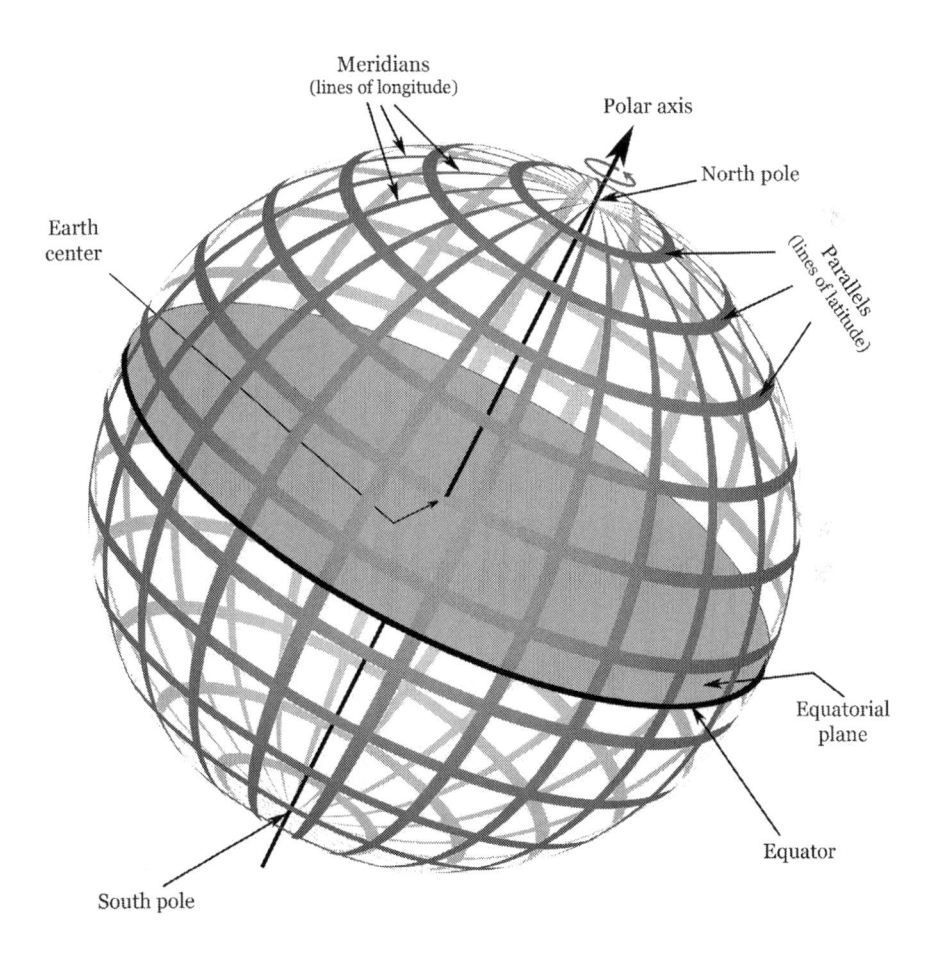

Ecliptic

Next, we will add one new feature to the diagram: the Ecliptic. As you saw in the diagram on page 208, the Ecliptic plane is the plane formed by the Earth ⊕ revolving around the Sun ☉. This sweeping movement of the Earth ⊕ from the Sun's ☉ perspective will form a flat plane, which we call the Ecliptic plane.

The Ecliptic plane slices the Earth ⊕ into two equal halves, and thus goes through the Earth's center. The line formed around the earth's surface by the Ecliptic plane is called the Ecliptic.

The diagram on the next page has the Ecliptic added. Because we are viewing the Earth ⊕ from the center of the Sun ☉, the Ecliptic appears as a straight horizontal line slicing the Earth ⊕ into two equal hemispheres. Just as the equatorial plane goes through the earth's center, so does the Ecliptic plane.

Celestial Geometry

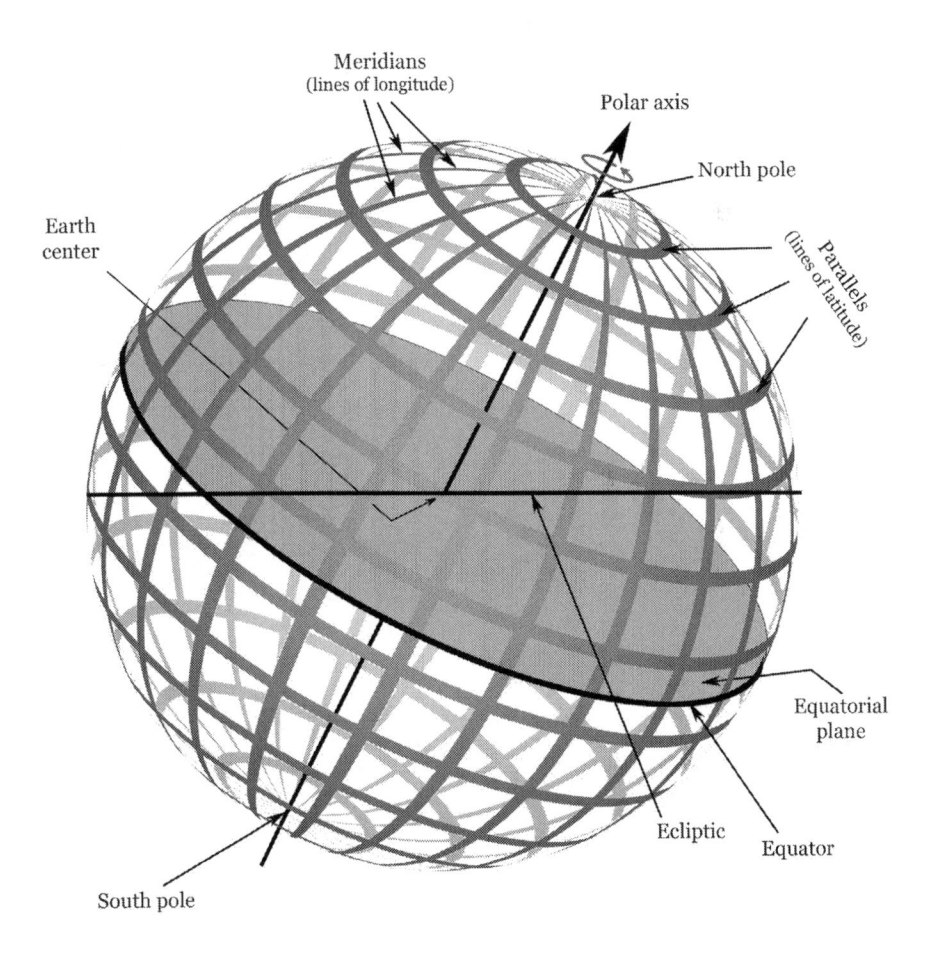

Birth Location

Next, we will add the birth location on the earth's surface. This is shown in the diagram on the next page.

I've picked a birth location at Washington, DC, U.S.A that is at a latitude of about 39° North. The time is 10:45 a.m. on May 5, 1990.

How do we know the diagram on the next page corresponds to a birth time in the morning and not the afternoon?

Imagine observing the Earth ⊕ spinning around its polar axis (counterclockwise when viewed from above the North Pole) for several hours. The birth location is fixed to the point on the earth's surface at the designated lines of latitude and longitude depicted in the diagram on the next page. As time moves forward, you will see the birth location move toward the right (and initially down a bit) until eventually, the birth point moves to the far right side of the Earth ⊕. This would correspond to sunset at this birth point time. As the Earth ⊕ continues to rotate, the birth point will be behind the Earth ⊕, and receive no sunlight. Eventually this birth point will appear on the far left side of the Earth ⊕, which corresponds to sunrise at this birth point time. In a few more hours, it will come back to the same position as shown in the diagram on the next page.

With this understanding, you can see that the birth point time was in the morning as it is on the left side of the Earth ⊕ from our vantage point at the Sun ☉.

Celestial Geometry

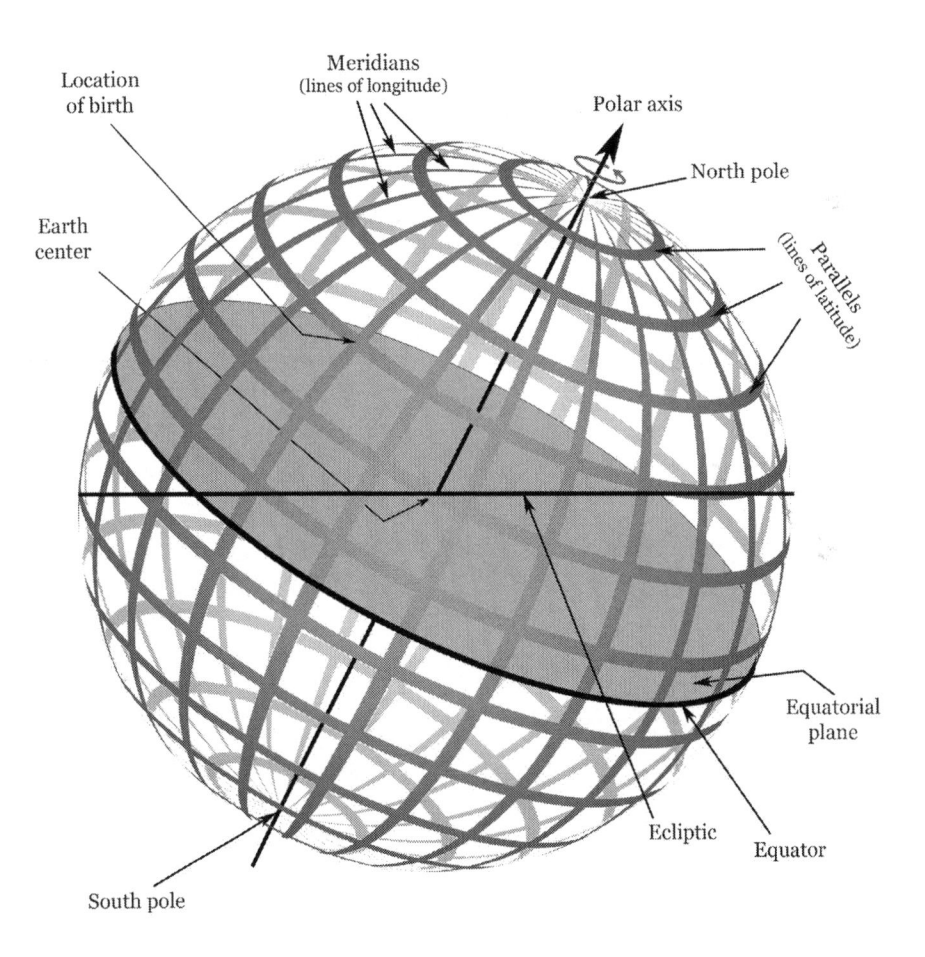

Zenith and Horizon Plane

The next line we will add is the Zenith. This is a line pointing straight up at the location of birth.

In the diagram on the next page, the Zenith is depicted as a line originating at the earth's center and passing through the earth's surface at the location of birth. From the perspective of the person born at this location, the Zenith would appear as a line straight up toward the center of the visible sky.

The Zenith is perpendicular to the earth's surface. The plane formed by the horizon at the place of birth is referred to as the Horizon plane and is shown in the diagram on the next page.

Geocentric Geometry

Calculations performed by astrology software programs are Earth-centered. Specifically, the birth location is moved to the earth's center. Then the calculations are performed from this new location. This simplifies the algorithms used to create a Natal chart. The error created by this repositioning of the birth location is negligible since the Planets are so far away from the Earth ⊕.

To accomplish this, we will move the Horizon plane to the earth's center without changing its orientation (perpendicular to the Zenith). This is shown on page 218. I've also added a label for the Horizon great circle, which is the circle around the earth's surface formed by the Horizon plane. Since this diagram is getting messy, I've eliminated the equator and equatorial plane as it no longer serves us going forward. This simplified diagram is on page 219.

Celestial Geometry

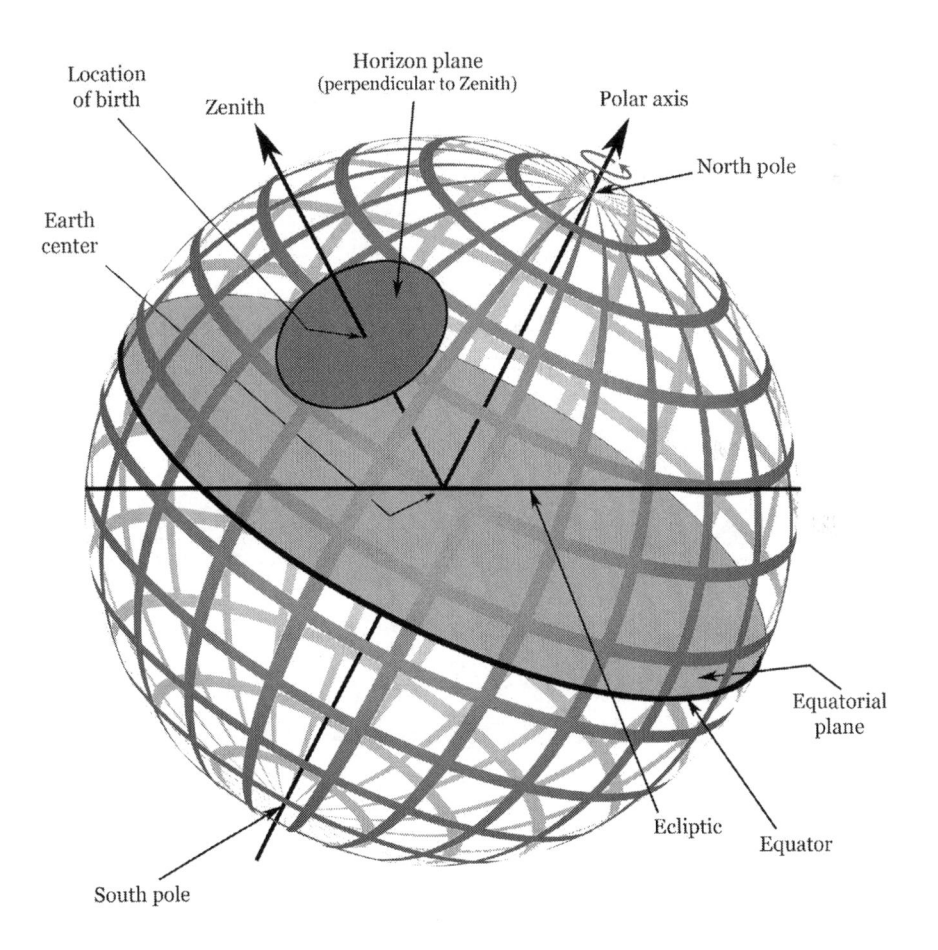

218

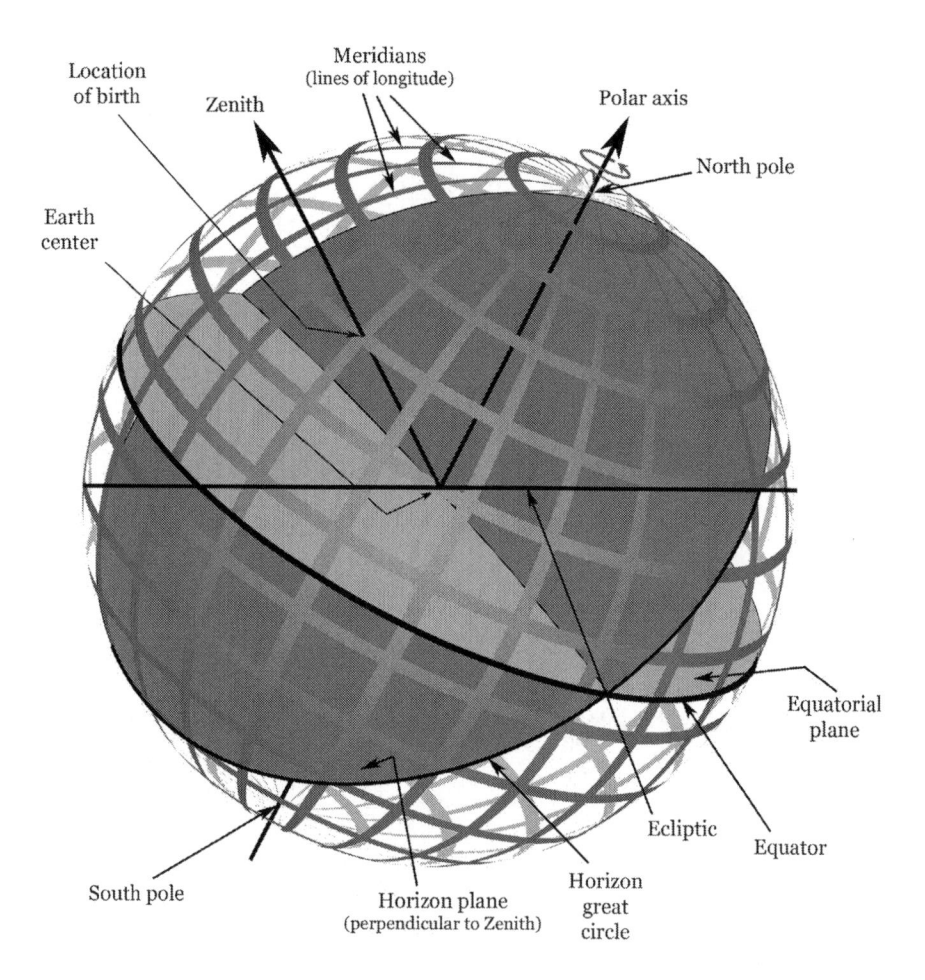

Celestial Geometry

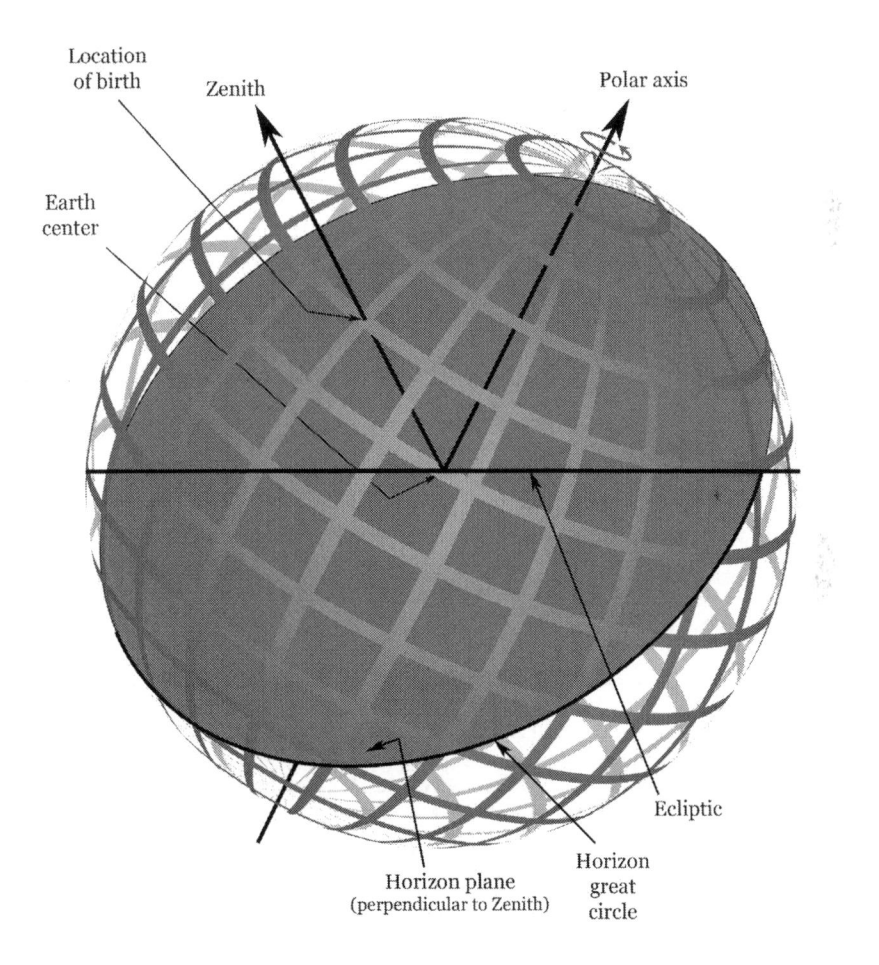

Ascendant A^s and Descendant D^s

We can now identify the points for the Ascendant A^s and Descendant D^s. These are the two points on the earth's surface where the Horizon great circle intersects the Ecliptic. I've added these points in the diagram on the next page. On the right side is the Ascendant A^s and on the left side is the Descendant D^s. Observe that the Descendant D^s is behind the Earth ⊕ from our vantage point.

Zenith-Ascendant Plane

We will create one last plane, which is the Zenith-Ascendant plane. This is a plane that passes through three points: the earth's center, the location of birth, and the Ascendant A^s (and the Descendant D^s by default). This is shown on page 222.

To put the Zenith-Ascendant plane in perspective, imagine standing at the birth location and pointing straight up along the Zenith. Now sweep your arm 90° to the Ascendant A^s on the eastern horizon. You just formed a 90° arc along the Zenith-Ascendant great circle. Similarly, you can point straight up along the Zenith, and sweep your arm 90° to the Descendant D^s on the western horizon. That will also form a 90° arc on the Zenith-Ascendant great circle.

Viewing a close-up at the birth location in the diagram on page 222, you see that the Zenith-Ascendant great circle does not go exactly east and west along the parallel (line of latitude), but deviates somewhat north of due east and south of due west. The Zenith-Ascendant great circle orientation varies during the day. Sometimes it points north of east, and at other times south of east.

221

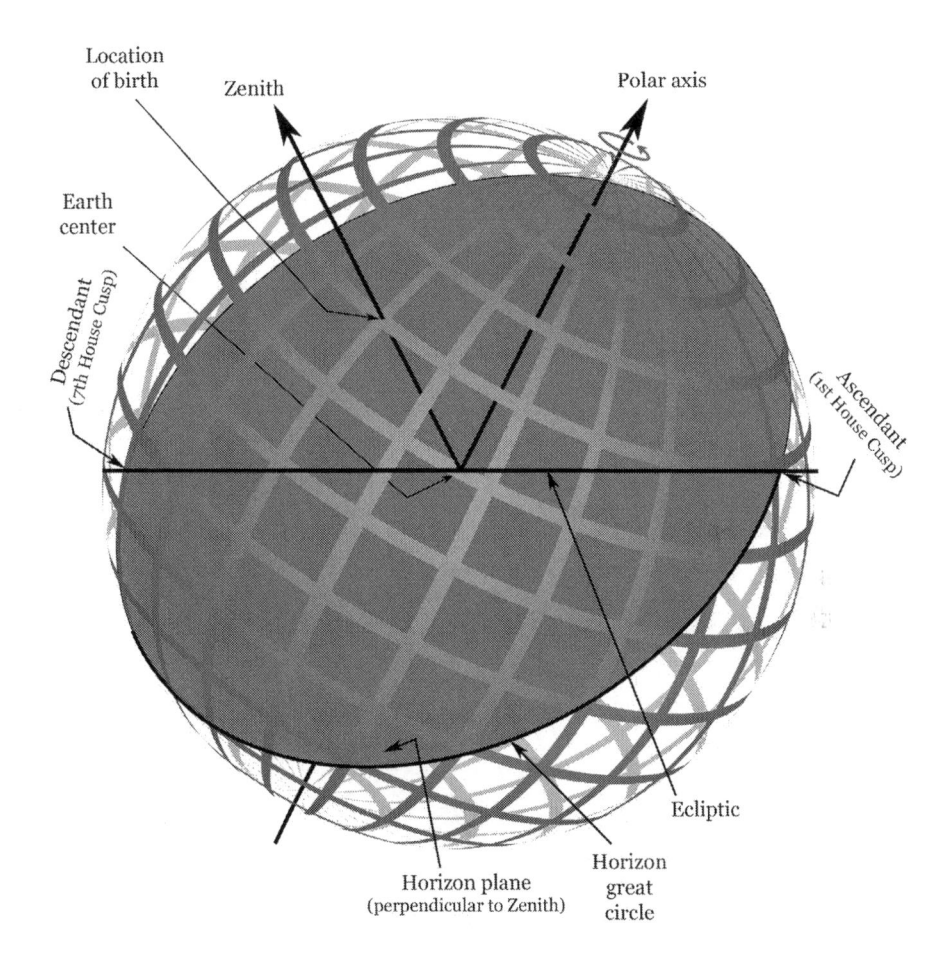

Celestial Geometry

Fast Track Astrologer

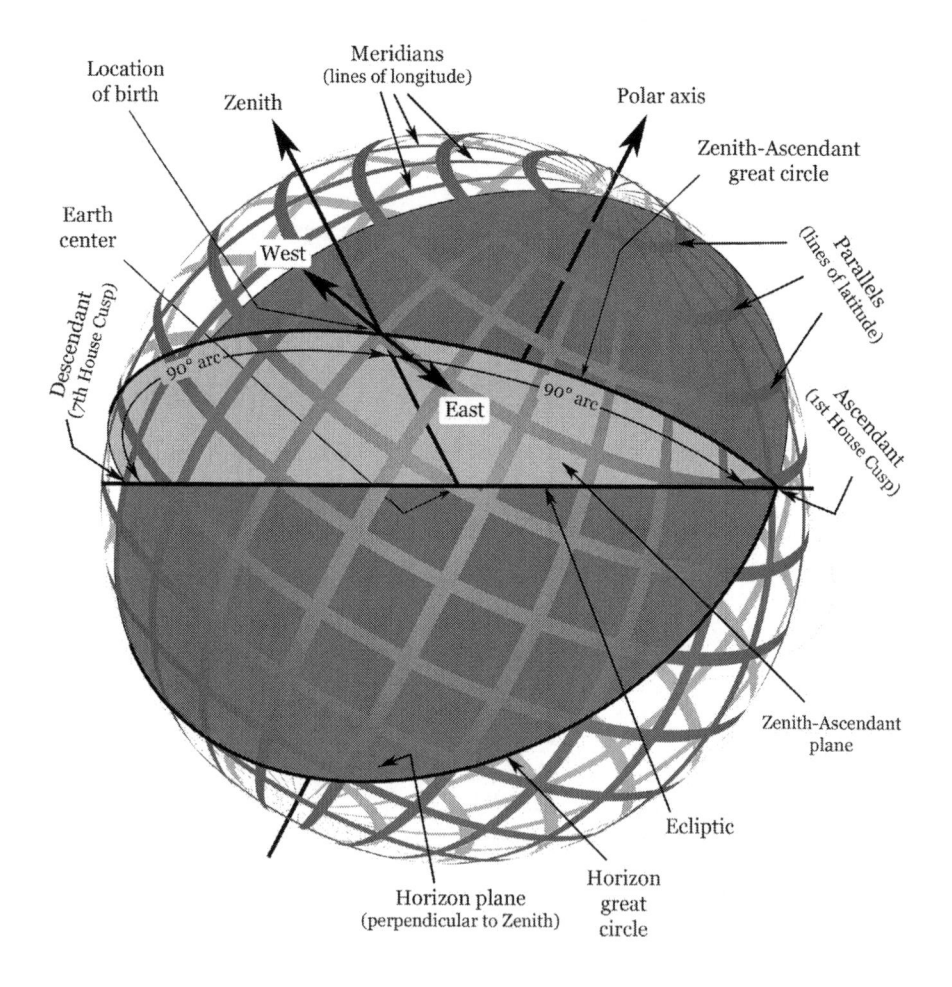

Midheaven M^c

We now have the points for the Ascendant A^s (1st House Cusp) and the Descendant D^s (7th House Cusp). Next, we will locate the Midheaven M^c (10th House Cusp), which will in turn also define the Imum Coeli I^c (4th House Cusp) since the Imum Coeli I^c is opposite the Midheaven M^c.

The diagram on the next page shows how we find the Midheaven M^c. We start at the location of birth and follow the north-south meridian line in a southerly direction until we intersect the Ecliptic. That point on the Ecliptic defines the Midheaven M^c. By default, we have also defined the Imum Coeli I^c, which is 180° from the Midheaven M^c.

Up to this point, we have not talked about House systems because all House systems define the Ascendant A^s (and by default, the Descendant D^s) and the Midheaven M^c (and by default, the Imum Coeli I^c) the same way.

Defining the intermediate Cusps (2nd, 3rd, 5th, 6th, 8th, 9th, 11^{th,}, and 12th House Cusps) is done differently by the varying House systems.

In the next part of this chapter, we will look at how the Krusiński House system defines the intermediate Cusps. As you will see shortly, the methodology used to determine the intermediate House Cusps using the Krusiński system is the same method we used to determine the Midheaven M^c. Fortunately, we will not need to create any new planes in order to proceed forward. We already have everything we need.

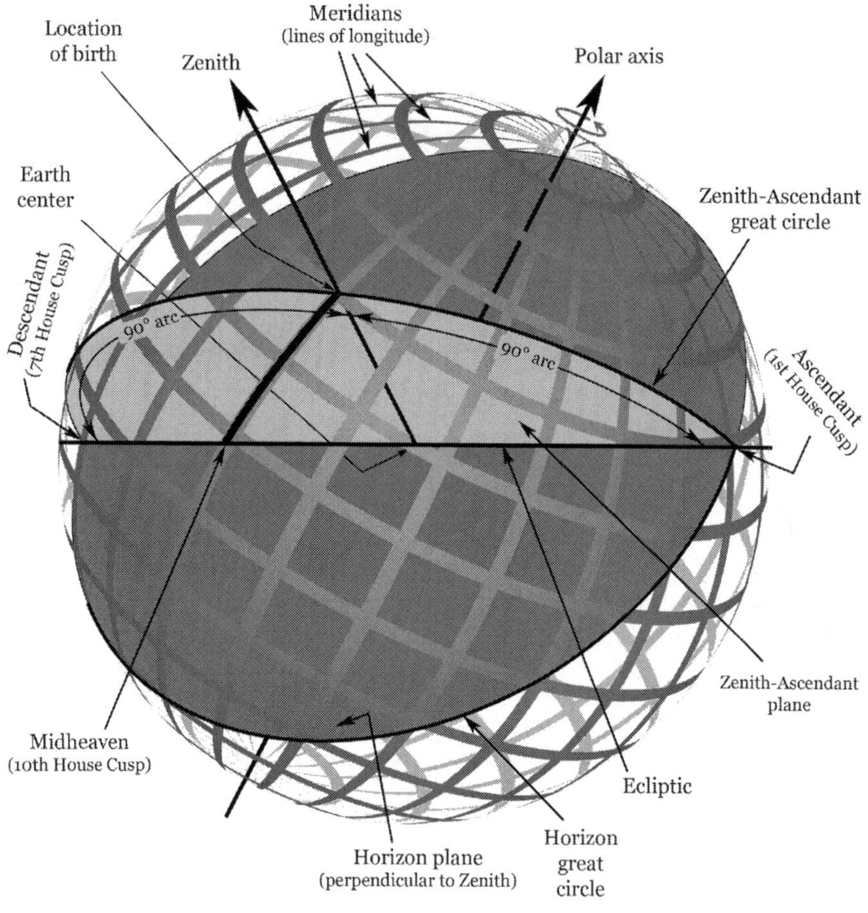
Meridians
(lines of longitude)
Location
of birth
Zenith
Polar axis
Earth
center
Zenith-Ascendant
great circle
Descendant
(7th House Cusp)
90° arc
90° arc
Ascendant
(1st House Cusp)
Zenith-Ascendant
plane
Midheaven
(10th House Cusp)
Ecliptic
Horizon
great
circle
Horizon plane
(perpendicular to Zenith)

Krusiński House System

With the Krusiński House system, we begin by taking the 90° arc from the Zenith to the Ascendant A^s on the Zenith-Ascendant great circle and dividing it into three 30° segments. Likewise, we take the 90° arc from the Zenith to the Descendant D^s and also divide it into three 30° segments. You can see this in the diagram on the next page.

From the perspective of the birth location, we are forming a 90° arc by pointing straight up (Zenith) and sweeping our arm toward the eastern horizon to the Ascendant A^s. We then divide this 90° arc into three equal arcs of 30°. We've now divided the left half of the visible sky (viewed from the birth location facing south) into three equal portions.

We follow the same procedure to divide the right portion of the visible sky into three equal portions by pointing straight up (Zenith) and sweeping our arm toward the western horizon to the Descendant D^s to form a 90° arc. We then divide this 90° arc into three equal arcs of 30°. We now have the visible sky divided into six equal portions. The portion of the sky behind the Earth ⊕ is, by default, also divided into six equal 30° portions.

To calculate the intermediate House Cusps, we follow the same procedure as we did to determine the Midheaven M^c. That is, we take the points along the Zenith-Ascendant great circle where the 30° arcs intersect this great circle, and follow each along the north-south meridian line until we intersect the Ecliptic. This is depicted in the diagram on page 227.

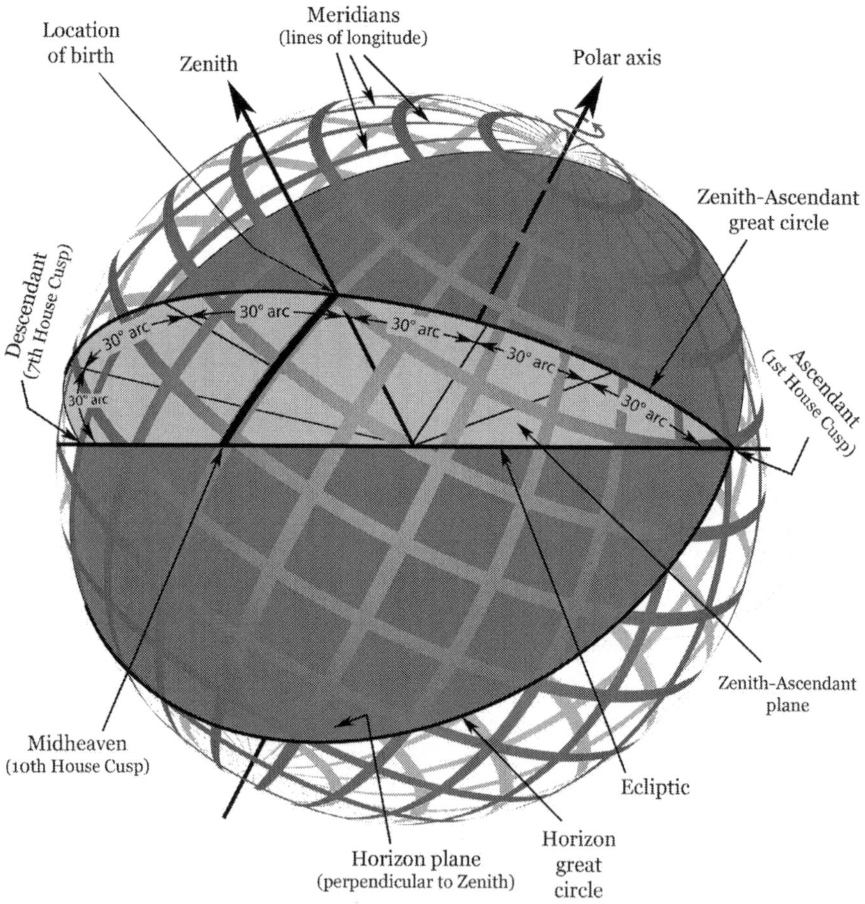
Location
of birth
Zenith
Meridians
(lines of longitude)
Polar axis
Zenith-Ascendant
great circle
Descendant
(7th House Cusp)
30° arc
30° arc
30° arc
30° arc
30° arc
30° arc
Ascendant
(1st House Cusp)
Zenith-Ascendant
plane
Midheaven
(10th House Cusp)
Ecliptic
Horizon plane
(perpendicular to Zenith)
Horizon
great
circle

227

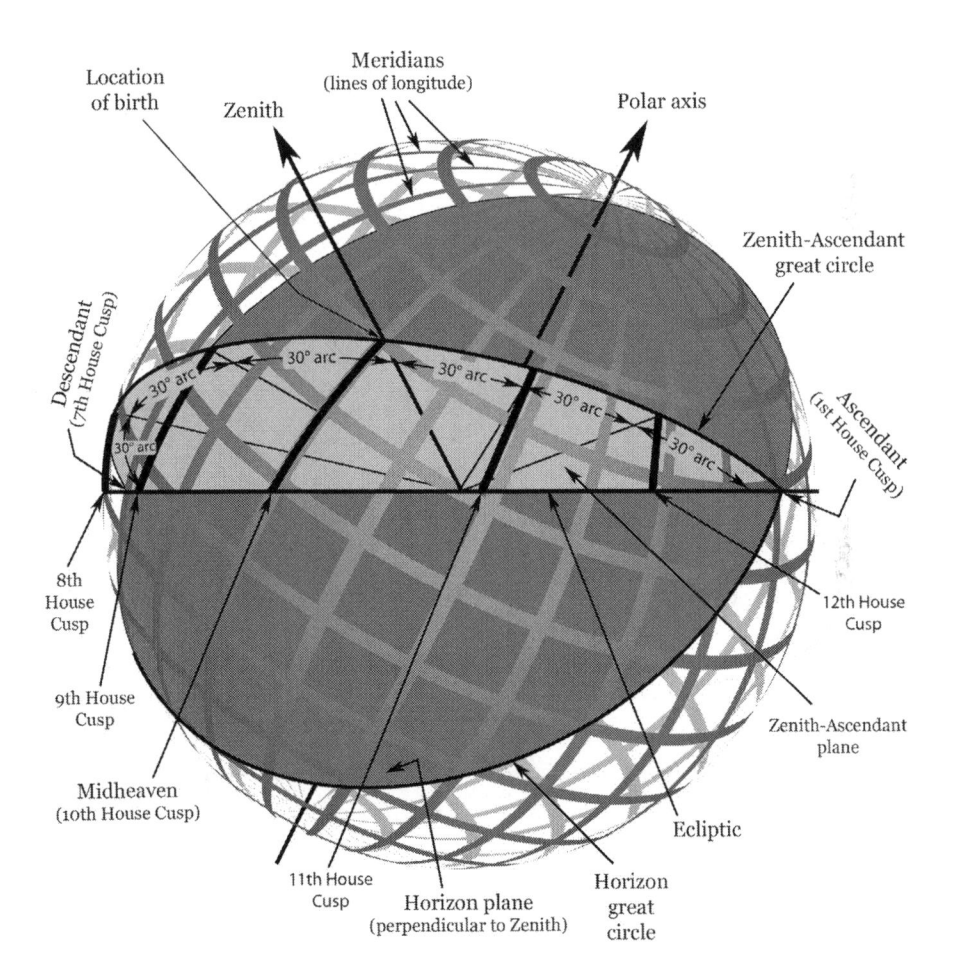

Celestial Geometry

We now have located the 8th, 9th, 11th, and 12th House Cusps (and by default the 2nd, 3rd, 5th, and 6th House Cusps).

Other House systems such as Koch and Placidus, determine the House Cusps by dividing the arc along the Ecliptic between the Ascendant A^s and the Midheaven M^c into three segments using parallel arcs to obtain the 11th and 12th House Cusps (and the 5th and 6th by default), and dividing the arc along the Ecliptic between the Midheaven M^c and the Descendant D^s into three segments to obtain the 8th and 9th House Cusps (and the 2nd and 3rd by default).

This approach seems incongruous to me because, in general, the angle of the arc along the Ecliptic between the Midheaven M^c and the Ascendant A^s is not 90°. For example, this angle is roughly 106° in the diagram on the previous page. The arc between the Midheaven M^c and the Descendant D^s is 74°. Later, I'll show you how I figured this out. Attempting to use formulations on an arc that is already distorted due to an earlier projection is still going to result in distortions.

Until I became aware of the Krusiński House system, I was uneasy in my astrology practice with all the House systems. It made no sense to me that the 3-D sky from the perspective of the birth location should be distorted using methods that deviated from the simplicity and beauty of all the other geometry associated with the Natal chart. I am comfortable and confident in the Krusiński House system because it is geometrically simple, uses a methodology consistent with the calculation of the Midheaven M^c (which everyone agrees with), and divides the visible sky into equal portions without distortion.

Sun on the Ecliptic

Before looking at the 2-D Natal chart that corresponds to the 3-D celestial diagram we created, we need to add one more very important point: where the Sun ☉ intercepts the Ecliptic.

We find the intercept of the Sun ☉ on the Eclipse by determining where the line from the center of the Sun ☉ to the center of the Earth ⊕ intersects the Ecliptic. Our vantage point in the 3-D celestial diagram is at the sun's center. Because of this, the Sun ☉ intercepts the Ecliptic at the same point on the 3-D celestial diagram as the earth's center. This is shown in the diagram on the next page. Please take the time to find this point as it is important for our next step.

Shortly, we will want to view the 2-D Natal chart from the same vantage point as the 3-D celestial diagram. To do this, we will need to find the points on the Natal chart that include our vantage point (sun's center), where the Sun ☉ intercepts the Ecliptic, and the earth's center.

Viewing the locations of the 10th and 11th House Cusps in the 3-D celestial diagram on the next page, notice that the Sun ☉ intercepts the Ecliptic in the 10th House and is very close to the 11th House Cusp.

Now we will contrast the 3-D celestial diagram (page 230) with the 2-D Natal chart (page 231).

230

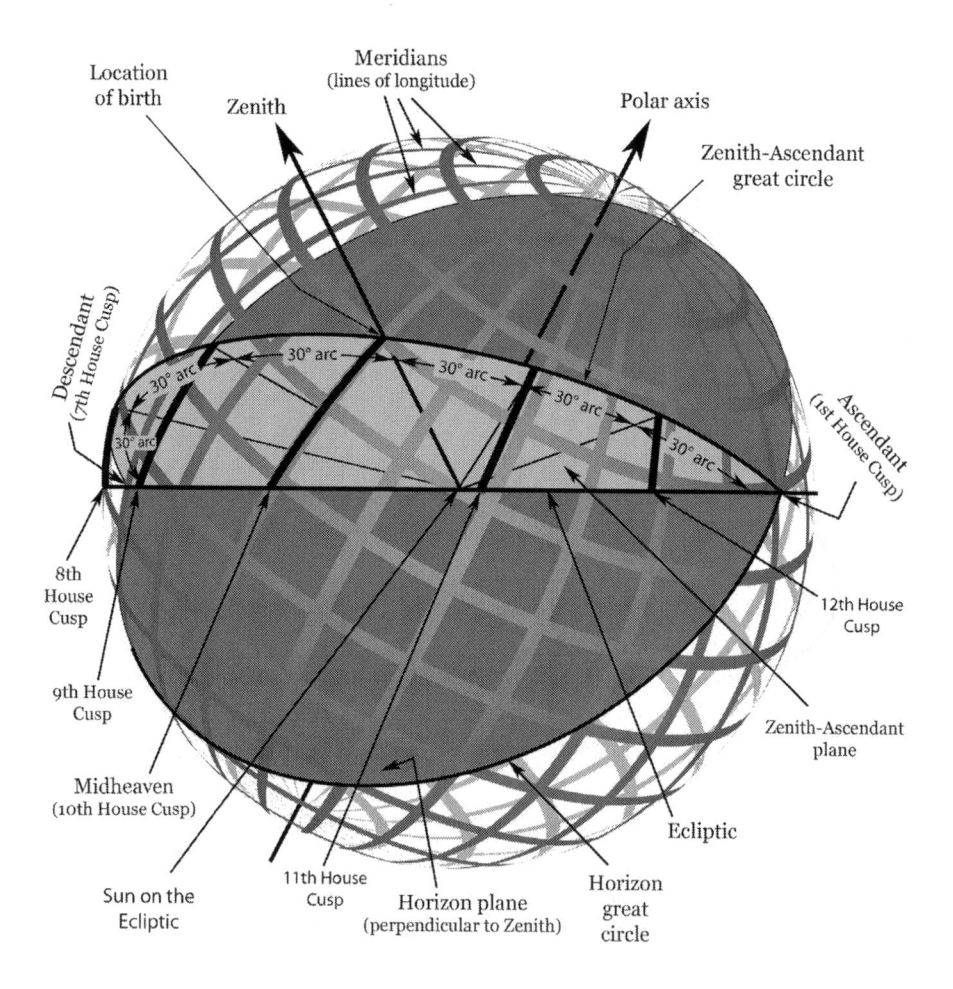

231

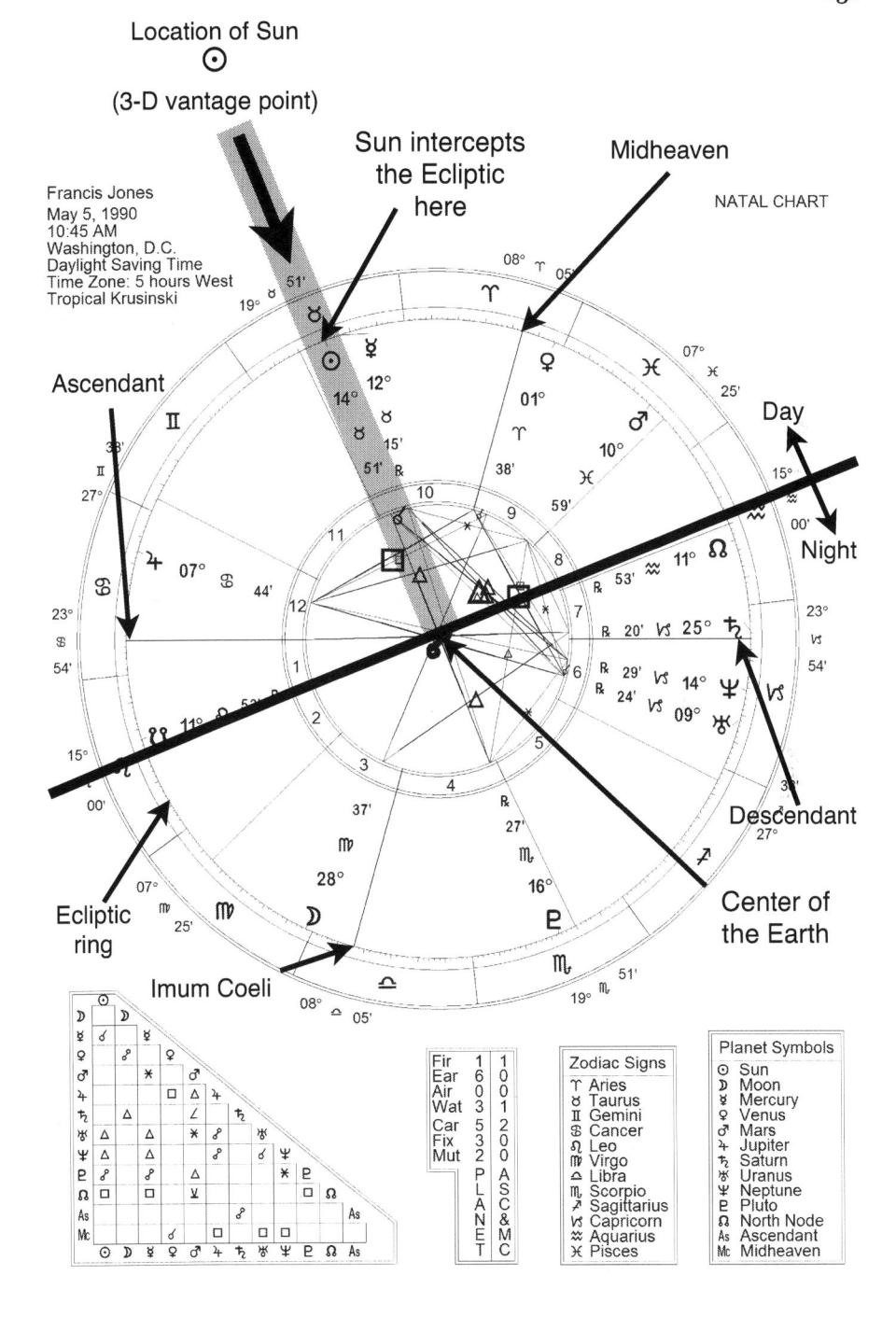

Celestial Geometry

3-D Celestial Diagram versus 2-D Natal Chart

Now we want to view both the 3-D (three-dimensional) celestial diagram and the 2-D (two-dimensional) Natal chart from the same vantage point. Then we can make comparisons. The previous two pages contain these two diagrams.

The center of a Natal chart represents the earth's center. The Ecliptic is represented by one of the outermost rings as marked in the Natal chart on the previous page. The positions of the Planets in the Natal chart indicate where the Planets cross the Ecliptic. The actual Planets are somewhere far outside the Natal chart. For example, the Sun ☉ intercepts the Ecliptic where the Sun ☉ is located in the Natal chart. The actual Sun ☉ is outside the Natal chart as depicted on the previous page.

Now, rotate the Natal chart so you are looking along the arrow from the Location of the Sun point (sun's center) to the center of the chart (earth's center). You are now looking at the 2-D Natal chart from the same vantage point as the 3-D celestial diagram. Notice the Sun ☉ intercepts the Ecliptic in the 10th House near the Cusp of the 11th House in both the Natal chart and the 3-D celestial diagram.

Viewing the Natal chart from the same vantage point as the 3-D celestial diagram, observe that the 10th House Cusp line (Midheaven M^c) is to your left and points down and to the left. In the 3-D celestial diagram, this is equivalent to the north-south meridian line going from the Zenith to the Midheaven M^c. Notice that this line also points down and to the left.

The black line I added to the Natal chart that is perpendicular to the shaded bar represents the dividing line between night and day on

Earth ⊕. Since the shaded bar from the Sun ☉ to the earth's center is perpendicular to this line, the half of the Natal chart closest to you (from the vantage point of the sun's center) will be bathed in sunlight, while the back half will receive no sunlight. Observe that the Ascendant A^s is receiving sunlight. In the 3-D celestial diagram, the Ascendant A^s is visible on the earth's surface, which means it is likewise receiving sunlight. The Descendant D^s in the Natal chart is in darkness because it is behind the black line perpendicular to the shaded line. Thus it is behind the Earth ⊕ from the vantage point of the Sun ☉. You can see that this is the case when viewing the Descendant D^s in the 3-D celestial diagram.

Earlier in this chapter, I mentioned that the angle along the Ecliptic from the Midheaven M^c to the Ascendant A^s is 106° and from the Midheaven M^c to the Descendant D^s is 74°. Here's how we figure it out. Viewing the Natal chart on page 231, we see that the Midheaven M^c is at 8° 5' Aries ♈, the Ascendant A^s at 23° 54' Cancer ♋, and the Descendant D^s is at 23° 54' Capricorn ♑. You can determine these two angles by calculating the angular distance from the Midheaven M^c to the Ascendant A^s, and the Midheaven M^c to the Descendant D^s. I'll leave it up to you to do the math.

If you were able to follow along in this chapter, you now have a better appreciation of how the 2-D Natal chart depicts the 3-D configuration of the Sun ☉ and Earth ⊕ at birth.

In the next chapter, we will take a look at the popular House systems and compare the effects on the intermediate House Cusps.

28 House Systems

There are a variety of House systems in use by astrologers. When I first learned astrology, this was an area that seemed glossed over in the literature. I found it confusing because Planets will reside in different Houses depending on the system being used. This is worth exploring further.

The two original House systems at the root of Western Astrology were known as the Whole Sign system and the Equal House system. These House systems are very easy to calculate, a necessity before the use of computers.

In the Whole Sign system, the Zodiac Sign encompasses the entire House. The 1st House always encompasses the Zodiac Sign at the Ascendant A^s. Karen's Natal chart on page 237 is calculated using the Whole Sign system. Notice that every House Cusp is at 0°. Because the Ascendant A^s is not at the beginning of the 1st House, its location is depicted on the chart. The same goes for the Midheaven M^c.

The Equal House system is the same as the Whole Sign House system, except the 1st House begins at the Ascendant A^s. Each House is 30° in size. Karen's Natal chart on page 238 is calculated using the Equal Sign House system. Notice that every House Cusp is at the same degree (21° 51'). Because the Midheaven M^c is generally not at the 10th House Cusp, its glyph is included in the Natal chart.

As our understanding of the cosmos expanded, numerous House systems were created in an attempt to divide the visible sky into equal segments, each with its own specific formulations based either on time or angle, and generally using geometric projections.

For example, in the early 1600s, the Placidus House system was developed and is probably the most widely-used system in practice today. You can view Karen's Natal chart using the Placidus House system on page 239.

A fairly recent system is the Koch (1964) House system. Its use has grown, particularly in Europe. You can view Karen's Natal chart using the Koch House system on page 240.

The newest "kid on the block" is the Krusiński House system, which was developed by Bogdan Krusiński in the 1990s. Its appeal is that it uses the same method to define the Intermediate Cusps as that used to determine the Midheaven M^c. Furthermore, it is the only House system that does not distort the sky from the perspective of the birth location. Its use has been increasing dramatically because of its simplicity and accuracy. You can view Karen's Natal chart using the Krusiński House system on page 241 (which is the same chart we have been using in earlier parts of this book).

237

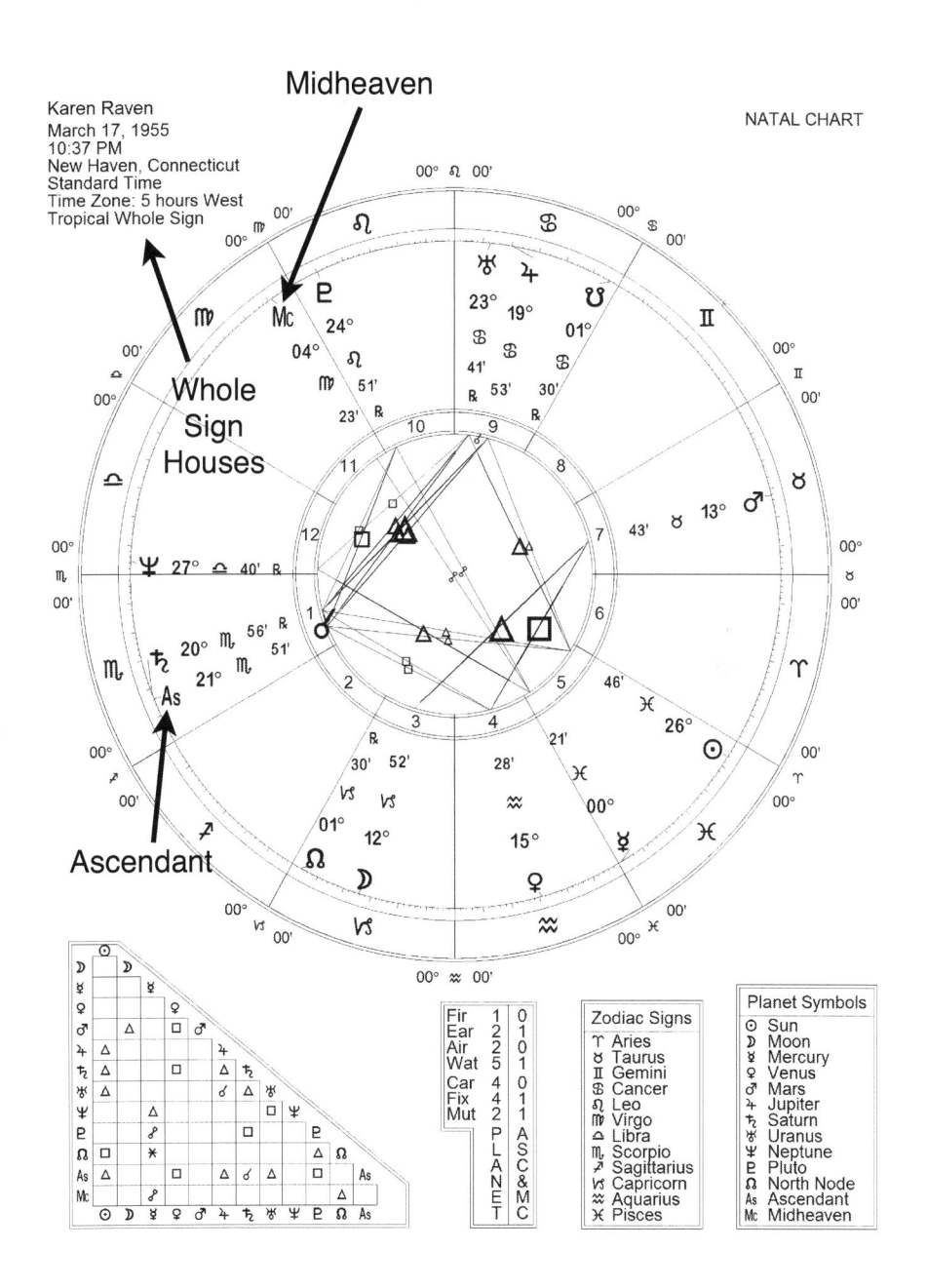

NATAL CHART

Karen Raven
March 17, 1955
10:37 PM
New Haven, Connecticut
Standard Time
Time Zone: 5 hours West
Tropical Whole Sign

Midheaven

Whole Sign Houses

Ascendant

	Zodiac Signs	Planet Symbols
Fir 1 0	♈ Aries	☉ Sun
Ear 2 1	♉ Taurus	☽ Moon
Air 2 0	♊ Gemini	☿ Mercury
Wat 5 1	♋ Cancer	♀ Venus
Car 4 0	♌ Leo	♂ Mars
Fix 4 1	♍ Virgo	♃ Jupiter
Mut 2 1	♎ Libra	♄ Saturn
P L A N E T	♏ Scorpio	♅ Uranus
A S C & M C	♐ Sagittarius	♆ Neptune
	♑ Capricorn	♇ Pluto
	♒ Aquarius	☊ North Node
	♓ Pisces	As Ascendant
		Mc Midheaven

House Systems

238

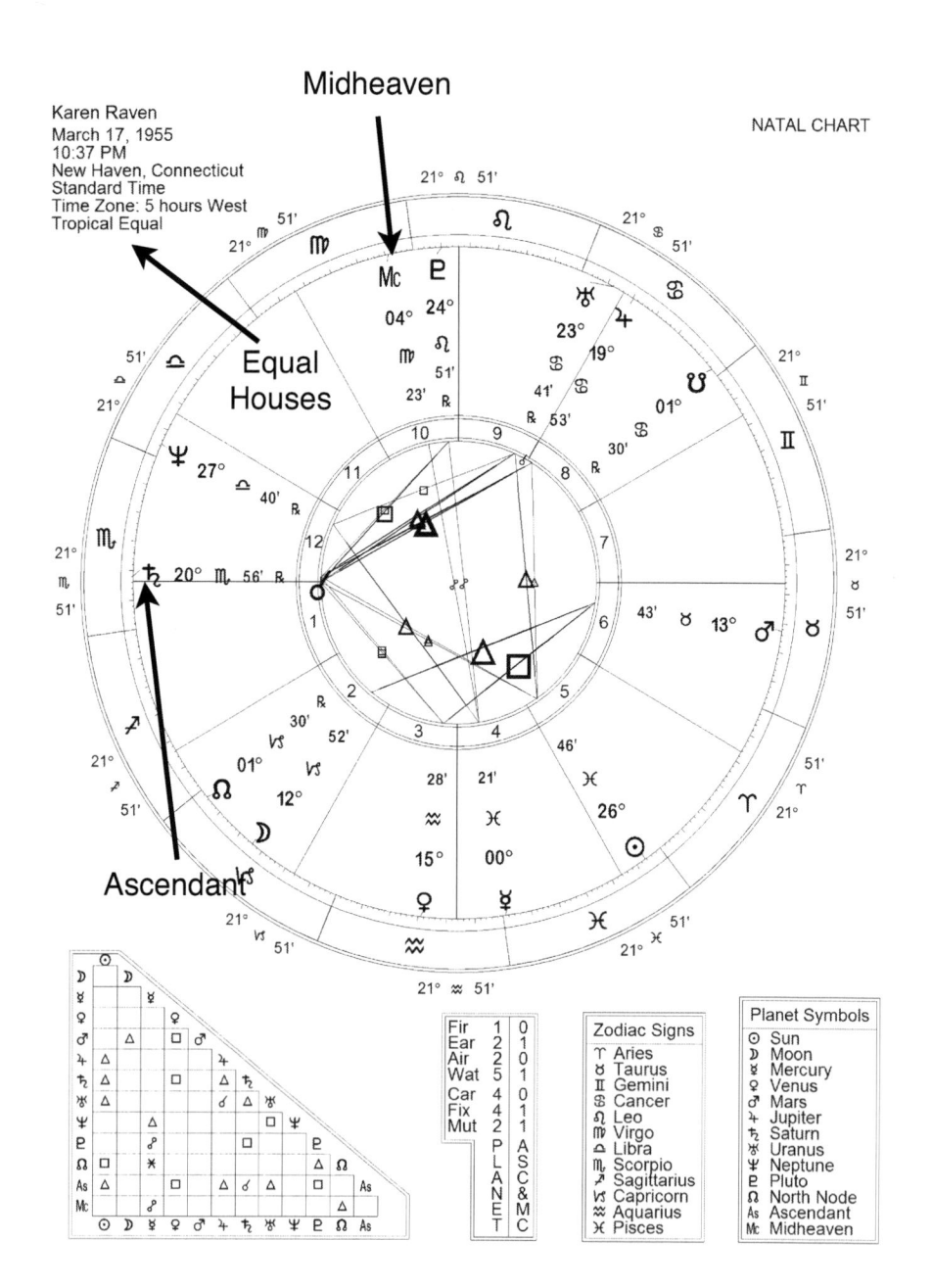

NATAL CHART

Karen Raven
March 17, 1955
10:37 PM
New Haven, Connecticut
Standard Time
Time Zone: 5 hours West
Tropical Equal

Midheaven
Equal Houses
Ascendant

	Zodiac Signs		Planet Symbols	
Fir 1 0	♈ Aries		☉ Sun	
Ear 2 1	♉ Taurus		☽ Moon	
Air 2 0	♊ Gemini		☿ Mercury	
Wat 5 1	♋ Cancer		♀ Venus	
Car 4 0	♌ Leo		♂ Mars	
Fix 4 1	♍ Virgo		♃ Jupiter	
Mut 2 1	♎ Libra		♄ Saturn	
	♏ Scorpio		♅ Uranus	
PLANET	♐ Sagittarius		♆ Neptune	
ASC&MC	♑ Capricorn		♇ Pluto	
	♒ Aquarius		☊ North Node	
	♓ Pisces		As Ascendant	
			Mc Midheaven	

Fast Track Astrologer

239

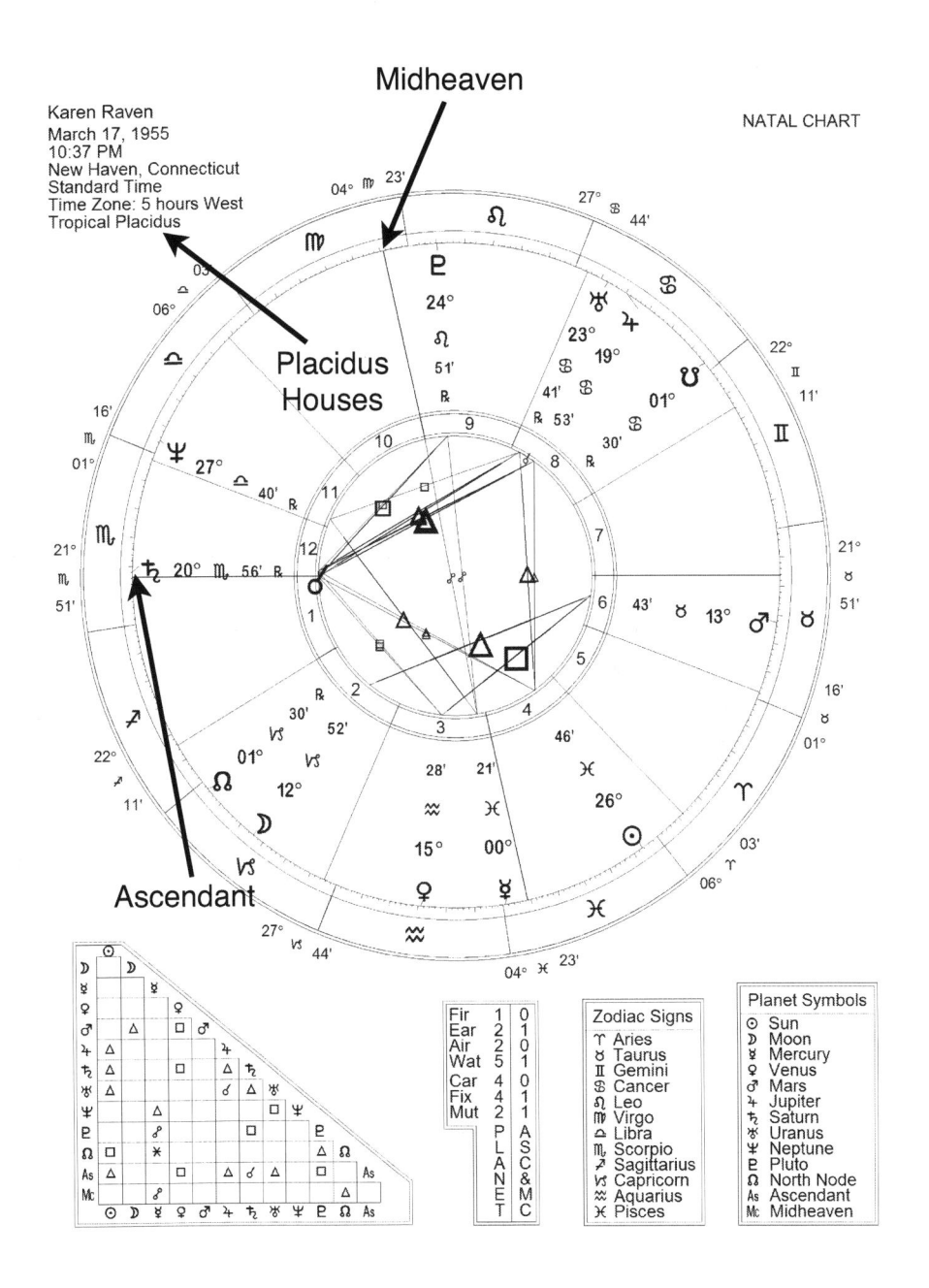

NATAL CHART

Karen Raven
March 17, 1955
10:37 PM
New Haven, Connecticut
Standard Time
Time Zone: 5 hours West
Tropical Placidus

Midheaven
Placidus Houses
Ascendant

	Zodiac Signs	Planet Symbols
Fir 1 0	♈ Aries	☉ Sun
Ear 2 1	♉ Taurus	☽ Moon
Air 2 0	♊ Gemini	☿ Mercury
Wat 5 1	♋ Cancer	♀ Venus
Car 4 0	♌ Leo	♂ Mars
Fix 4 1	♍ Virgo	♃ Jupiter
Mut 2 1	♎ Libra	♄ Saturn
P A	♏ Scorpio	⛢ Uranus
L S	♐ Sagittarius	♆ Neptune
A C	♑ Capricorn	♇ Pluto
N &	♒ Aquarius	☊ North Node
E M	♓ Pisces	As Ascendant
T C		Mc Midheaven

House Systems

240

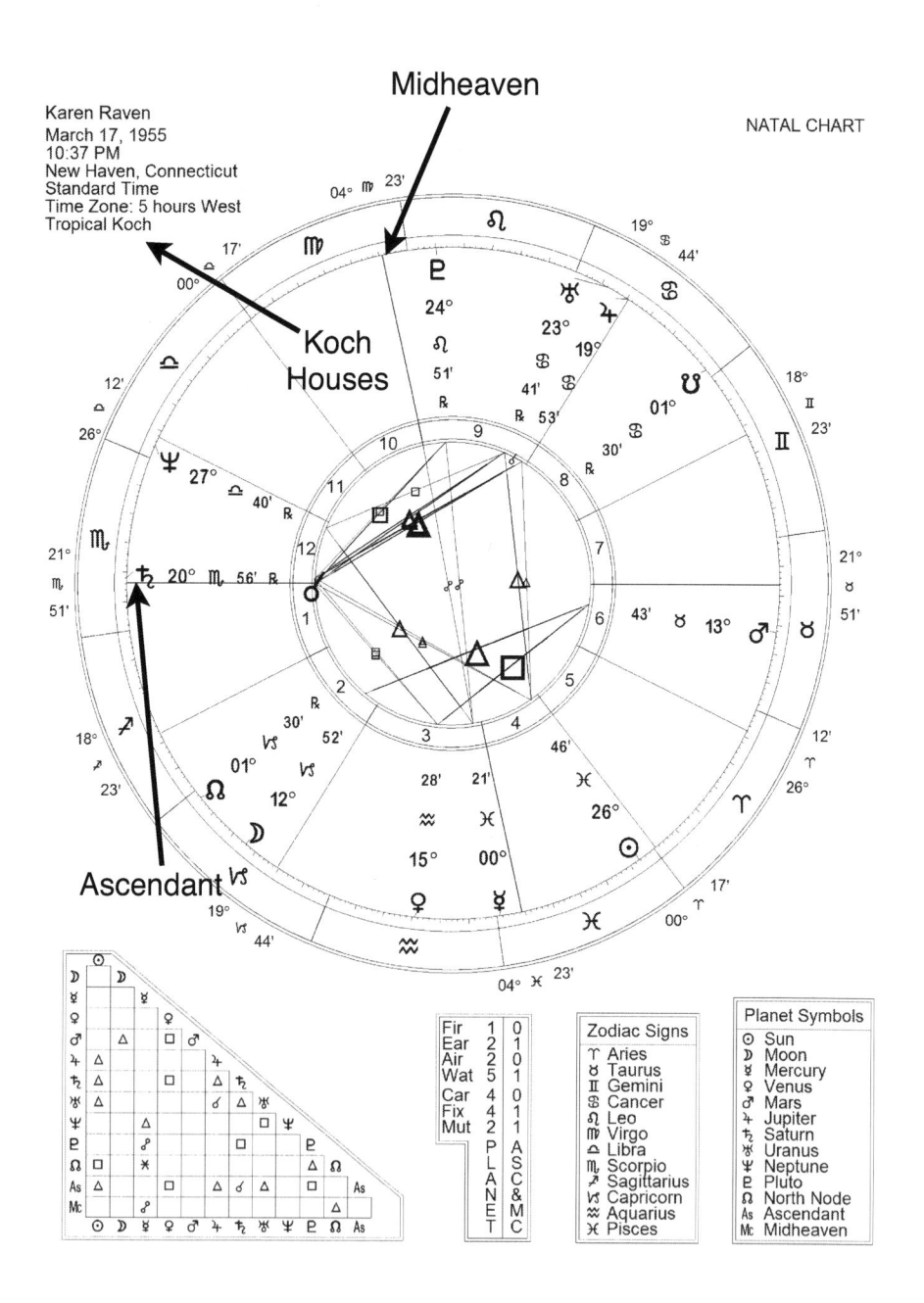

Karen Raven
March 17, 1955
10:37 PM
New Haven, Connecticut
Standard Time
Time Zone: 5 hours West
Tropical Koch

NATAL CHART

Midheaven

Koch Houses

Ascendant

Fir	1	0
Ear	2	1
Air	2	0
Wat	5	1
Car	4	0
Fix	4	1
Mut	2	1

PLANET / ASC&MC

Zodiac Signs	
♈	Aries
♉	Taurus
♊	Gemini
♋	Cancer
♌	Leo
♍	Virgo
♎	Libra
♏	Scorpio
♐	Sagittarius
♑	Capricorn
♒	Aquarius
♓	Pisces

Planet Symbols	
☉	Sun
☽	Moon
☿	Mercury
♀	Venus
♂	Mars
♃	Jupiter
♄	Saturn
♅	Uranus
♆	Neptune
♇	Pluto
☊	North Node
As	Ascendant
Mc	Midheaven

Fast Track Astrologer

241

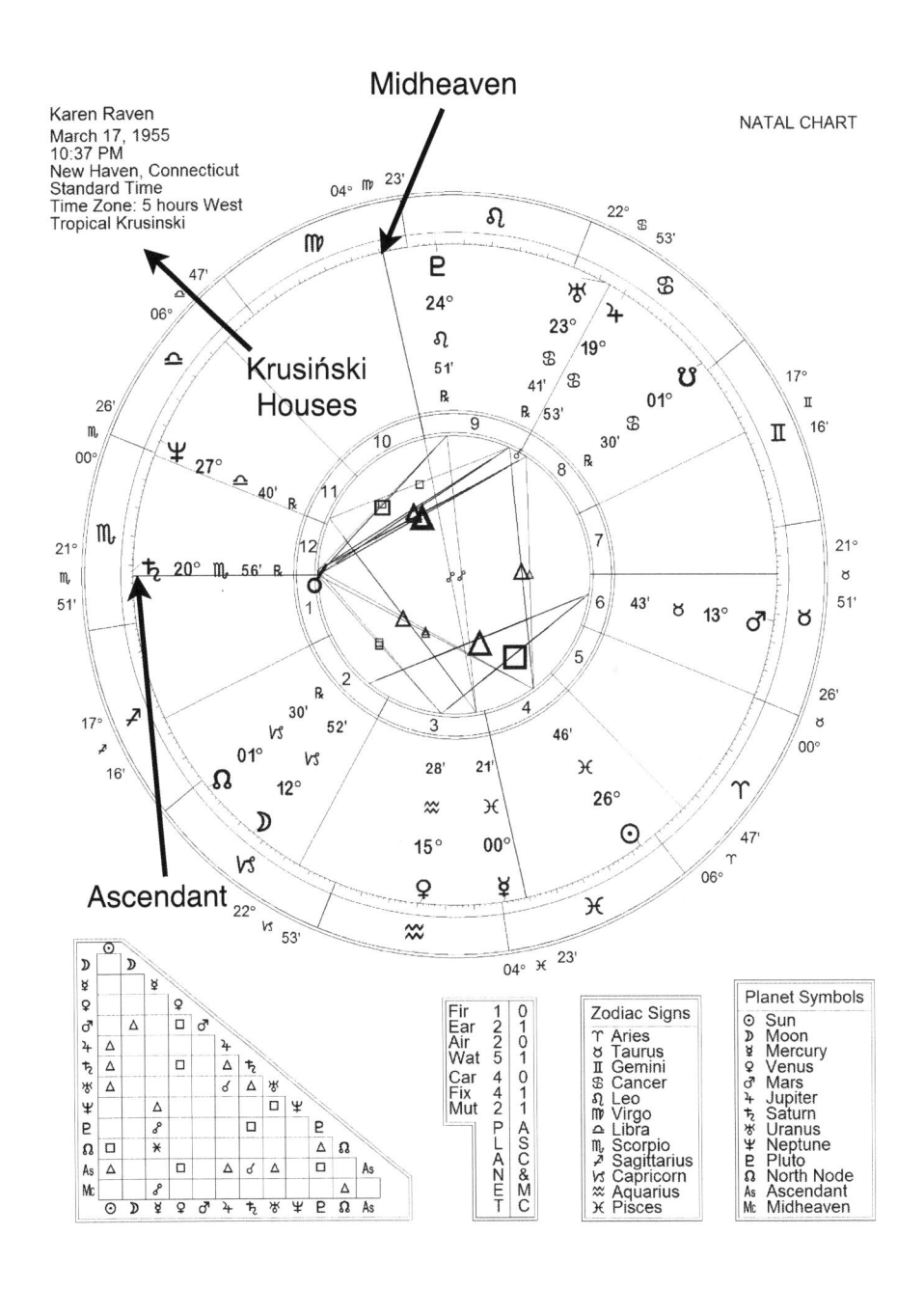

Midheaven

Karen Raven
March 17, 1955
10:37 PM
New Haven, Connecticut
Standard Time
Time Zone: 5 hours West
Tropical Krusinski

NATAL CHART

Krusiński Houses

Ascendant

	Fir	1	0
	Ear	2	1
	Air	2	0
	Wat	5	1
	Car	4	0
	Fix	4	1
	Mut	2	1
		PLANET	ASC&MC

Zodiac Signs
♈ Aries
♉ Taurus
♊ Gemini
♋ Cancer
♌ Leo
♍ Virgo
♎ Libra
♏ Scorpio
♐ Sagittarius
♑ Capricorn
♒ Aquarius
♓ Pisces

Planet Symbols
☉ Sun
☽ Moon
☿ Mercury
♀ Venus
♂ Mars
♃ Jupiter
♄ Saturn
♅ Uranus
♆ Neptune
♇ Pluto
☊ North Node
As Ascendant
Mc Midheaven

House Systems

Each of the five Natal charts on the previous pages look somewhat different. The Placidus, Koch, and Krusiński House systems are quite similar to each other (identical Midheaven M^c, Descendant D^s, Imum Coeli I^c, and Ascendant A^s; and Intermediate House Cusps that only differ by a few degrees) while the Equal and Whole Sign House systems are quite a bit different.

The tables on pages 243 and 244 provide a summary of the overall differences between the five Natal charts. The table on page 243 has a list of the locations of the House Cusps, and the table on page 244 has the Planet House placements for each of the five House systems.

Viewing the table on the next page, you can see that the 1st, 4th, 7th, and 10th House Cusps for the Placidus, Krusiński, and Koch House systems are identical and always will be identical. The remaining House Cusps for the Krusiński system are for the most part close to or between those of the Placidus and Koch House Cusps. According to research done by Bogdan Krusiński, the Koch House Cusps are closer to the Krusiński House Cusps at higher latitudes and the Placidus House Cusps are closer to the Krusiński House Cusps at lower latitudes.

Looking at the Planet House placements in the table on page 244, we see that in most cases, the Planets are in the same Houses in these three House systems. However, the Planet placements in the Equal and Whole Sign systems are quite different.

House Cusps

House	Placidus	Krusiński	Koch	Equal	Whole Sign
1st	22 ♏	22 ♏	22 ♏	22 ♏	0 ♏
2nd	22 ♐	17 ♐	18 ♐	22 ♐	0 ♐
3rd	28 ♑	23 ♑	20 ♑	22 ♑	0 ♑
4th	4 ♓	4 ♓	4 ♓	22 ♒	0 ♒
5th	6 ♈	7 ♈	0 ♈	22 ♓	0 ♓
6th	1 ♉	0 ♉	26 ♈	22 ♈	0 ♈
7th	22 ♉	22 ♉	22 ♉	22 ♉	0 ♉
8th	22 ♊	17 ♊	18 ♊	22 ♊	0 ♊
9th	28 ♋	23 ♋	20 ♋	22 ♋	0 ♋
10th	4 ♍	4 ♍	4 ♍	22 ♌	0 ♌
11th	6 ♎	7 ♎	0 ♎	22 ♍	0 ♍
12th	1 ♏	0 ♏	26 ♎	22 ♎	0 ♎

Planet Placement in Houses

Planet / Personal Point	Placidus	Krusiński	Koch	Equal	Whole Sign
Sun ☉	4th	4th	4th	5th	5th
Moon ☽	2nd	2nd	2nd	2nd	3rd
Mercury ☿	3rd	3rd	3rd	4th	5th
Venus ♀	3rd	3rd	3rd	3rd	4th
Mars ♂	6th	6th	6th	6th	7th
Jupiter ♃	8th	8th	9th	8th	9th
Saturn ♄	12th	12th	12th	12th	1st
Uranus ♅	8th	9th	9th	9th	9th
Neptune ♆	11th	11th	12th	12th	12th
Pluto ♇	9th	9th	9th	10th	10th
Ascendant Aˢ	1st	1st	1st	1st	1st
Midheaven Mᶜ	10th	10th	10th	10th	11th
North Node ☊	2nd	2nd	2nd	2nd	3rd
South Node ☋	8th	8th	8th	8th	9th

Bogdan Krusiński performed a statistical comparison of the Krusiński House system with other House systems. His analysis used approximately 5,000 Natal charts. The Koch House system differed from the Krusiński House system by an average of two Planets. That is, on average, there were two Planets that appeared in different Houses when contrasting the two systems. Comparing the Placidus with the Krusiński House systems, the difference was two-and-a-half Planets on average.

The net effect of all these different House systems is that a Planet may show up in a particular House using one system and in the next higher or lower House when using a different system.

I have used the Whole Sign, Placidus, and Koch systems in the past, and have never been comfortable with any of them, or any other House system with the exception of the Krusiński system.

I use the Krusiński House system for two reasons:

1. The geometrical foundation of the Krusiński House system is built on the same methodology as that used to determine the Midheaven M^c. With this method, the sky from the perspective of the birth location and time is divided further into 12 exactly equal portions. The Intermediate Cusps are then found by following the north-south meridian lines until they intercept with the Ecliptic, which is the same method used to determine the Midheaven M^c. This approach stays true to the sky being divided into 12 equal portions and then forms the intermediate House Cusps without introducing any additional geometry.

2. The majority of astrologers currently use either the Placidus or Koch House system, and frequently they use both systems because they both work well. The statistical comparison of these

two House systems with the Krusiński House system results in a small effect (two to two-and-a-half Planets on average are in different Houses). This is comforting to me, given the vast collective experience of astrologers finding both the Koch and Placidus House systems to be useful and accurate. Unfortunately, the Koch and Placidus House systems distort the sky from the perspective of the birth location. The Krusiński House system does not.

In actuality, the House system chosen by an astrologer is not a big deal because in situations when a Planet is near the border of two Houses, experience has shown that the Planet has an emphasis in both Houses.

I encourage you to experiment with a variety of House systems and choose the one that works best for you.

Final Thoughts

I hope you have found this book helpful in developing your understanding of astrology and inspiring you to delve further into this useful discipline. I invite you to visit my astrology web site at www.usefulastrology.com. I periodically write interesting blogs and also offer astrology consultations using the methods in this book.

House Systems

Appendix

Useful Tables

Planets			
Planet / Personal Point	**Glyph**	**Average Periodicity**	**Approximate Rotation Rate w/r to Zodiac**
Sun	☉	365.26 days	1° per day
Moon	☽	27.2 days	1° per 2 hours
Mercury	☿	88 days	1° per day*
Venus	♀	225 days	1° per day*
Earth	⊕	23 hrs 56 min	1° per 4 minutes
Mars	♂	1.9 years	3.5° per week
Jupiter	♃	11.9 years	2.5° per month
Saturn	♄	29.5 years	1° per month
Uranus	♅	84 years	4° per year
Neptune	♆	165 years	2° per year
Pluto	♇	248 years	1.5° per year

* Because ☿ and ♀ are inside Earth's ⊕ orbit, they appear, on average, to move with the Sun ☉ from Earth's ⊕ perspective.

Personal Points and Other Luminaries

Planet / Personal Point	Glyph	Average Periodicity w/r to Zodiac	Approximate Rotation Rate w/r to Zodiac
Ascendant	A^s	23 hrs 56 min	1° per 4 minutes
Midheaven	M^c	23 hrs 56 min	1° per 4 minutes
Descendant	D^s	23 hrs 56 min	1° per 4 minutes
Imum Coeli	I^c	23 hrs 56 min	1° per 4 minutes
North Node	☊	18.6 years	1.5° per month
South Node	☋	18.6 years	1.5° per month
Chiron	⚷	51 years	7° per year
Ceres	⚳	4.6 years	6.5° per month
Pallas	⚴	4.6 years	6.5° per month
Juno	⚵	4.4 years	7° per month
Vesta	⚶	3.6 years	8° per month

Appendix: Useful Tables

Key Words for Planets and Personal Points

Planet or Personal Point	Glyph	Key Words
Sun	☉	Your main actor, coming out in the world
Moon	☽	Nurturing, receiving, feeling
Mercury	☿	Thinking and communicating
Venus	♀	Attracting and relating, sensuality
Mars	♂	Initiating, getting what you want, passion
Jupiter	♃	Expanding, projecting optimism
Saturn	♄	Structuring, controlling, promoting realism
Uranus	♅	Breaking free, being unique, social change, rebel
Neptune	♆	Growing spiritually, transcending the ego
Pluto	♇	Transformation, using power, sexuality
Ascendant	As	Personality you portray to others
Midheaven	Mc	Characteristics of your career and reputation
North Node	☊	Areas for lifetime growth that are not instinctual
South Node	☋	Areas for lifetime growth that are instinctual

Zodiac Signs

Zodiac Sign / Glyph	Element	Quality	Polarity
Aries ♈	Fire	Cardinal	Masculine
Taurus ♉	Earth	Fixed	Feminine
Gemini ♊	Air	Mutable	Masculine
Cancer ♋	Water	Cardinal	Feminine
Leo ♌	Fire	Fixed	Masculine
Virgo ♍	Earth	Mutable	Feminine
Libra ♎	Air	Cardinal	Masculine
Scorpio ♏	Water	Fixed	Feminine
Sagittarius ♐	Fire	Mutable	Masculine
Capricorn ♑	Earth	Cardinal	Feminine
Aquarius ♒	Air	Fixed	Masculine
Pisces ♓	Water	Mutable	Feminine

Zodiac Sign Characteristics		
Zodiac Sign	**Glyph**	**Characteristics**
Aries	♈	Pathfinder, action-oriented, spirited
Taurus	♉	Predictable, pragmatic, sensual, practical
Gemini	♊	Quick, communicative, collector of knowledge
Cancer	♋	Feeling, intuitive, nurturing, giving & receiving
Leo	♌	Creative, fun, ego balance, magnanimous
Virgo	♍	Improvement-focused, discriminating, service
Libra	♎	Harmony, balance, relationship-oriented
Scorpio	♏	Exploring the hidden depths, use of power
Sagittarius	♐	Wide-ranging, philosophical, distant ventures
Capricorn	♑	Structured, ambitious, achiever, disciplined
Aquarius	♒	Innovative, altering social paradigms, original
Pisces	♓	Spiritual connectedness, idealistic, visionary

Rulers of Zodiac Signs

Zodiac Sign	Ruling Planet(s)
Aries ♈	Mars ♂
Taurus ♉	Venus ♀
Gemini ♊	Mercury ☿
Cancer ♋	Moon ☽
Leo ♌	Sun ☉
Virgo ♍	Mercury ☿
Libra ♎	Venus ♀
Scorpio ♏	Pluto ♇, Mars ♂*
Sagittarius ♐	Jupiter ♃
Capricorn ♑	Saturn ♄
Aquarius ♒	Uranus ♅, Saturn ♄*
Pisces ♓	Neptune ♆, Jupiter ♃*

* Before the outer Planets were discovered, Mars ♂, Saturn ♄, and Jupiter ♃ were the Rulers of Scorpio ♏, Aquarius ♒, and Pisces ♓, respectively. These three Planets are now referred to as the Traditional Rulers.

Appendix: Useful Tables

| **Areas of Life for each House** ||
House	Areas of Life
1st	How you convey yourself to other people
2nd	Possessions, how you earn money, self-confidence
3rd	Your thinking and communicating, short-term travel
4th	Home, psychological roots, family patterns
5th	Creativity, recreation, hobbies, pleasure, fun, romance
6th	Daily routines and habits, health attitudes
7th	Close relationships, influence, diplomacy, intimacy
8th	Cycles of death and rebirth, resource sharing, sexuality
9th	Long-distance travel, philosophy, higher education, ethics
10th	Career, reputation, status, achievement
11th	Your dreams and aspirations, friends and associations
12th	Your inner sanctuary and how you care for it

Natural Rulers of Houses

House	Natural Ruler(s)
1st	Mars ♂
2nd	Venus ♀
3rd	Mercury ☿
4th	Moon ☽
5th	Sun ☉
6th	Mercury ☿
7th	Venus ♀
8th	Pluto ♇, Mars ♂*
9th	Jupiter ♃
10th	Saturn ♄
11th	Uranus ♅, Saturn ♄*
12th	Neptune ♆, Jupiter ♃*

* Before the outer Planets were discovered, Mars ♂, Saturn ♄, and Jupiter ♃ were the Natural Rulers of the 8th, 11th, and 12th Houses, respectively. These three Planets are now referred to as the Traditional Natural Rulers.

Appendix: Useful Tables

Aspects		
Aspect	**Glyph**	**Angle**
Conjunction	☌	0°
Opposition	☍	180°
Trine	△	120°
Square	□	90°
Sextile	✶	60°
Semisquare	∠	45°
Sesquiquadrate	⚼	135°
Semisextile	⚺	30°
Inconjunct	⚻	150°

Appendix: Useful Tables

Made in the USA
Columbia, SC
05 November 2020